SCRATCHBUILDING & KITBASHING
Model Railroad Stations

EDITED BY BOB HAYDEN

STATIONS IN TRADITIONAL MATERIALS	**2**
Flagstop station	2
Building Lizard Head	7
A wood station for Timber City	10
A shelter for any station	18
STUDIES IN STYRENE	**22**
Ticket to Tomahawk	22
Recombination station	30
STATIONS BUILT TO LAST	**42**
A small brick station	42
Mail-order station	50
Hermosa Beach freight station	61
STATIONS BUILT TO FIT	**65**
Alturas depot	65
Two-level station	72
COMPLETING THE STATION SCENE	**82**
Baggage-handling equipment	82
Train-order signals	87
Station signs	90
Variety in station platforms	94
Scratchbuilders' glossary	98
Index of techniques	100

COVER SCENE: Passengers converse with the station agent between trains at Lake Beulah, a quiet lakeside station on a narrow-gauge branch line. The photo was taken by Dave Frary on his HOn30" gauge Carrabasset & Dead River Railway. Complete details of the design and construction of this "mail-order station" begin on page 50.

ART DIRECTOR: Lawrence Luser
LAYOUT: Mike Schafer, William Scholz
CONTINUITY: Donnette Dolzall, Mike Schafer

Kalmbach k BOOKS

© 1978 by Kalmbach Publishing Co. All rights reserved. This book may not be reproduced in part or in whole without written permission from the publisher, except in the case of brief quotations used in reviews. Purchaser may have photocopies of drawings made locally as an aid to modelmaking, but is prohibited from distribution of copies of the drawings to others. Published by Kalmbach Publishing Co., 1027 North Seventh Street, Milwaukee, WI 53233. Printed in U.S.A. Library of Congress Catalog Card Number: 77-86282. ISBN: 0-89024-533-9.

Flagstop station

Classic techniques for building a small station with high-quality, inexpensive Strathmore board

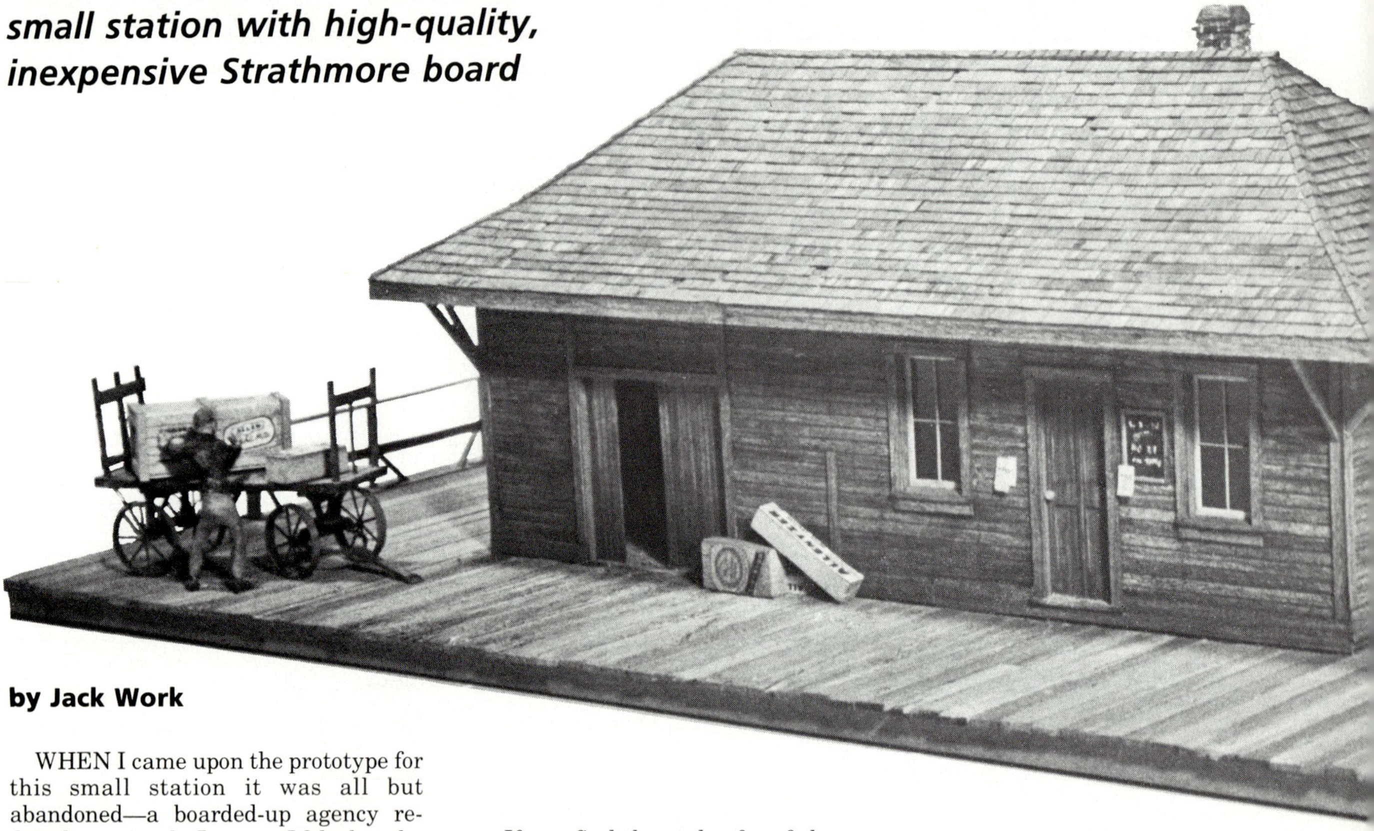

by Jack Work

WHEN I came upon the prototype for this small station it was all but abandoned—a boarded-up agency reduced to a simple flagstop. I felt that the boarded-up look was novel and eye-catching, and because I knew I would eventually need more than one small station on my pike, I decided to construct two variations of the building, saving time by laying both out at once. It is common practice for the prototype railroads to standardize on structures. Thus, one of my variations is a duplicate of the abandoned prototype, while the other model shows the same building in busier times.

Surprisingly enough, the mere addition of sashes and "glass" to replace the boarded-up windows makes a world of difference. The "busy" station has life and reason compared with the tired and deathlike appearance of the other. My other additions consist of a brick chimney, a notice board near the office door, and a planked platform in place of the gravel one serving the prototype.

Construction is simple, especially of the model without windows and chimney. If you find the style of roof shown confusing to lay out, you could easily change it to a two-sided gable affair and simply peak the end walls to suit. My text describes methods for construction in HO scale; material sizes are easily altered for other scales using the proper scale ruler, since all dimensions are stated in scale sizes.

The prototype building was painted entirely one color, the usual "railroad red," except for the shingled roof, which had never been painted and had weathered to varying shades from gray to blackish-brown in an overall patchy effect. The structure had no window sashes to serve as a coloring guide, so I developed my own color scheme and painted them cream yellow. All materials were precolored, which helped to attain a weathered appearance as well as a certain degree of neatness.

Walls

If the wall material you are using around your windows is less than 4 scale inches thick, you must first decide on a method to increase the thickness to 4". My model has walls of four-ply Strathmore board, which is 2" thick in HO. Fig. 1 shows how I framed the inside of the window openings with 2 x 4 stripwood, and reinforced this framing with additional 2 x 4's cemented against the framing members on the back side of the window openings. The alternate method is to simply use 2"-thick filler (wood or card) behind the wall, but I feel the technique shown is neater.

The method you choose will determine the size of the window openings. The first method requires that the openings be 4" larger each way than shown in fig. 1 to allow for the 2 x 4 strips. If you use the second method, the dimensions for the openings can be taken right from the drawing.

Lay out all four walls end-to-end on Strathmore board according to the dimensions shown in fig. 1. A drawing board and instruments are handy for this work, but a small metal square will substitute nicely. After the wall areas are laid out, locate the window and door positions and scribe in the individual wallboards. Then color the siding with a thin stain of your favorite paint applied with a cloth pad. I used a roof brown color to which I added a little each of gray and white, along with thinner.

If you are modeling the building with boarded windows, leave the window areas blank when you scribe the walls. Then scribe in the window boards so they are slightly out of alignment with the wall sheathing to give the impression that the windows were boarded up

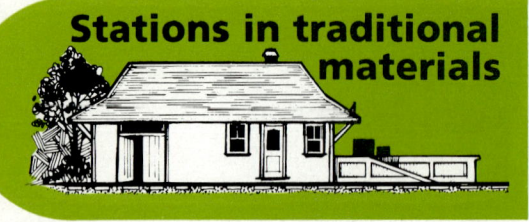

Stations in traditional materials

All photos by the author.

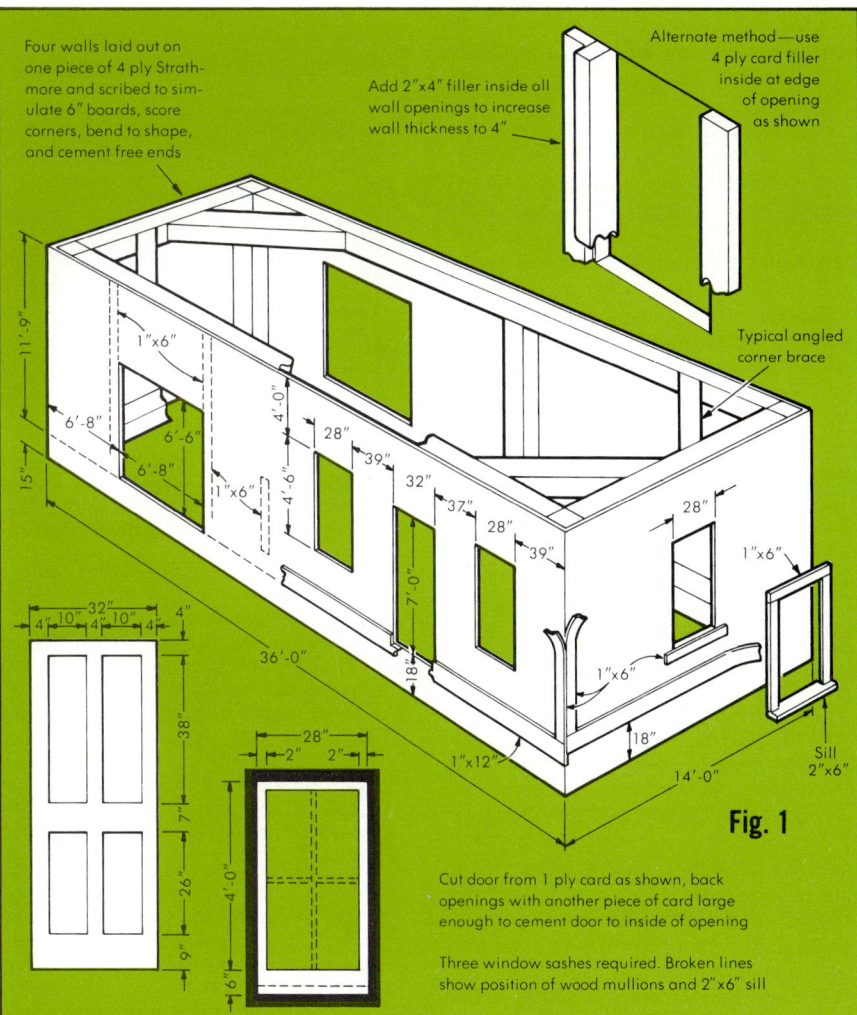

separately. The windows in the long wall of the prototype are boarded horizontally, while the one in the end shows vertical boards.

The prototype station sits 2 to 3 feet below track level. This requires a deeper wall than shown in fig. 1, where only 15" is below the dashed line which represents the platform level. My models are built according to the figure.

After coloring the walls, cut the window and door openings with a sharp knife, remove the excess material around the wall edges, and score the three wall corner joints so they may be bent to form a box as shown. Do not join the free corners yet.

Windows and doors

Cut and add the filler material to increase the wall thickness at the window and door openings now. You may have a pet method of window construction, but here's mine for those who wish to try it. First lay out the window sashes, fig. 1, on precolored one-ply (for HO) Strathmore stock. The sashes have 2' x 3'-10" openings and enough excess material to allow for cementing behind the wall opening, shown by the solid black area in the drawing. Remember to locate the mullion positions on the edge of each sash, thus dividing the glass area into four equal segments.

After completing the sashes, prepare the mullions by sanding a piece of $1/32$" (actual) sheetwood to one-third its original thickness. Choose a soft, straight-grained piece about an inch square, which is enough to provide dozens of mullions without making the sanding job tedious. Stain the wood to match your sash color and then lay a sharp knife or razor blade along the wood, with the grain, and press down to trim away a mullion about as wide as it is thick. Cut enough mullions for all the sashes, using your eye as a gauge. There will be oversize pieces, but they can be discarded with little lost effort.

Measure the mullion lengths on your sashes, cutting them to fit. Cement thin clear plastic glass material behind the sash openings and add the wood mullion strips. Install the vertical strips full

Stations in traditional materials

3

length, then place the two short horizontal pieces, aligning them with the marks made previously on the sash edges.

I prefer a thinned down contact-type cement for adding the mullions. Apply a thin coat to the edge of the mullion with a small brush and place the piece on the "glass" surface. Too much cement will result in deposits that mar the glass, but a little experimentation and practice will give you an idea of the correct consistency and amount of adhesive required for a neat job. Once you master this technique for making mullions you'll probably never return to the old methods of painting lines on the glass or using thread, neither of which is easier or neater. Besides, wood more closely resembles prototype mullions.

Cement the completed sashes behind the wall openings with 2" showing on each side and across the top. This should leave 6" showing on the bottom, half of which will be covered by the angled 2"-thick sill.

Make a door, fig.1, from one-ply card cut and backed with more card to form panels. Again, allow extra material around the finished door for cementing area. Cut the window and door sills from 2 x 8 wood, allowing sufficient width to trim for a proper overhang of the framing boards beneath each sill. The sills should extend 1" beyond the 5½" window and door framing on each side; window sills should be 3'-4" long, door sills 3'-8". Add the sills to the windows and doors, notched to fit into the opening and against the sash or door.

If you have wood thin enough to represent 1" boards and you like working with this material, cut it into 5½"-wide strips for the window framing. That 5½" dimension may sound rather fussy; however, you can ensure the correct size by simply transferring measurements from your scale rule to the work using dividers.

I made my window, door, corner, and base trim on a sheet of precolored two-ply card, and used a steel straightedge to cut the boards to width. Before installing the trim, touch up the raw white edges and ends of the cut boards with stain so that no painting will be required once they are in place.

Basic assembly and floor

The building walls are completed on the outside with color, doors, windows, and all trim except for the corner and bottom boards which will be added

Stations in traditional materials

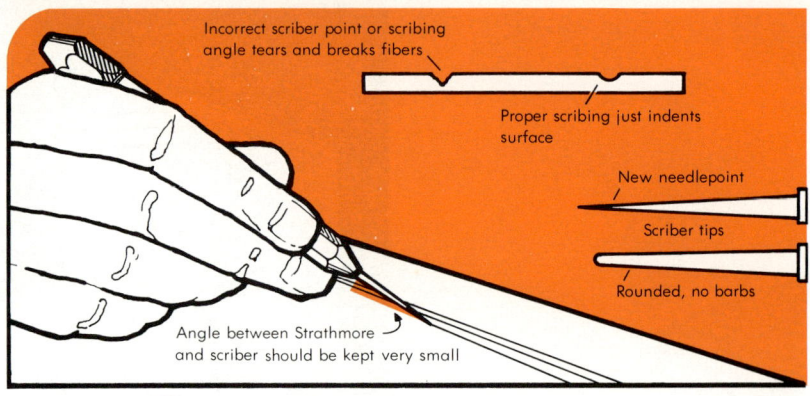

STRATHMORE CONSTRUCTION

Strathmore bristol board is a quality artists' material and drafting paper very well suited to modelwork. A pressed paper, it comes in one-, two-, three-, four-, and five-ply thicknesses; each ply is .005" thick. Two surface finishes are made; the machine-smoothed high, or plate, finish is best for modeling. Strathmore board comes in 23" x 29" and 30" x 40" sheets, and is available at stores that sell artists' materials or drafting supplies. It is less expensive than commonly used sheetwood.

Strathmore is quite different from everyday cardboard. It is much less likely to warp, cuts neatly and holds an edge well, takes paints and stains readily, and is easy to form, glue, and laminate. Unlike wood, it will not split, but it does have grain. When Strathmore is to be bent or laminated around a curve, the grain should be parallel to the axis of the curve. Determine the direction of the grain by flexing the sheet; it will bend easily one way, and it will be much stiffer the other way (against the grain).

Cutting

Strathmore cutting tools should have very thin blades—thick blades push material aside and produce beaded and beveled edges. Single-edge razor blades are thin enough, and are extremely sharp. When the part of the edge that does the actual cutting becomes dull it can be broken off with a pliers to produce a new edge.

The work surface is also important to accurate cutting. It should be a heavy, medium hardness material such as pressed board (Masonite, Beaverboard) or heavy cardstock—hard enough that the pressure of a cutting stroke does not push the Strathmore into the work surface. Do not use wood as a cutting surface; your cutting instrument will tend to follow the wood grain and ruin the edge.

For straight cuts, use a steel ruler or straightedge to hold the Strathmore firmly against the cutting surface, and cut through the stock with several light strokes rather than a single heavy one. For curves, cut the material freehand, leaving some excess, and use fine sandpaper to smooth the curve to finished shape. Inside curves can be sanded by wrapping sandpaper around a dowel slightly smaller than the finished radius of the curve. All cut edges should be lightly sanded with fine grit paper to remove burrs or beads.

Gluing and laminating

Almost any adhesive suitable for porous materials can be used with Strathmore. White glues are useful for joining small areas and for cementing wood bracing or trim parts. Contact-type adhesives work best for gluing prepainted surfaces, and should be used where absolute neatness is required. For joining large Strathmore surfaces and for laminating one sheet to another use a slow-drying acetate cement like Ambroid or household cement. These will penetrate the surfaces to be joined for a good bond, but will not warp or delaminate the plies as would large amounts of white glue.

Scribing and staining

Only a few simple tools and techniques are needed to effectively scribe and stain Strathmore to represent a board surface. Make a scriber by inserting a large sewing needle into a pin vise and rounding the point with sandpaper so that it will not tear the surface of the paper. Hold the scriber at a very small angle to the material and draw it along, indenting but not tearing the paper. A couple of practice pieces will teach you how much pressure to apply.

Strathmore is easily colored, but stay away from water-based paints and stains that involve soaking the material. After your surface is scribed and ready for color, use a small piece of absorbent fabric to spread and rub a thinned flat lacquer or enamel paint stain into the surface. Try to merely tint the Strathmore while building up color in the scribed grooves, but do so without developing an opaque coating—with a little practice, you'll quickly master the technique.

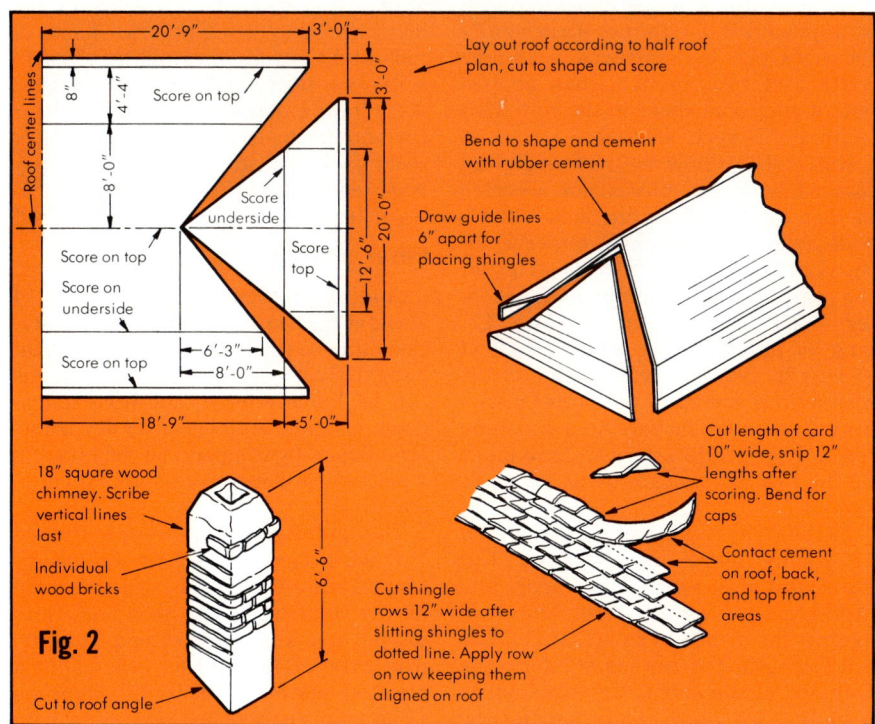
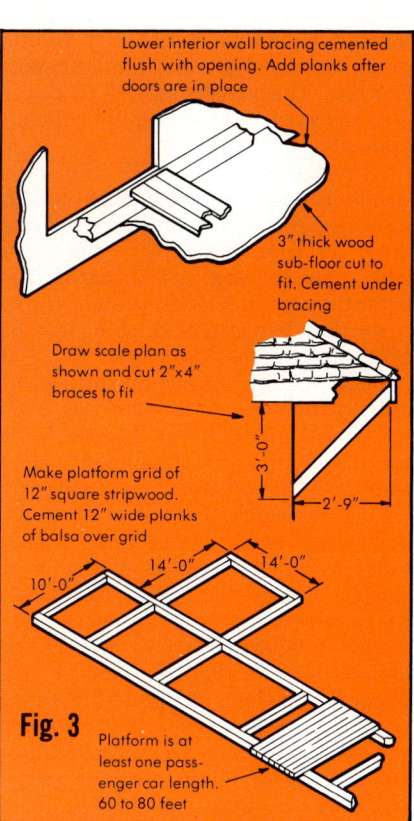

later. Now reinforce the walls by cementing stripwood bracing to the back. I used pieces about 12" square along the top and bottom edges of each wall, and one vertical brace near the center of each long wall. Once the cement on these braces has set, bend the walls to form the rectangular building and join the free ends with a 12 x 12 brace at the inside corner.

Note in fig. 3 that the top edge of the bottom 12" brace is flush with the freight-shed door opening, and that a heavy cardstock or 3"-thick sheetwood floor is cemented below this. Measure the length and width inside the walls at the bottom and cut a floor for a neat fit that will help to hold the building square. After cementing this in place, add angled corner braces from one wall to the adjoining wall at the top, fig. 1. One brace across the building between the long walls will prevent the walls from warping.

Freight doors and trim

The freight-shed doors are made by scribing lines on 3" centers on Strathmore stock cut oversize to allow for gluing to the walls. I left the front set of doors partly open on my "open" model, and although they do not operate, you could make them movable by using the floor planks on the inside and a sill on the outside to form a channel in which the door could run.

If you leave any of the doors open, install floor planking inside to complete the realism. Add this planking before the roof is in place, cementing lengths of 12"-wide planks cut from 3"-thick balsa across the building on top of the wall braces. The planking need only extend as far as you can easily see through the open doors; and remember that it will be quite dark inside after the roof is on. I added a cardstock partition at the center of my structure with unboarded windows to keep light from showing through the office onto the freight-shed floor.

Install trim boards at each corner and around the bottom of the exterior of the station. Again, use thin wood or two-ply card and cut 5 ½" widths for corner trim and 12" widths for all or most of the bottom boards around the building. These boards varied somewhat in width on the prototype station, so you can use the photos as a guide.

Station roof

I used two-ply card for the roof material. This may seem quite flimsy, but it takes on sufficient strength as it is bent and cemented into roof form and fastened to the building. Fig. 2 shows a half plan of the roof layout. Note that the fascia trim boards along the outer roof edge have been included in the roof layout for simplicity. Lay out the roof carefully as shown and score all lines as indicated, including those on the reverse side.

Cut the roof to shape and separate the two smaller end pieces from the main portion. After bending to shape, cement these in place to complete the four-sided roof, fig. 2. The roof can be assembled without clamps or formers by using a contact-type adhesive applied to both edges of each seam. Allow the adhesive to dry for several minutes before joining the edges. I found it unnecessary to reinforce the roof interior, but the outside fascia trim boards require some stiffening. Cement the 6" edge of scrap 6 x 10 stripwood against the back of the long trim boards. To reinforce the corner joint, cement the ends of the wood butting against the short end fascia.

Brush away any lint or dust particles from the inside of the window glass and cement the roof assembly in place on the walls, allowing an even overhang all around.

It has been said many times that our models are viewed most often from above; thus roof detail is probably more important than any other part of the model. Use individual shingle strips to achieve a realistic roof, especially if your model is to be in or near the foreground of your layout. The procedure for shingling a roof is neither difficult nor time consuming once a system is worked out to prepare and apply the shingle strips.

Start by staining a sheet of single-ply Strathmore or bond paper that in size is slightly more than double the roof area to be covered. I found that a 9" x 12" (actual) sheet was ample for the two roofs on my models. Rub-stain the paper in a very streaky fashion with a black-gray stain overall, then follow up with

Stations in traditional materials

more pronounced streaks of lighter grays, earth colors, and small amounts of white. The streaks should all run in one direction and be quite crudely applied.

Next, use dividers to mark off 6"-wide bands running perpendicular to the streaks of color. To save time and effort, draw the first line 6" from the paper edge, skip the next set of marks, and draw the next line 12" from and parallel to the first. Repeat this skipping method all the way across the paper.

Begin making individual shingles by slitting the paper to the first line, 6" in from the edge. Use your sharpest knife for this job, and vary the shingle widths from 2" to 15". After you have made slits all the way across the edge of the sheet, go back and shorten the lengths of a few of the shingles at various places in the row for a realistic weathered appearance.

The shingle row is now ready to be detached from the sheet of shingle paper. Lay a straightedge on the second 6" markings and trim off the shingle row. Now you have a 12"-wide shingle strip slitted for half its width at irregular intervals. Continue making these strips, but stop now and then to apply some of them to the roof to avoid monotony.

Guidelines drawn 6" or 12" apart on the roof material are helpful in placing the shingle rows so they remain level and evenly spaced as the shingle laying progresses toward the peak of the roof. It is especially important that the rows be evenly spaced on a hip roof like the one on this station, where the rows are continuous and must match at each corner. The guidelines are easiest to draw when the roof is being laid out on the drawing board.

My favorite cement for shingle application is a contact adhesive thinned with paint reducer or thinner to the consistency of heavy cream. Coat a portion of the roof, the entire back of each shingle strip, and the front upper portion above the slits where the shingle strip will be overlapped by the next row with cement. This cement can be applied with a small brush either before or after the strips are cut to length for the roof, because the thinner evaporates rapidly and the shingles are thus easily handled. In either case, coats of dried cement adhere readily to each other.

In laying the shingles, most rows can be applied full length, but occasionally the rows can be shortened a shingle width and split in two, then applied with a gap somewhere in the row. This technique is very effective.

Fig. 2 shows how the roof ridges are covered with cap pieces, an accepted method in wood shingling jobs. Cut 6"-wide strips of the shingle material for the corner caps and 10"-wide strips for the peak. Score these strips on their center lines, mark them off into 12" lengths, apply contact cement, and cut to length. Bend the cap pieces on the scored lines and apply to the roof in lapping fashion as shown. As a finishing touch, I used a thin gray stain to touch up the raw white edges of each shingle row.

Fashion a brick chimney from an 18"-square length of stripwood. Cut horizontal grooves spaced 3" apart into the stripwood with a razor saw held against the blade of a small square. Use a full length of stripwood and form the chimney at one end so the excess stock may be used as a handle during the process. Scribe in the vertical brick lines with a needle, taper the top as shown, fig. 2, to simulate a mortar cap, and add a row of ornamental bricks with small bits of wood just below the cap. Drill a hole into the top of the wood strip and square it off with a sharp knife to represent the flue. To prevent filling in the sawcuts, color the entire chimney white with thin paint, then touch brick-colored paints to individual bricks with a small pointed brush. Vary the brick colors by using several shades of reds and browns, intermixing them to achieve a weathered brick appearance. As a final touch, paint the top mortar cap and the inside of the chimney a dark sooty gray, and streak a very thin gray wash down over the bricks and downward from the chimney over the roof.

Final details

Add angle braces made from 2 x 4 stock at each corner, fig. 3. Hang a station nameboard from thin wood or metal hanger straps on each end; these signs can be hand-lettered, cut from magazines, or made with decals or dry transfers. Paper signs should be cemented to a piece of card or wood to make them 1" thick.

The prototype station was fronted with a filled gravel platform retained by large square timbers. I used this style for my structure of the abandoned prototype, but since my second building was to represent another era, I built a planked platform for it, fig. 3. Some 12"-square timbers formed grid fashion and lap-jointed support 12"-wide planks cut from 3" balsa sheet.

The blackboard for train movement notices is made from a small gray-black piece of card framed with thin wood strips. Hang a few bulletins made from tissue paper with pencil scribbles on the wall, add some cartons, crates, and benches, and drop in a figure or two to enliven the scene in anticipation of the next passenger-train arrival.

Stations in traditional materials

All photos, MODEL RAILROADER: A. L. Schmidt unless otherwise credited.

Building Lizard Head

An unusual timber structure built board by board from stripwood

by Len Madsen

IN its last years, the now defunct 3-foot-gauge Rio Grande Southern of Colorado used this former section house for its station at the summit of Lizard Head Pass after the original station burned down. The station is not difficult to model, and it will fit into many model layouts—standard-gauge as well as narrow-gauge—as it is only 22 x 30 feet.

The prototype was built of 6 x 12 timbers notched at the ends and joints like logs in a cabin. The roof was shingled with wood, and two brick chimneys completed the building. The interior walls were papered and the ceiling was plastered.

Sides

To begin construction of Lizard Head station, cut 6 x 12 timbers to length for each side and notch the ends. Cut the timbers that border the door and window openings slightly oversize. Stack the timbers for one side and measure its height. Lay out the side, including openings, on stiff paper. Start with the bottom timber and cement it in place on the paper. Add each succeeding timber, letting the oversize pieces stick out into the door and window openings. The window openings extend through the top timber; a cap strip will be added later. Trim off the surplus paper backing.

Lay out the adjoining wall in the same way, fitting each piece to its mating timber. Follow the same procedure for the third and fourth sides. If you cut the timbers of the north and south sides square and oversize, cut them off to the proper roof pitch now. If you have assembled the sides carefully, they should fit well. Sand any ill-fitting notches with an emery board.

I recommend an acetate-base cement, such as Ambroid, for this work since the wood and paper wall may tend to curl slightly. If it does, wet it with lacquer thinner to soften the cement, place the sides on a flat surface, and weight them. When dry, add the 2 x 8 cap, allowing the extra 2" to extend inside the walls.

Prepaint and partially weather the sides. The prototype had dirty yellow walls with dark brown trim. Wash-coat the yellow very lightly all over and keep adding washes until you achieve the desired appearance.

Working windows and doors

The next step is to frame the windows and doors. The widths of the openings are shown on the sketches, but heights will vary depending on your supply of timbers. Measure the openings and make pattern blocks of scrap wood—one for the window openings and one for the door openings—that will measure exactly the right height and width.

Sand the openings until the pattern blocks are a light press fit. When you have enlarged all openings, cut the framing lumber to size, prepaint it, and frame one window and one door. Sand down your patterns so that they will again be a light press fit in the framed openings. This appears to be a lot of extra work, but when you start putting in the doors and windows, the preparation pays off. Minor variations in measuring and cutting are more easily corrected on a piece of solid work than on a small frail insert.

Install the balance of the door and window trim as shown in figs. 1 and 2, using your patterns again to insure a good cement fit. Don't cement the door sill down yet.

The doors are three-piece laminations of two-ply Strathmore bristol board. Cut one lamination with panels, the second lamination solid but a scale 2" narrower, and the third plain, full width. Place a length of wire in the space left by the narrow second lamination, fig. 1, and cement the three laminations together. Clip the wire off 2" longer than the door on the bottom and slightly longer on the top. Add a clipped pin for a doorknob. Check the fit in the door opening and clip the upper end of the wire into the hole in the top of the door opening. Slip the door sill in place, catching the bottom end of the pivot

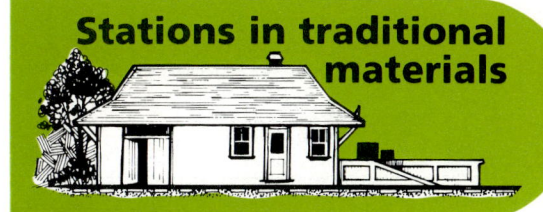

Stations in traditional materials

wire in the groove in the sill. Cement the sill down. Add small strips of paper or wood for door stops.

Make windows by cementing strips of precolored two-ply Strathmore bristol board onto a piece of acetate, fig. 2. When the cement is dry, cut the windows apart in pairs of upper and lower sash. Then check the fit in each opening, sanding the double sash where necessary. If the windows are to be operating, sand the sash until you get a very light press fit, then cut it in half and cement the upper half against the outer trim board. Add a filler strip below this sash to make an outer sash stop. Cement the lower window to the filler strip. If you want operating windows, cement a 1 x 4 to the back of the wall as an inner stop after the window is in place. Before the cement dries completely, open and close the window several times to be sure no cement has gotten into the tracks.

At this stage your careful preparation begins to pay off: Since the openings are equal in dimension, the windows can be laid out on the bristol board and cut apart, and very little fitting will be required.

Assembly and roof

Center and cement a 6 x 12 to each end from a point 12" below the peak to the floor line. Assemble the sides into a box by carefully applying cement to the corners on the inside of the notches. Set the building on a flat surface and check for squareness. Cut a ridgepole of 6 x 12 and cement it between the end walls, fig. 3. Cut another 6 x 12 to fit between the end braces and cement it in place above the tenth board. Omit this piece if you don't intend to detail the interior. The ceiling fits below this piece and under the 2" extension of the cap strip.

Cut the ceiling from two pieces of two-ply Strathmore board and notch the pieces to clear the end wall braces. Cut the inside walls and center partition board with 6 x 12 spacers, fig. 4. Cut the floor out of a piece of scribed siding and cement it on a simple framework that will fit snugly inside the walls.

Paint the walls and ceiling and add interior detailing, fig. 4. If you choose to light the building, paint the walls black first and then recoat with a pastel color.

Install floor, partitions, and ceiling. Do not cement. It's not necessary, and it is easier to make changes if you don't use cement.

Make the roof out of sheetwood and paper or wood shingles. Cement the roof in place and add 2 x 4 side trim and 2 x 6 end trim against the walls. Add cap strips and install the chimneys. Make the chimneys from balsa, carved or papered with yellow brickpaper.

Final details

Add the platforms next. Cement a 6 x

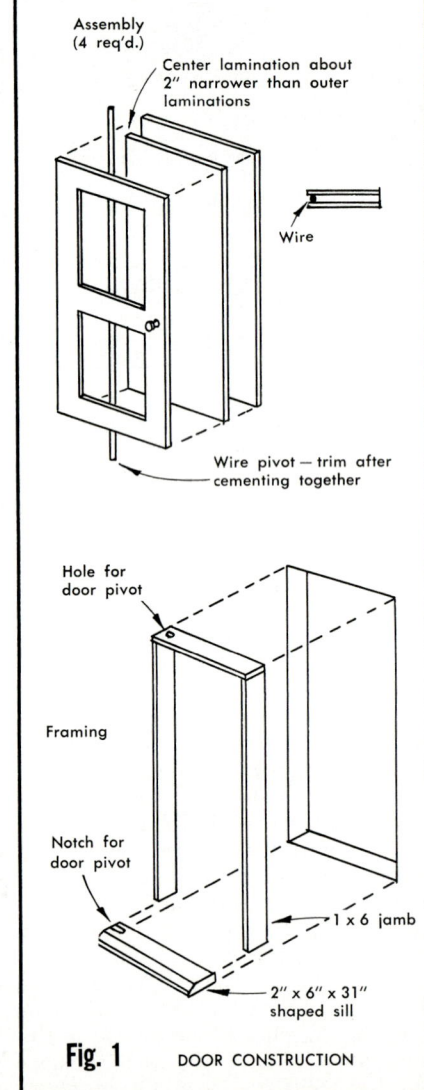

Fig. 1 DOOR CONSTRUCTION

Stations in traditional materials

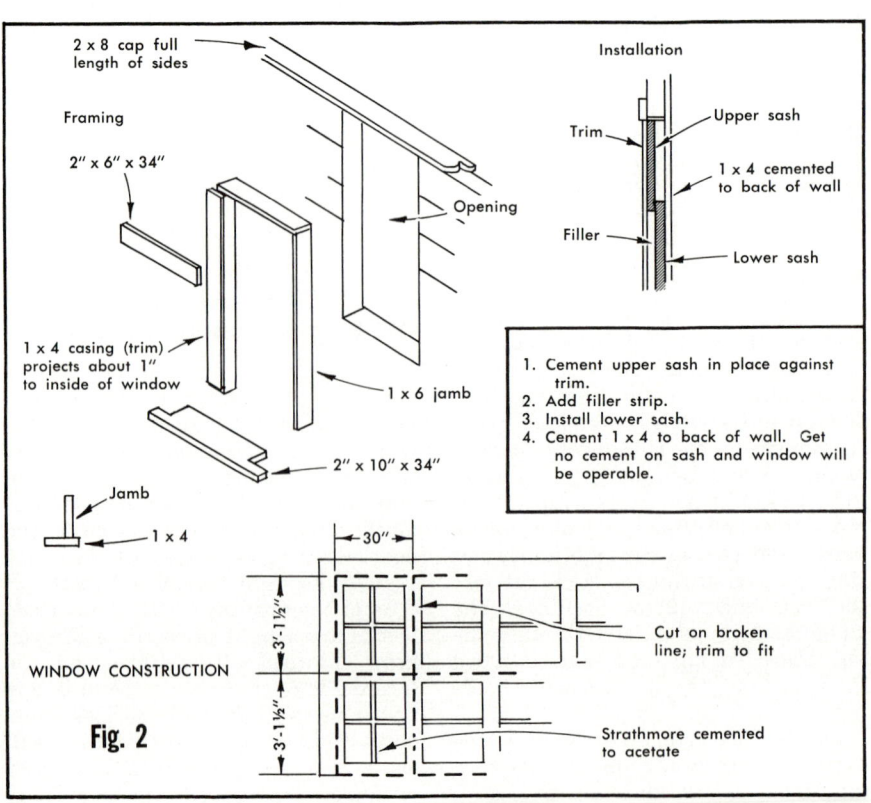

Fig. 2 WINDOW CONSTRUCTION

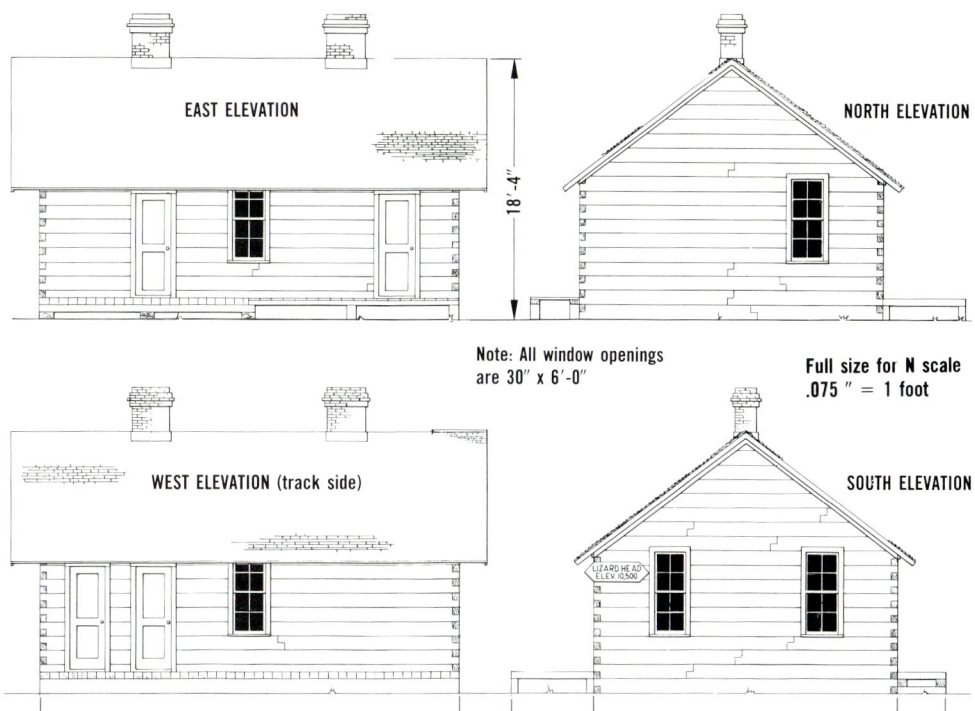

12 cut to length to the bottom of the west wall (the track side of the structure). Block out another 6 x 12, 6 feet from the wall, and add 6 x 8 planks along the top of this frame. The east wall platform is of two different sections: the south half, made of 6 x 8 timbers, and the north half, made of 2 x 10 planks with a 4 x 8 stringer to level the platform. This half rests on 8 x 8 posts. Weather the platform with thin black washes.

The station is now complete, except for touchup and additional weathering. Set the building in place and cement wood strips around it, then remove the building and add scenery up to the wood strips. This procedure makes the station easy to service if you install lights. The prototype is situated in a shallow valley, sparsely grassed. There are no trees within a quarter mile of the station. I used a commercial scenery mix and darkened it with oil colors. I daubed patches of cement on the scenery, and used brown flock on the patches. Washcoat the flock with a dirty tan by spraying and it will appear to be dying grass. Add the trackwork (I used individual ties and code 70 nickel silver rail) and reinstall the structure, and the summit station is complete.

A STRUCTURE OF MANY USES

The small structure that served as the Rio Grande Southern representative at desolate Lizard Head Pass (elevation, 10,250 feet) in Colorado was used variously as a station, section house, and emergency shelter until the railroad closed its doors in 1951. Therefore, if you like its design but don't envision the structure as a station on your pike, consider it for use as a section bunk house, a yard office, or other backwoods branchline purpose.

More prototype data and plans are featured in Kalmbach's RAILROAD STATION PLANBOOK.

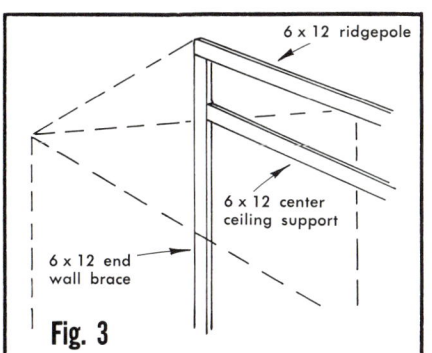
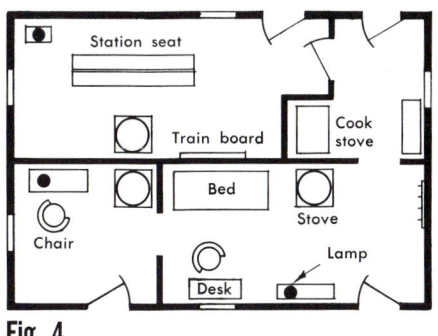

J. W. Maxwell

Stations in traditional materials

All photos by the author.

A wood station for Timber City

A detailed presentation of techniques for modeling in wood

by Ben King

HALF a century ago most rural communities depended on the railroad for passenger, mail, express, and freight service. Perishables such as milk, eggs, and meat—and even live chickens—were shipped to city markets from the tiniest lineside hamlets. Each town had its own station, and while no two seemed alike, many followed certain classic lines: Most were frame structures, and most were painted in two or three colors. When my Timber City & North Western layout needed a station for Timber City, I designed and built this small structure with characteristic rural station features in mind. The station is small—only 15 by 30 feet—and will fit into any layout.

Materials and paint

The materials used for this project were milled sheetwood with scale 3" scribing for all wall parts, 9" scribed stock for the underside of the roof, scale 6" stripwood angle for trim, and Strathmore bristol card for window sash. I cut most of the materials into parts before assembly, and many pieces were made oversize and trimmed later. I did all cutting with a sharp single-edge razor blade working against a steel rule. All wood parts were painted before assembly. I used white glue throughout the project. Edges and part faces that were to be glued were not painted, as paint weakens the glue bond.

I used Floquil paints. The wainscot and gable valances were made Pullman green, waist and upper wall panels, depot olive, and the trim, tuscan red. The interior is a buff color made with Floquil mud, and the floor was swabbed with a mixture of 1 part black to 20 parts Dio-Sol thinner.

Preparing the stock

I work slowly; it took me nearly 75 hours to build this station, in many sittings of two hours each. My model is built in HO scale, but construction techniques in other scales are the same except as material thicknesses affect trimming and parts cut to fit. All dimensions are given in scale feet and inches; to work in a scale other than HO take measurements from the drawing with an HO rule and use a rule in your scale to transfer these measurements to your materials.

Start by preparing your materials in long strips. Cut the wainscot panel stock across the scribing lines to make 110 running feet of the material. Note that while the drawing shows the wainscot 36" high (including the two trim strips), the scribed section must be cut shorter than 36" because it tucks under the angle stock; my wainscot strips came out just 30" high. Paint the

Stations in traditional materials

10

wainscot stock on the face only, brushing in the direction of the scribing. The wainscot is not cut to length until needed, so put it aside for now.

Cut the waist panels to size on all four edges and paint them, and cut and paint the two long upper wall panels. Make the upper end wall gables in two layers, fig. l; the bottom layer should be made from horizontally scribed sheetwood that is cut long enough to extend into the peak of the roof. The two matching end pieces must be cut exactly alike. To do this, make a template of thin cardstock or styrene for use as a cutting guide. Paint the exposed part of these gable pieces the same color as your upper wall. Cover the upper portion of each gable with a valance of vertically scribed wood. This piece should be serrated at the lower edge and painted a contrasting color for a gingerbread effect. Precise measurement is mandatory here; how you finish this piece will make a great deal of difference in the final appearance of the model. Use white glue to laminate the two gable pieces, then place them under weight on a flat surface so they will dry without warping.

Prepaint about 600 scale feet of 6 x 6 stripwood angle for trim. If you work carefully, many parts can be cut to length together. However, the two doorjambs, E and F in fig. l, must be cut overlength and trimmed when the wall is assembled.

Dry assembly of walls—then gluing

Arrange all parts for the rear wall, fig. 1, face down on a flat surface. You will need to use pieces of angle for temporary leveling shims under the outer edges of panels A and D. Place a small weight on each panel to hold it in place, and after making sure the two windows and the door are spaced correctly, check overall dimensions.

When all parts are properly aligned, lay a bead of glue along each seam to be joined. Don't try to put the glue between the edges—it's not necessary and may come through on the finished side. Cut two 12 x 12 corner blocks the full height of the wall and glue them flush with the ends, fig. 1. Only after the glue has set on the corner blocks is the wall assembly rigid enough to be handled. Trim the bottoms of the doorjambs.

Assemble the front wall next, using the same procedure. The opening for the bay window is made like a large doorway. Do not build the bay window yet. Assemble the two gable end walls, and place a corner angle trim at each edge, fig. 1.

Cut the floor from 6"-thick sheetwood with 6" scribing running lengthwise. Cut 12" x 12" notches at the corners to clear the corner fillers, and paint the floor. Trial fit the walls and floor and glue them together as follows: Apply a

bead of glue to the edge of one corner filler and assemble a side and end, using the floor as a square. Do the same for the other side and end. When the glue has set on these assemblies, apply glue to two of the floor edges and press the floor into place in one of the assembled corners. Apply glue to the other two floor edges and to the remaining corner filler surfaces and press the other walls in place. This completes the basic wall assembly.

Bay window

Begin constructing the bay window, fig. 2, by making two floors from 6" scribed sheetwood and painting one of them. The second floor will be used as a gluing jig later. Next make the three wainscot panels using the prepainted 6" angle stock. Cut the wainscot panels oversize and trim them to fit; cut the mitered edges with a razor blade by holding the blade broadside to the panel end at the desired angle and pressing it through the material. Glue the panels to the floorpiece, and clean the paint from the corresponding gluing surface (bay window-opening angle trim) of the front wall by gently scraping with a razor blade; do not dig into the wood, though, because it is not necessary to

Stations in traditional materials

11

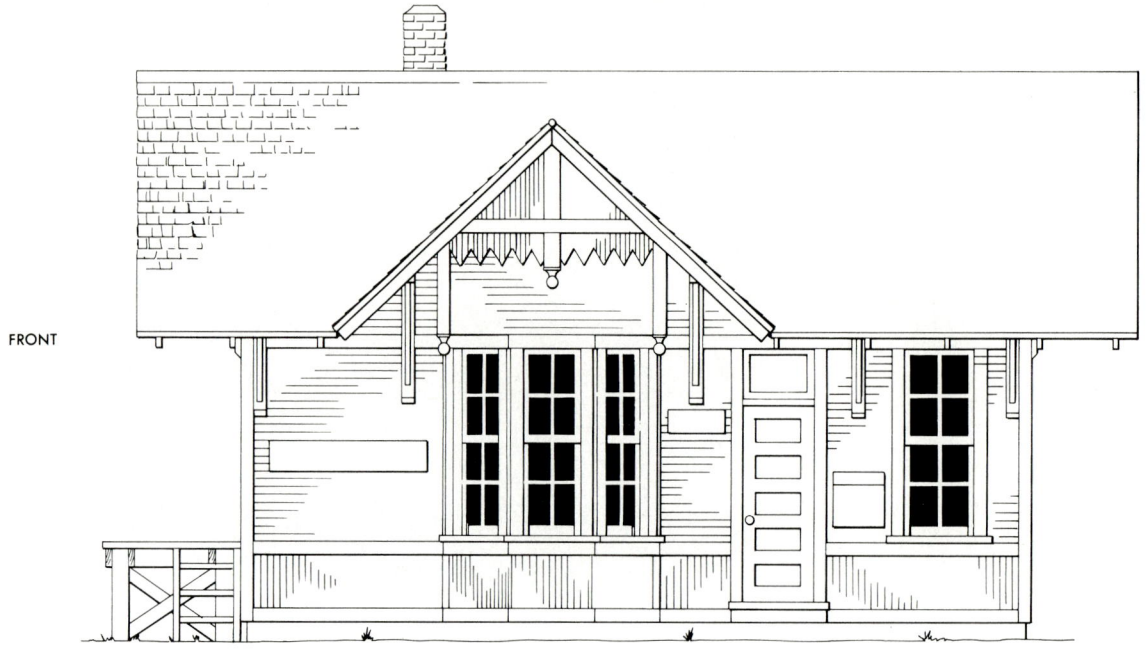

FRONT

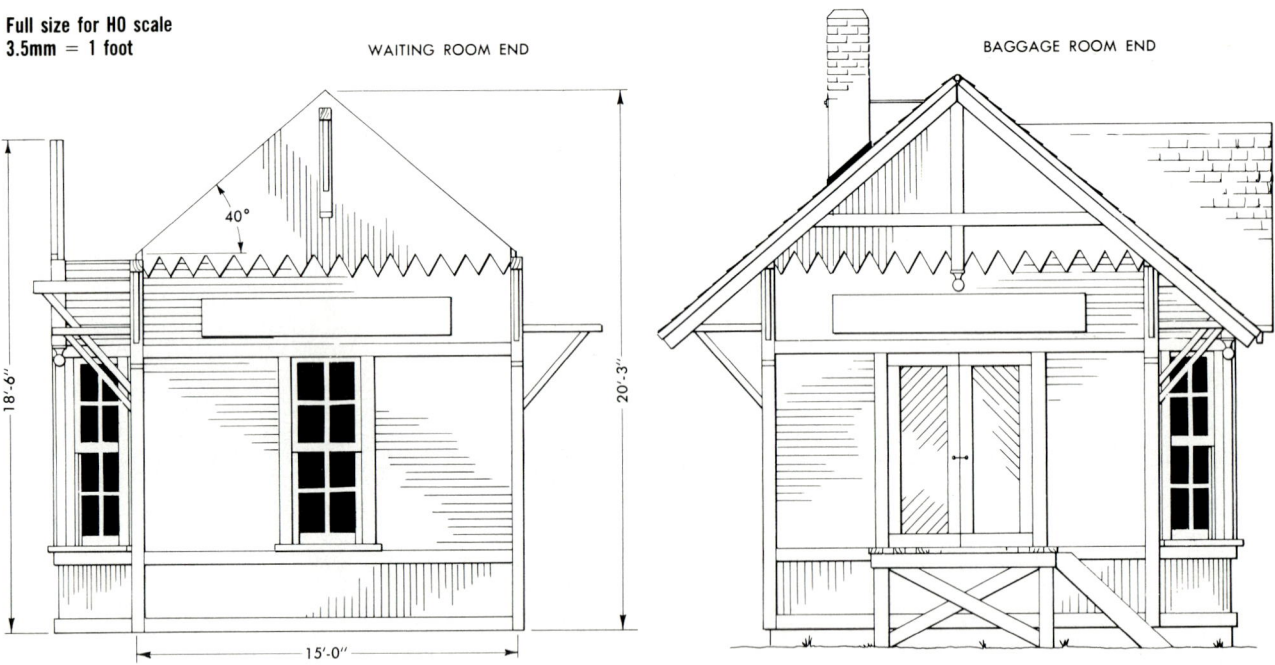

Full size for HO scale
3.5mm = 1 foot

WAITING ROOM END

BAGGAGE ROOM END

remove all traces of paint. Glue the bay window wainscot assembly to the building.

Make the bay window gable end next. It has a 42-degree pitch, so make a different gable template for it. Laminate the bay gable valance as you did the other gable ends. Cut the side, back, and bottom panels and paint the scribed sides of all except the back one. Glue this assembly together.

Fit the second bay window floorpiece with angle trim as shown in fig. 2; this is the top part for the bay window frames. Center this subassembly and glue it in place under the bay gable. Cut two 12 x 12 wall stiffeners the height of the main wall and glue them in place just inside the bay window opening, using the trim as a guide. Scrape the paint from the back of the bay gable and the gluing surface on the front wall and glue the bay gable in place. After the glue is dry, prepare the bay window framing by carefully cutting six pieces of trim stock to achieve a press fit between the upper trim on the wainscot panels and the trim that makes the top of the window frames. Fit the center window frame first, and put a dab of glue on the inside of the angle trim at top and bottom. Do the same for the other two windows.

Prepaint 50 feet of 3 x 12 stock with trim color on one side and the edges. Cut windowsills 4 feet long and notch them to fit each window. Scrape paint from the base panel trim at the bottom of each window before gluing the sills in place on all windows, then touch up any trim that needs it.

Baggage room wall and floor

If you plan to add interior detail, install the baggage room wall and floor now, fig. 3. First add a 12 x 12 gluing block to the back wall directly across from the front wall stiffener nearest the baggage end of the station. Cut the baggage room floor from 6" scribed sheetwood, notched to clear the 12 x 12

Stations in traditional materials

12

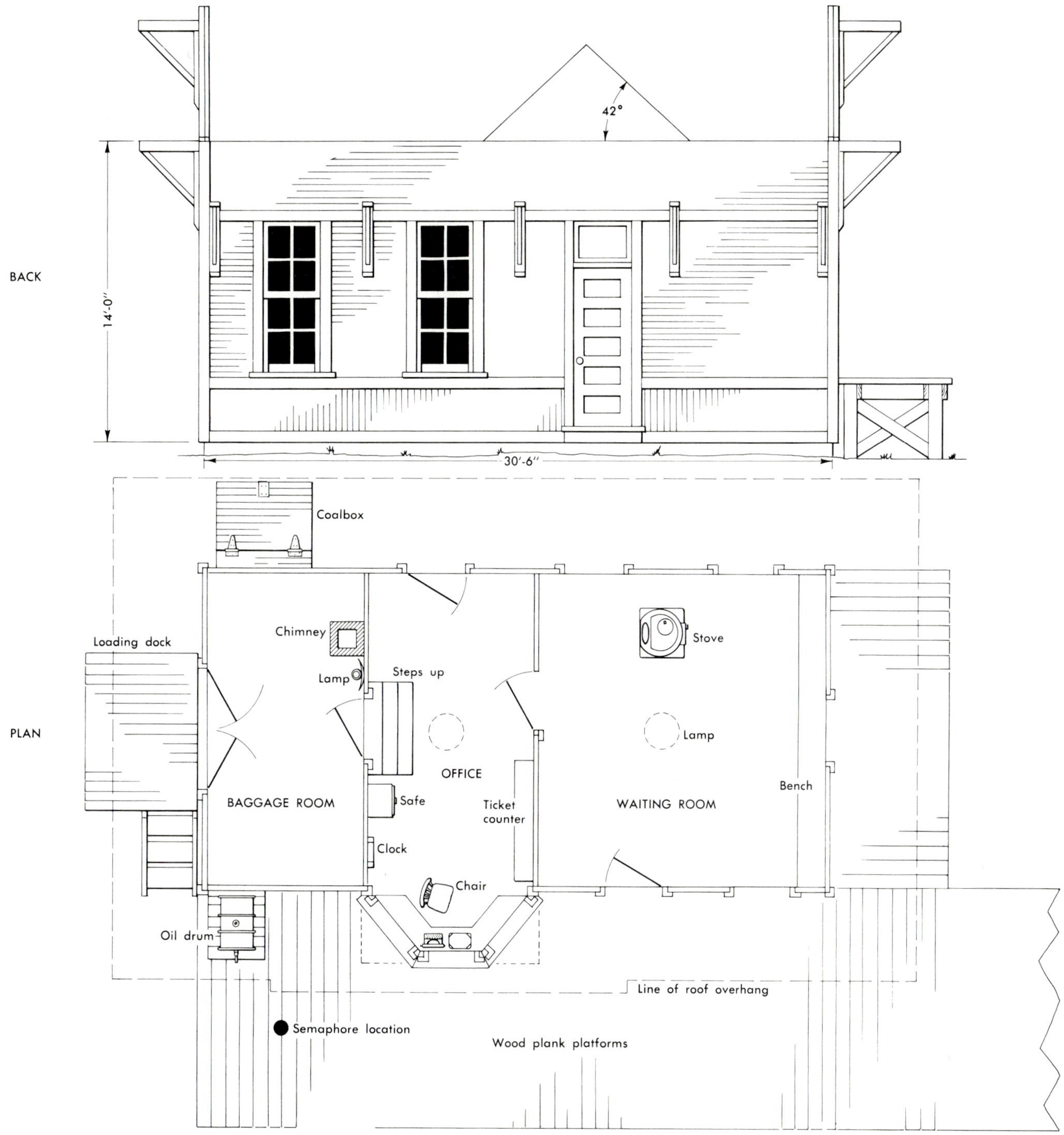

blocks, and stain it. Cut two 24"-high risers from scrap 6" stock and cement them to the main floor at the edges of the baggage room, then glue the baggage floor to them.

Cut the interior baggage room wall, including the door opening, and paint the scribed side. Add a 12 x 12 stiffener to the top edge, and frame the doorjamb with prepainted angle trim. Paint the rear side of the wall leaving a 12" strip along each outer edge for glue; when the paint is dry, cement the wall in place. Cut the door sill from prepainted 3 x 12 and glue in place.

Roof

Cut the large pieces needed for the roof, fig. 4, from 3"-thick, 9" scribed siding, and rule the unscribed side of the stock with lines spaced 9" apart as shingle positioning guides. Paint the underside (the scribed surface) with your upper wall color, and while this dries cut two roof stiffeners from 6"-thick stock using your 40-degree gable angle template as a guide. These stiffening blocks should be a snug fit inside the gable walls, as the roof will not be glued in place.

Glue the stiffening blocks between the roof halves, and when the glue has set on the stiffener joints turn the roof upside down and run a small bead of white glue along the full length of the inside ridge. After this bead has set, place the roof on the building.

Make the gable roof over the bay window from the same materials as the main roof, and trial fit the parts where they will intersect the main roof. Be sure that the ridge is level and that the gable pitch matches the bay window. Glue the gable roof in place on the main roof.

Detailing

Begin detailing the structure by simulating rafter ends with 3 x 6 stock. Prepaint 300 running feet of stock on

Stations in traditional materials

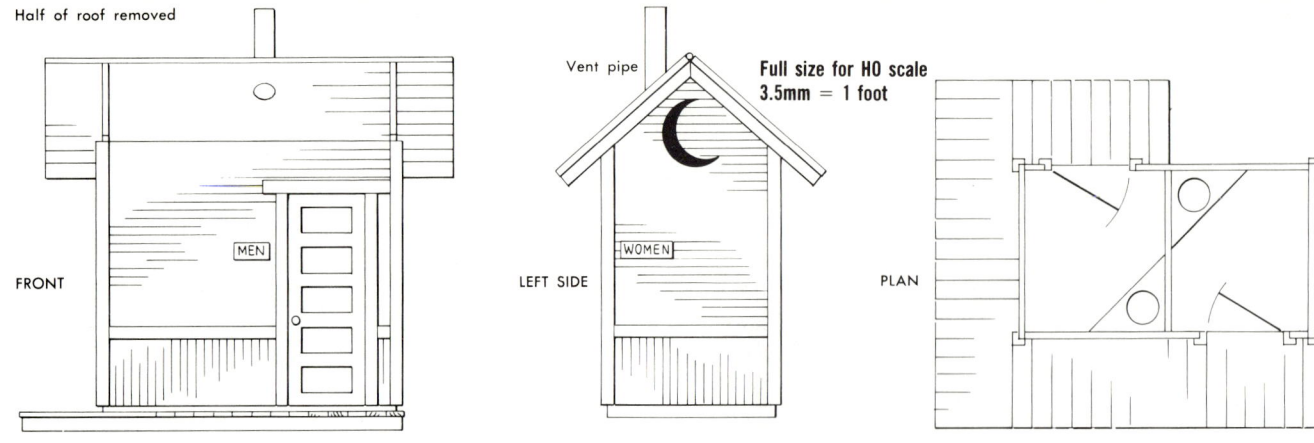

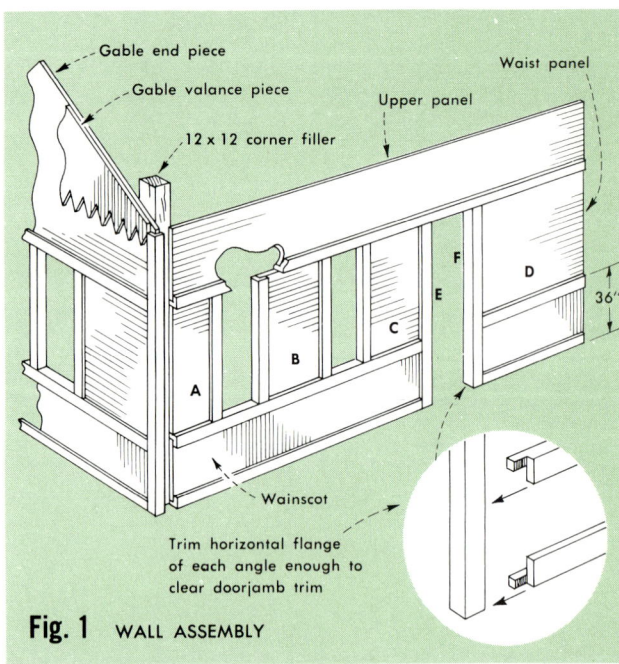

Fig. 1 WALL ASSEMBLY

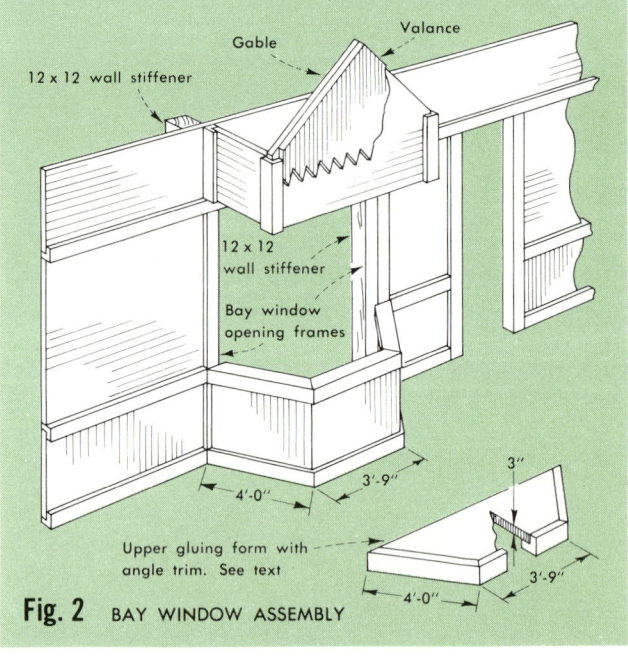

Fig. 2 BAY WINDOW ASSEMBLY

both flanks and one edge, and while the paint dries prepare the cutting guide shown in fig. 5. On a sheet of paper draw two lines crossing at a 90-degree angle and a third line at 40 degrees. Use this guide to cut one end of the rafters, but leave the pieces long so they can be trimmed in place. The six rafters that go under the gables are long; all others are dummies—they stop at the building walls. These short ones are best glued in place with the building upside down and the roof in place. This way, the 50-degree angled ends butt against the walls and help keep the roof aligned. Mark the positions and use a rubbery contact cement like Goo, Pliobond, or Weldwood to install the rafters.

After all rafters—including the two over the bay window—are in place, install the ornamental framing in the gables. You will need 100 feet of prepainted 6 x 6 stock. Cut the two horizontal span pieces for the end gables first, again using the crossed-line cutting guide. Cut each end to a 40-degree angle, using the other side of the 90-degree angle to make a sharper point than for the rafter ends. Cut a notch 3" deep and 6" wide into the center of the horizontal span timber to accept the vertical timber. Cut the vertical pieces oversize, and measure up from the bottom of the pieces 3 feet and cut a notch 3" deep and 6" wide. Saddle the horizontal and vertical pieces together with a dab of glue, square them up, and let the joint dry on each assembly. Make the smaller bay window decorative framing the same way.

Install the ornamental framework by trimming the upper end of the vertical member until all three framing ends touch the roof, then glue in place. The ball at the bottom of the vertical framing is made from a scale handrail stanchion filled with glue and filed round. Drill a hole into the end of each vertical, glue the stanchion in place, and paint it the same color as the trim.

Also place a ball at each corner of the bay window soffit.

Make the chimney from 18 x 18 stock; you can carve and paint the bricks as I did, or cover the wood form with brick

Stations in traditional materials

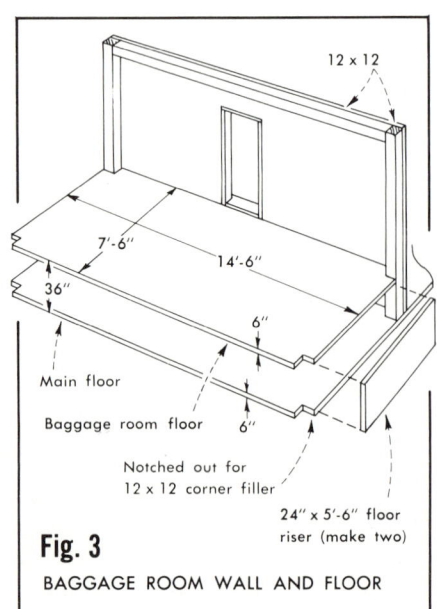

Fig. 3 BAGGAGE ROOM WALL AND FLOOR

14

MODELING SUGGESTION

By nature we tend to make parts one at a time as we need them while assembling a structure. However, don't overlook the possibility that some other way might be more fun and produce a better model. In this story the author does not do the obvious thing next. He paints most parts before gluing them together—even before cutting them to size. Sometimes he doesn't cut a piece until it has been installed. He assembles the station walls and floor before installing the bay window. Try these ideas on several structures. Once you discipline yourself to think "Would this assembly or trimming job be better done now or later?" you may find ways of modeling that are more fun and that work better.

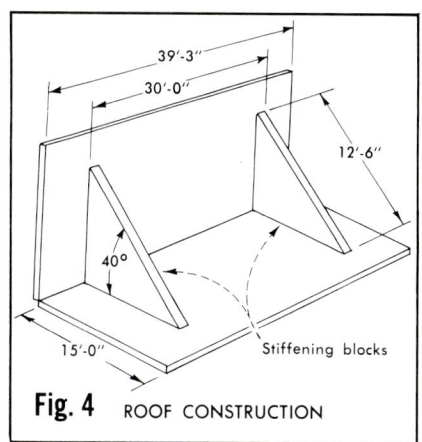

Fig. 4 ROOF CONSTRUCTION

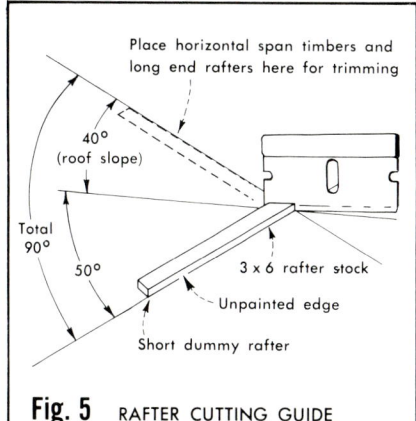

Fig. 5 RAFTER CUTTING GUIDE

Stations in traditional materials

15

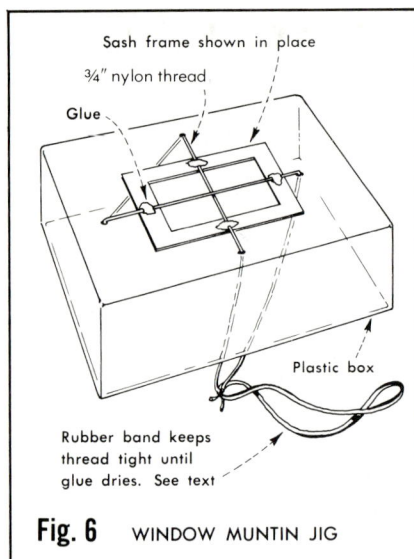

Fig. 6 WINDOW MUNTIN JIG

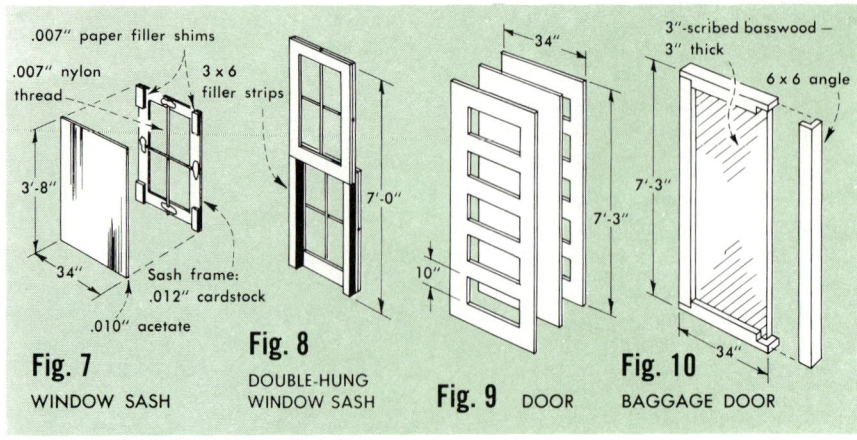

Fig. 7 WINDOW SASH

Fig. 8 DOUBLE-HUNG WINDOW SASH

Fig. 9 DOOR

Fig. 10 BAGGAGE DOOR

paper or embossed brick sheet. For realism, add a sooty flue to the top of the chimney by heating a 9"-square metal bar red hot and pressing it into the wood. Cut a 40-degree angle on the bottom end of the chimney, drill a 1½"-diameter hole through it for the wire chimney brace, and add the piece to the roof.

Next, shingle the roof. I used slate-gray-colored bond paper cut into slotted strips and applied over the roof guidelines; commercial shingles can also be used.

Window sash

There are a number of ways to make window sash. While I feel my method works well in HO scale, if you are modeling in a different size I suggest you make a trial assembly before committing yourself for all 14 sashes. Cut the sash frames from 1" Strathmore stock and paint the outside faces with the trim color.

Next make a jig for assembling and gluing the sash frames, fig. 6. Scratch two lines at right angles on the top of a small clear plastic box. Drill four holes—two on each of the lines—through the plastic. The holes should be large enough to accept your muntin material, and spaced to clear a sash frame. Run a scale ¾"-diameter thread through the holes to form a cross, tie the ends to a rubber band, and pull the thread tight by wrapping the rubber band around the box and hooking it over the box latch.

To use the jig, put a sash frame, painted side down, under the threads and align it. Put a dab of household cement over the thread to hold it to the sash frame, fig. 6. After the cement dries, cut away the excess thread and paint the thread muntins with the trim color.

Next comes glazing. Glue four ¾" paper shims (the same thickness as the thread diameter) to the back of the sash frame—one in each corner, fig. 7. Cut a window pane the same size as the sash frame from thin clear plastic, put dabs of contact-type cement on each of the four shims, and press the sash onto the window pane to complete the subassembly.

The bottom sash of a double-hung window is inside the upper sash; for a closed window put the bottom edge of the upper sash frame over the upper edge of the lower frame, fig. 8. Cut two prepainted 3 x 3 filler strips to the length of the bottom sash and glue them to the front side of the bottom sash, the same distance apart as the inside dimension of the window frame.

Glue together the upper and lower sashes, and position them over the inside of the window frames, resting on the sill. Work from inside the building and use a toothpick to put six small dabs of white glue around each window sash assembly to hold it to the frame.

Doors

Make three doors, fig. 9, from prepainted 1"-thick cardstock glued together with a contact-type adhesive. Use the head of a small pin for a doorknob, or turn your own from brass. I glued the back door closed and the inside baggage room door partly open, but made the front door movable so that it can be opened to show the ticket office, but closed for certain photos. To build a movable door, cut a length of a 1½"-diameter wire 6" longer than the door at both top and bottom, and glue it to the

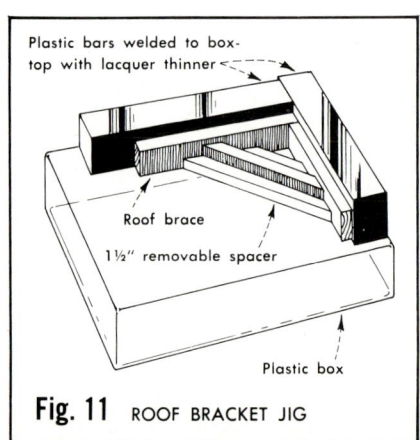

Fig. 11 ROOF BRACKET JIG

Stations in traditional materials

16

edge of the door as a long hinge pin. Drill a hole in the floor for the bottom extension, and fit a notched scrap of 3 x 6 above the door.

Do not install movable doors until you have installed the transom windows. Make the transom windows from Strathmore stock frames and clear plastic window glazing and glue them in place using the doors as positioning guides. Make the two outside baggage room doors from sheetwood scribed on 3" centers. Lay out these doors so that the grooves run at 45-degree angles, 90 degrees to each other. Paint the door panels the upper wall color and frame them with prepainted 6" angle trim before installation, fig. 10.

Final details

The braces under the eaves are each made of three pieces. All of the vertical and most of the horizontal members are 3 x 6 stock; the horizontal members at the gabled end corners and on each side of the bay gable are 6 x 6. Do not prepaint any of the horizontal or vertical stock because the paint would weaken the glued joints, but prepaint about 175 feet of 3 x 3 for the diagonal pieces. Draw crossed lines at 45 degrees and use the sketch as a cutting guide.

Construct a jig, fig. 11, to assemble the roof braces. Because white glue does not stick to plastic, make the jig from small plastic bars glued to the top of a plastic box. Mark the positions for the braces on the walls with a pencil, and notch the upper trim on the front and back walls to clear the vertical brace members. Place the roof on the building and make sure it is seated properly, then glue the roof braces in place, using your pencil marks and the roof as a guide. Use a contact adhesive, and remember that the braces must fit up against the roof to look right.

I made my station signs photographically, but would recommend decals or dry-transfer lettering for those without access to a darkroom. The station platform is made from stained 3 x 9 planks, but brick, cement, cinder, and even gravel platforms were common at this type of station.

Two grain-of-wheat bulbs—one high over the waiting room and the other over the ticket office—do a fine job of lighting up the interior of my station. These bulbs should be kept high enough so they can't be seen through the windows, but if you want the effect of kerosene lamps, hang two or three bulbs about 7 feet from the floor so they *can* be seen. Connect this low string of bulbs in series so they burn with a dim yellow glow, and consider adding small shades to better their appearance. A warm yellow kerosene platform lamp will also add realism; connect it in series with the dim bulbs inside to further reduce the voltage for a pleasing glow.

Complete your station by building up a kerosene drum and coalbox, adding interior detail, and considering a train-order signal for the front platform. I glued my station platforms—along with the one for the outhouse—in place on my layout, but left the structures portable so that they can be removed for track maintenance and general cleaning.

Stations in traditional materials

17

All photos by the author unless otherwise credited.

A shelter for any station

It can be a wayside halt all by itself, a platform opposite a main building, or a shelter on a remote track in a terminal

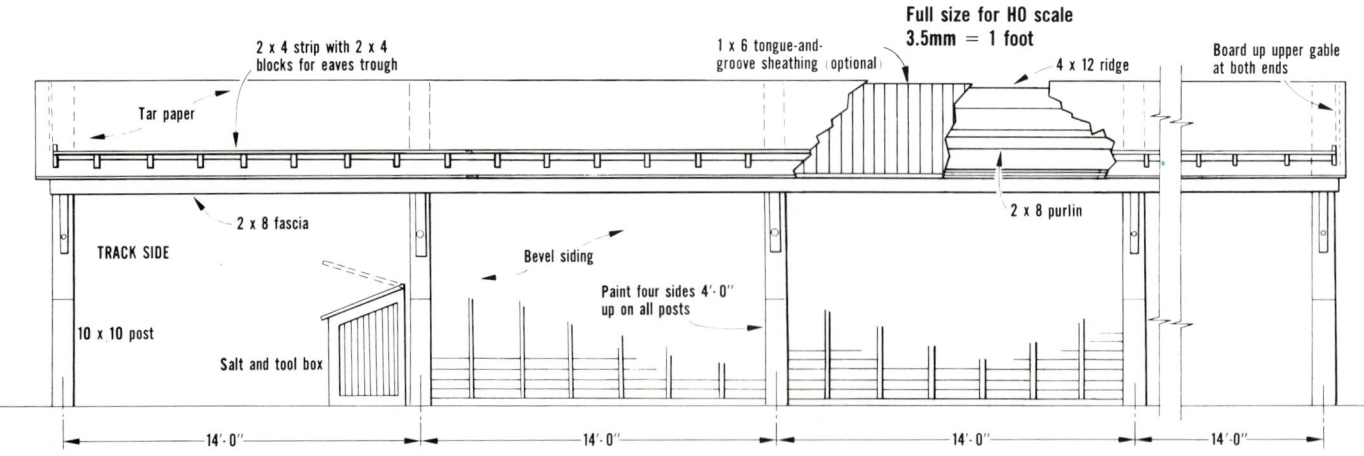

Stations in traditional materials

by F. L. Hendren

HERE'S a structure every pike can use—perhaps several of them—in any shape, size, or color that suits your fancy and space. The design is based upon a standard Chicago, Burlington & Quincy (now Burlington Northern) Chicago commuter division prototype at West Hinsdale, Ill., and similar structures are found everywhere. They are usually located across the tracks from a larger station building, especially on double-track lines. If you run an interurban line you can use shelters like this one in pairs, one structure on each side of the track.

These passenger shelters are still

18

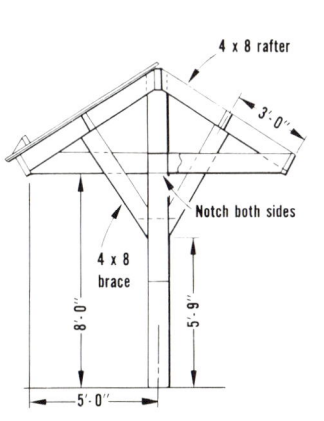

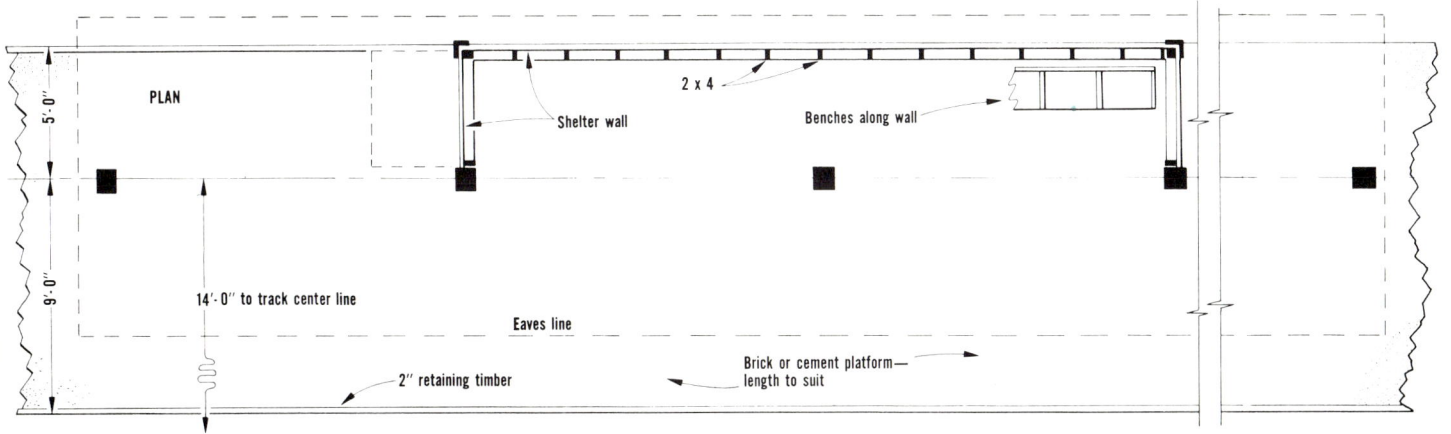

doing their job in commuter service near large cities. They give commuters a place to huddle under on a rainy or snowy or windy morning. Even with dieselization and the demise of passenger service, such a shelter will still provide a bit of atmosphere in the form of a wayside relic.

I resorted to the scrapbox to select materials for this project. I chose some hefty timbers like 10 x 10 posts, and 4 x 6, 4 x 8, and 4 x 12 stock. These sizes can be varied, depending on your supply; but remember, build it good and solid so you won't ever have to call the repair crew to prop it up. This kind of thinking explains why many a trackside shelter is still standing.

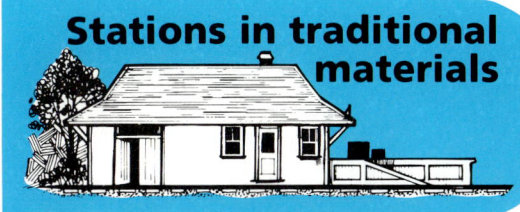

Stations in traditional materials

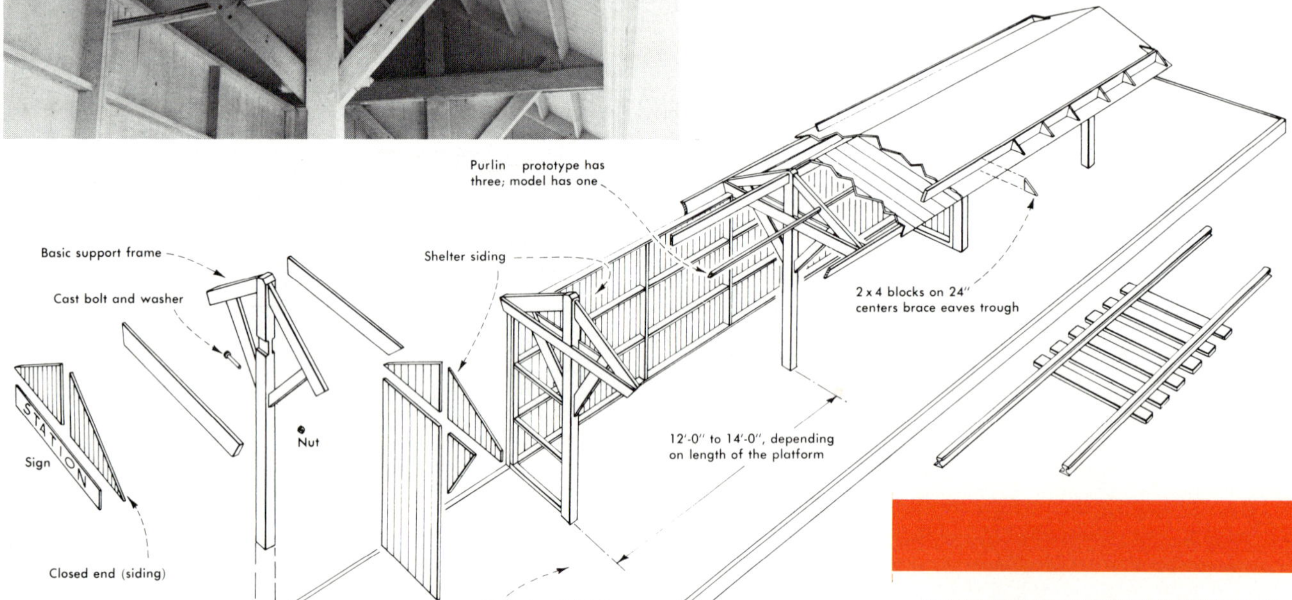

A NOTE ON WEST HINSDALE

This tiny shelter was only one part of the passenger facilities at West Hinsdale, Ill., a commuter stop 18 miles west of Chicago on the Chicago-Aurora main line. A substantial station with upstairs quarters stood on the other side of the tracks until the 1960's. Drawings for the main station are in Kalmbach's **RAILROAD STATION PLANBOOK**.

Stations in traditional materials

Robert Bullerman.

20

After selecting your lumber stock, lay out a post and truss pattern suited to your modeling scale. Cut the timbers to length over your drawing. Pin or cement scrap blocks in place on the drawing to form a jig so the supporting units will be exactly alike. You need a minimum of five roof posts with trusses for each shelter you plan to build here, so the common pin jig (see sidebar) is a timesaver here.

Use any smooth-surface material 12" to 18" thick as a base for the platform. Cut it straight or gently curved to fit your trackside space. The platform can be of brick, blacktop, cement, wood, or gravel. If you simulate gravel, build a creosoted timber enclosure to confine the loose material. I used balsa painted dark gray, edged with strips stained black. Using a sharp knife, cut postholes in the platform on 14-foot centers to fit the roof supports. Be sure all posts stand vertical and at the same height, and cement the supports firmly in place.

Next tie the supports together with a ridgepole and add purlins and fascia boards. In the photo of the prototype structure you will notice three purlins as well as the fascia on each side of the center post. Since only a stray ant would ever be able to check this point on a model, I show only one purlin on the drawing. If you're building for a contest, follow the photo and include all the purlins and other small parts.

If your pike represents a southern railroad through swamp country, you can build the roof now to complete the structure. However, if your railroad represents a more northerly prototype where rain turns to snow and howling blizzards sweep across the prairie, you should add some windscreen walls for passenger protection.

To do this, create one long wall by paneling in two or three bays and two short end walls using a simple 2 x 4 frame covered with board siding. This step should be completed before putting on the roof. If you add the windscreen walls you should also include the tool and salt box.

The roof consists of tongue-and-groove siding covered with tar paper. I used Strathmore bristol board painted black. An interesting part of the prototype is the eaves trough and downspout system. Here the old CB&Q structure builders outdid themselves. A plain 2 x 4 was laid along the eaves and braced with 2 x 4 blocks on 2" centers, tarred in place: a bit primitive, perhaps, but economical and efficient. After installing the roof, paint the station and add station signs. Then spot passenger figures here and there: They can be standing or lolling on a bench. A few ads or posters cemented to the inside back wall of the shelter will add a realistic touch.

The color you paint your wayside shelter is up to you. When I took the photos the shelter was ivory trimmed in dark green; it is likely to be a different color the next time the maintenance crew comes down the line. If you have a standard color for railroad structures, by all means use it. However, using a separate color for trim adds to the detail effect of the model and helps make the railroad seem less compressed.

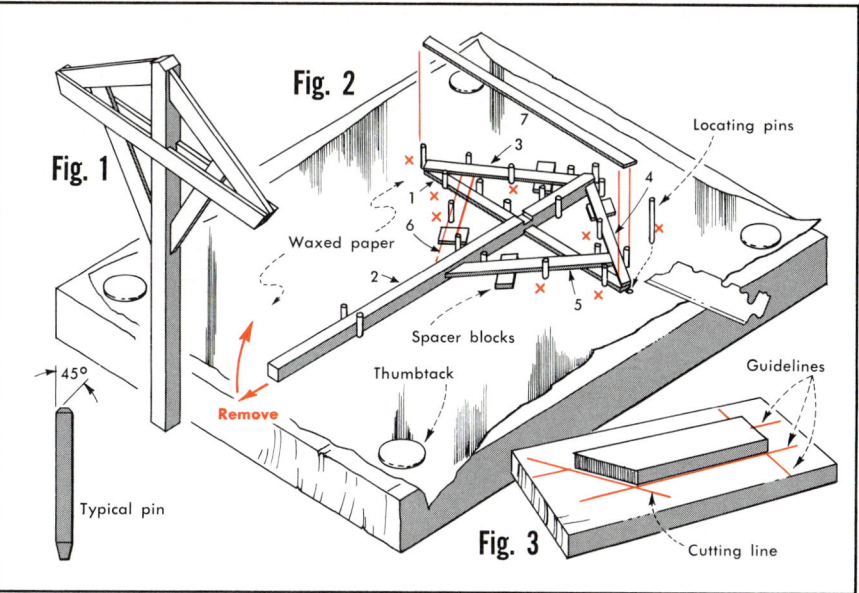

MAKING A PIN JIG

Jigs are used extensively in industry to hold parts during assembly and manufacture. They allow a large number of identical pieces or assemblies to be produced.

One of the simpler ones is a pin jig. It consists of a number of pegs secured in holes in a plate or a block of wood. The pegs hold pieces to be assembled until cement or solder sets. Metal pins in a hardwood block are a suitable combination, but any combinations of metal, wood, and plastic can be used to suit individual requirements. Common pins that can be pushed into wood are often adequate. Wood can be used even when soldering, providing there isn't so much heat applied that the wood is damaged.

The base of this jig is a flat wood block, preferably hardwood. Lay the support out on the board full size. To secure the pieces, drill holes that are slightly smaller than the pin diameter for a press fit. Use a drill press if you have one so the holes will be perpendicular. Pins 1/16" in diameter are large enough for most jobs. Cut the heads off the pins and chamfer the top edges to remove any burrs that could keep the assembled piece from being removed easily.

If you are going to use cement, tack down or tape waxed paper over the wood base and drive the locating pins through it. The only other parts required are spacer blocks or pads which hold various assembly members in place. In the case shown, these blocks are equal to the thickness of pieces 1 and 7 in fig. 2. I prefer metal spacers, since metal pieces will lie flat of their own accord; paper and wood spacers are easily dislodged.

All parts can be precut to size. Fig. 3 shows a simple cutting template consisting of lines drawn on a block of wood. The pieces are laid in place and trimmed with a cutting instrument. A more elaborate jig for this purpose would provide small blocks of wood to position the pieces.

Part 1 in fig. 2 is positioned first. Then part 2 is cemented to it. Parts 3, 4, 5, and 6 are added, using spacer blocks to hold them at proper height. Part 7 is cemented in place last. Use cement sparingly.

If the jig is not too complicated, finished pieces can be lifted straight out. However, there are sometimes so many components that the assembly cannot be removed without damage unless you make several pins removable. In the sample, those marked X could be made a little loose by drilling the associated holes slightly larger.

Cement sometimes oozes from the joints and affixes the assembly to the jig. The purpose of the waxed paper is to prevent this from happening. If, however, part of the assembly adheres to the jig, break a double-edge razor blade to the shape shown in fig. 2 and slide it under the joint to loosen the assembly.

Stations in traditional materials

All photos by the author.

Ticket to Tomahawk

Scratchbuilding an eye-catching station with a material that combines the virtues of metal with the workability of wood and card

by Alan Armitage

AS buildings go, my Thunder River Railroad's depot at Tomahawk is not an especially prepossessing or magnificently imposing edifice. But something about it—perhaps some quality of composition in its design, a certain indefinable character in its style—has made the structure a longtime favorite of mine. In all my years of chasing trains, no other station has quite captured my fancy like this one.

The design for the model was taken from Boston & Maine's Greenwood station, which formerly served the B&M Portland Division at Wakefield, Mass. In the old days the structure trembled to the thunder of P-4 Pacifics, T-1 Berkshires and the glorious R-1 Mountain types with their deep baritone chimes. In more recent times the growling rumble and blatant voice of F7's rattled the windows.

Though I have no definite knowledge of just when the station was built, my guess would be somewhere around the turn of the century. I have no drawings of the prototype dimensions, only recollections, so I cannot vouch for precise accuracy in the model. As you may notice, I have taken a few liberties with the design to suit my purposes, but I tried to retain the essence of the architecture as well as the general configuration of the building.

The original structure was strictly a commuter station and had no baggage room. I added baggage facilities with doors at the west end of the station. I

Studies in styrene

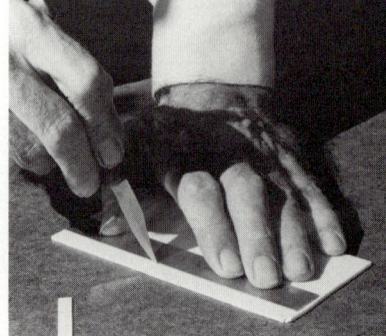
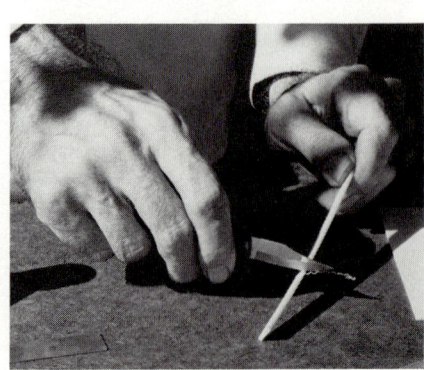

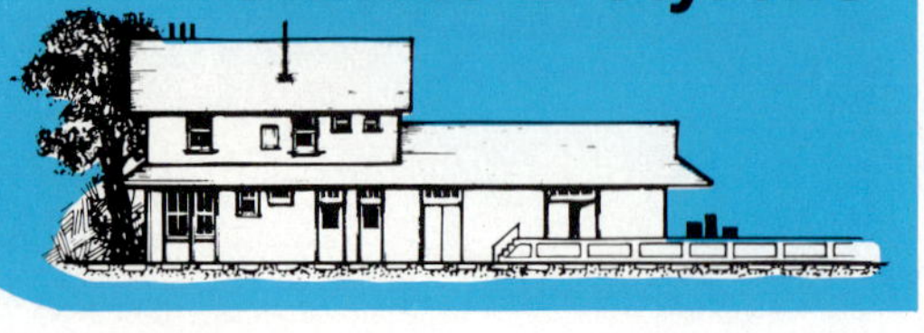

22

was not happy with this arrangement, however, so I changed the drawing to show sliding baggage doors at the west end of the station front. You can build the station as it was originally by merely repeating the detail on the east end in mirror reverse.

Drawings are printed full size for HO and N scales, with dimensions in scale feet and inches for the convenience of those modeling in other scales. Decimal dimensions in the text and on the figures refer to the stock thicknesses used on my HO model.

Working with styrene

My instructions are based on the use of polystyrene, a common plastic. Although you may substitute other materials, they will require a slightly different approach, so plan your fabricating procedures according to the demands and limitations of the material you choose. If styrene is new to you, I strongly urge that you give it a try. In more than 20 years of model making I have never used a more versatile, workable material. Almost anything on your railroad—buildings, cars, and even locomotives—can be made better and easier from polystyrene. Projects in styrene can be done in less time and with less effort than projects in other materials, and the finished product will be a clean-cut model with sharp detail.

Styrene cuts easily, scribes beautifully, has no grain, and can be drilled and tapped more readily than metal. Moisture and atmospheric change have no effect on styrene, a characteristic strongly favoring its use in the humid basements where many model layouts are found. While styrene can be machined like metal, hand tools are all that are required for most projects. A sharp knife with a thin blade, a metal straightedge, dividers, drills, tweezers, files, and an easy-to-make scribing tool are all you'll need for Tomahawk station; most of these are probably already on your workbench, and we'll make the scribing tool when we need it. Styrene is soft and tends to "load up" your files, so keep a file card handy to clean them, and choose files that have fairly coarse teeth.

One of the nicest things about styrene is the ease and rapidity with which individual parts can be produced once you are familiar with the material. Thin stock can be cut with a knife on a hardwood cutting board. Thicker sizes should be scored with several cuts and then snapped with the fingers or broken in a vise. After breaking the stock along the scored line the edge will be rough, but it can be smoothed and squared with a knife or file. Cutting with a knife leaves a raised burr on each side of the cut because material is forced aside by the blade (this is the reason for the thin blade), but the burrs are quickly shaved away by scraping with the edge of a knife held at a right angle to the edge.

The best adhesives for styrene work are solvents; they bond by softening the mating surfaces to actually weld them together. The liquid styrene cement sold in hobby shops is a solvent, and it comes with a brush in the cap. Methylethylketone, called MEK or simply ketone, is an industrial solvent that works well

Studies in styrene

and fast, and you may be able to purchase a small amount at a solvent supply house (check your Yellow Pages). The thick styrene cement sold in tubes is useful only for attaching small parts to an already-painted model, and is messy and slow-drying compared to solvents.

Solvents are potent chemicals, so be careful with them around children, and don't use them in a small room without adequate ventilation. Avoid breathing the fumes and keep the liquid away from your eyes. An ideal dispenser for the solvent is a small bottle with a brush in the cap, set into a wood block to prevent spilling. The brush should be small so that you can control the amount of liquid applied to the joint. Capillary action draws the liquid between the surfaces and bonds them almost instantly, although the bond will not harden for a while. Fabrication proceeds as fast as you can make parts, because there is no waiting for joints to set up and no clamping.

For the Tomahawk station you will need high-impact styrene sheet in the following sizes: .010", .015", .020", .040", and .060". These, and .080" stock, are the most useful thicknesses for model work. Styrene is available at many hobby shops, and through plastics supply houses in many cities. Smooth, opaque white sheet stock is best for our purposes. (It is also available in round rod form, ideal for making either hand or machine turnings.)

Wall units

I started this project with the wall unit construction, a lengthy task calling for careful and accurate workmanship because of the numerous joints and subassemblies. Groups of panels make separate wall units; two are shown in fig. 1. The templates show the exact outline size for these wall units, allowing for the overlap and thickness of material specified for HO construction. However, certain inconsistencies are bound to occur in cutting the parts. Any excess can be taken out of wall C to keep the building square. Template A, black, is flopped left-to-right to get the proper window position for the two righthand corners of the station sides. Templates J and K are also flopped for opposite end corners.

I suggest making the walls in pairs (north and south, east and west), matching them for size and squareness. To avoid errors in assembly, mark each

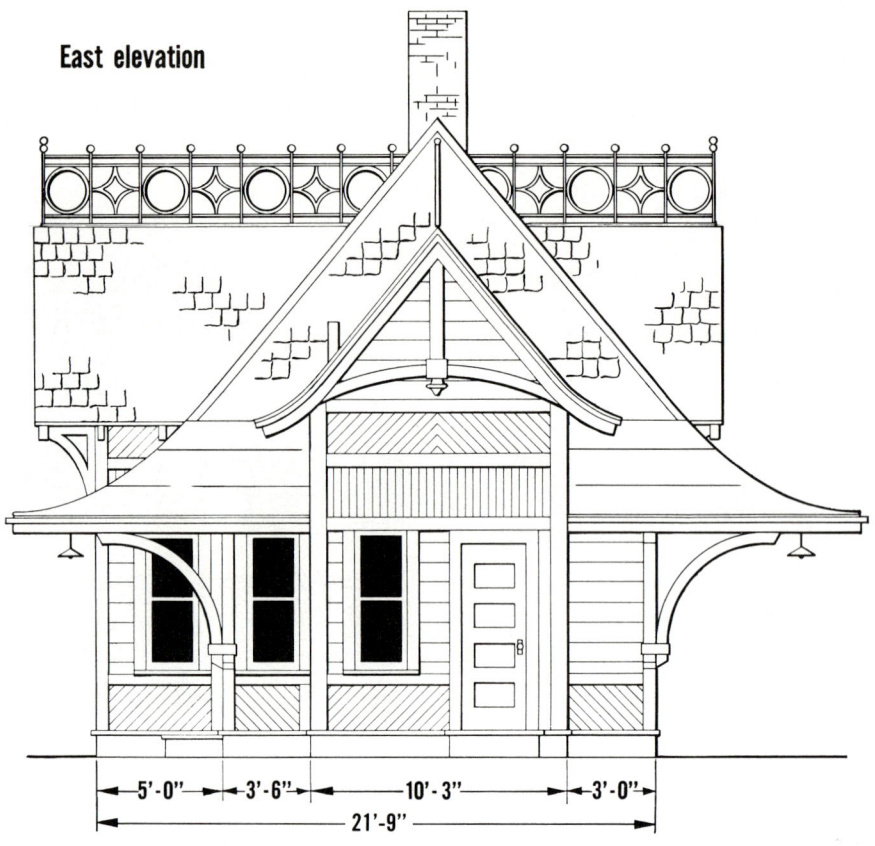

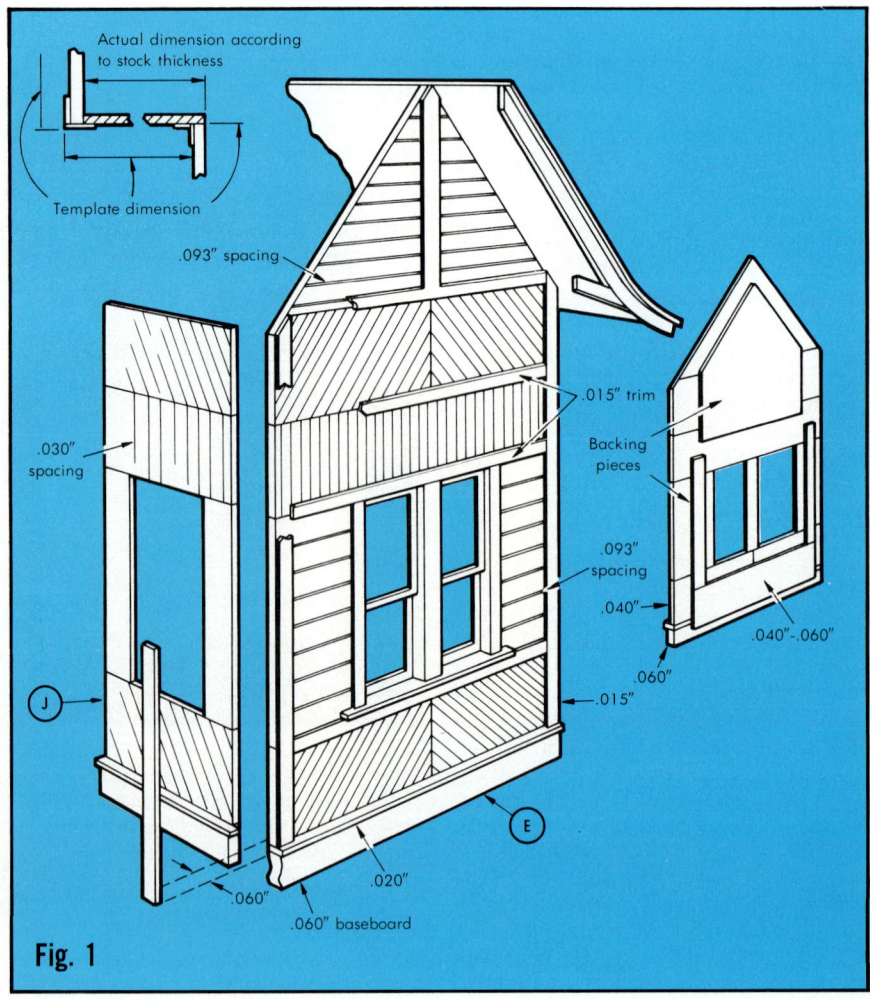

Studies in styrene

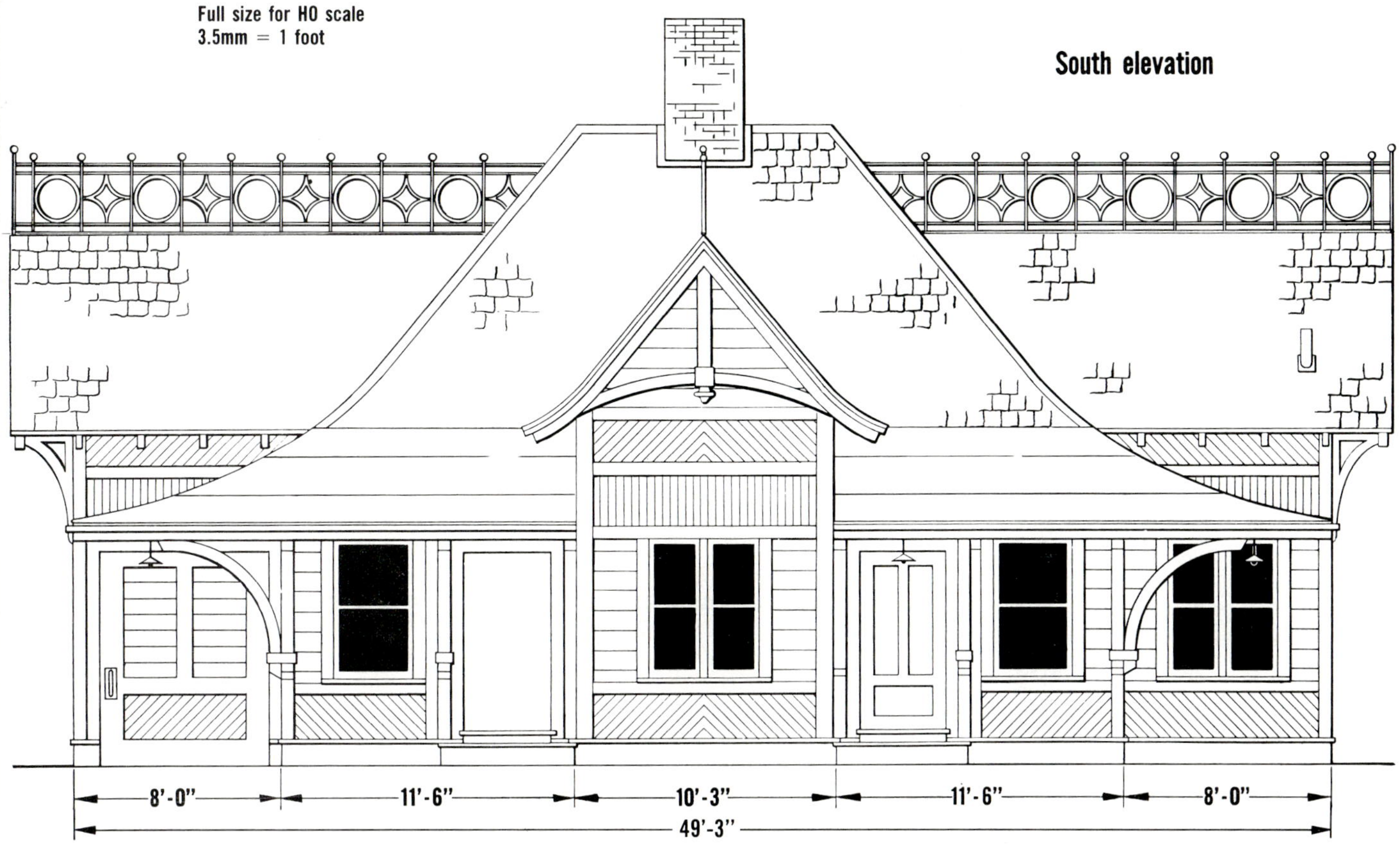

Full size for HO scale
3.5mm = 1 foot

South elevation

8'-0" 11'-6" 10'-3" 11'-6" 8'-0"
49'-3"

with the template letter plus letters SE, SW, etc., for southeast, southwest, etc., quarters of the depot.

Scribe the various types of paneling required on .040" stock. This demands careful layout, then close attention to the layout during the scribing operation in order to achieve evenly spaced grooves. Mark off the spacing by "walking" dividers along one edge of the plastic, pressing the points into the stock as you go. Rub your finger over the holes when you have finished. The dust and dirt from your hands will make the marks readily visible.

This is where that special scribing tool comes into use, so make one as shown in fig. 2 from a dental pick (like mine), a large needle, or an old round file. Grind as shown so the tool will remove material instead of just pushing it aside as an ordinary scriber would do. Make sure the angles of the cutting edges are the same on both sides, so the tool won't tend to pull off to one side in use. Keep the scriber sharp by honing it from time to time, and remove any slight burrs on the edges with a suede brush.

A little practice will show you how to get the best results with the scribing tool. Tape the styrene to a board with a straight edge and use a square as a guide to scribe the grooves as evenly as possible. Don't dig too deep, or the grooves will be too wide. Try to apply equal pressure with each stroke.

The 45-degree-angle grooves run both ways on the paneling, so scribe enough material of each type. You can always find a use for excess scribed stock. Cut the various panel parts and butt-join them with a touch of solvent where they rest against each other. Do the assembly on a sheet of waxed paper laid over the plan. The joints between panels are lapped with styrene strips. It is important that the diagonal scribing run in the proper direction below the window sills and in the gable ends. Note that while the diagonal scribing makes a symmetrical pattern on each side bay and at the west end, the scribing runs in one direction to the door at the east end as shown in the drawings and photos. Complete each wall subassembly, including trim and window sashes, fig. 3, but omit the clear plastic "glass" until the model has been painted. Peel the paper from the

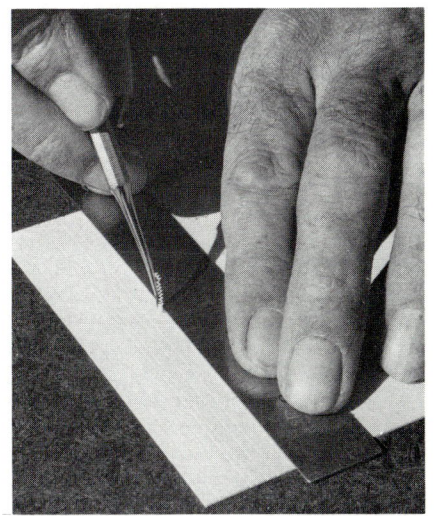

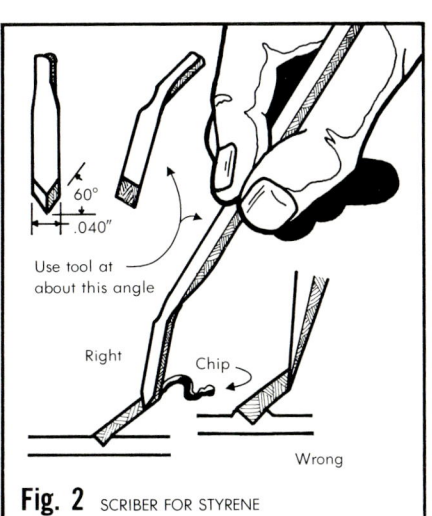

Fig. 2 SCRIBER FOR STYRENE

Studies in styrene

25

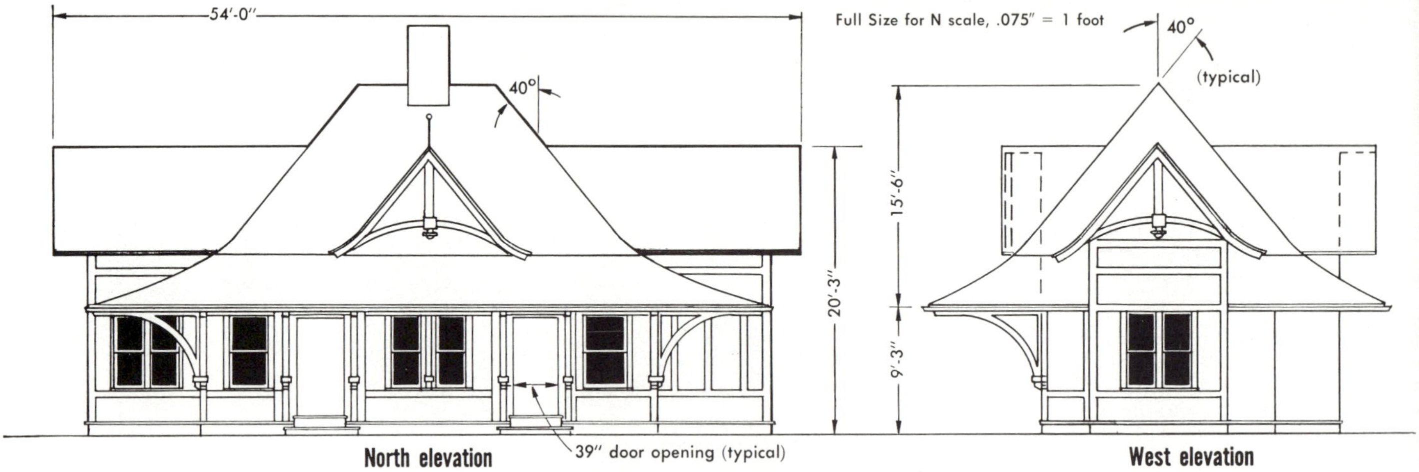

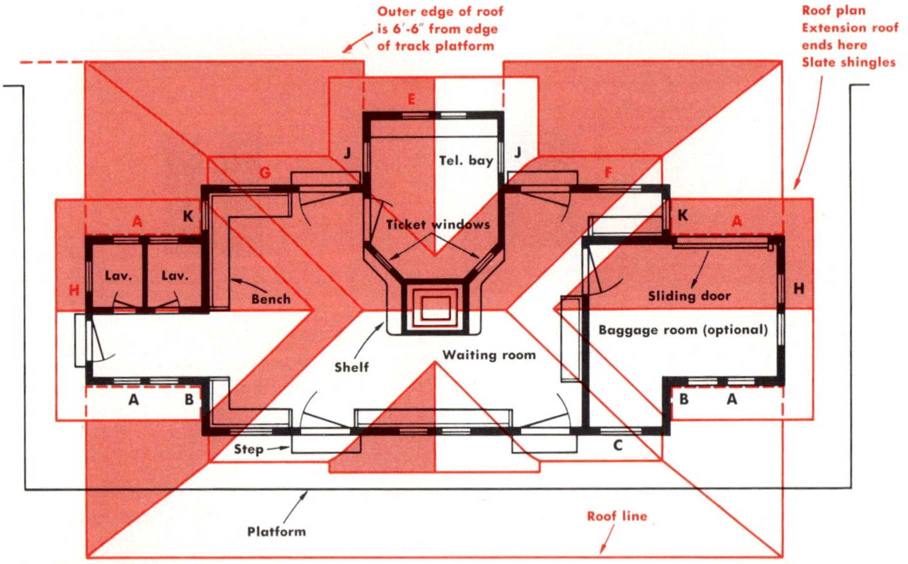

North elevation — 54'-0", 40°, 20'-3", 39" door opening (typical)

Full Size for N scale, .075" = 1 foot

West elevation — 40° (typical), 15'-6", 9'-3"

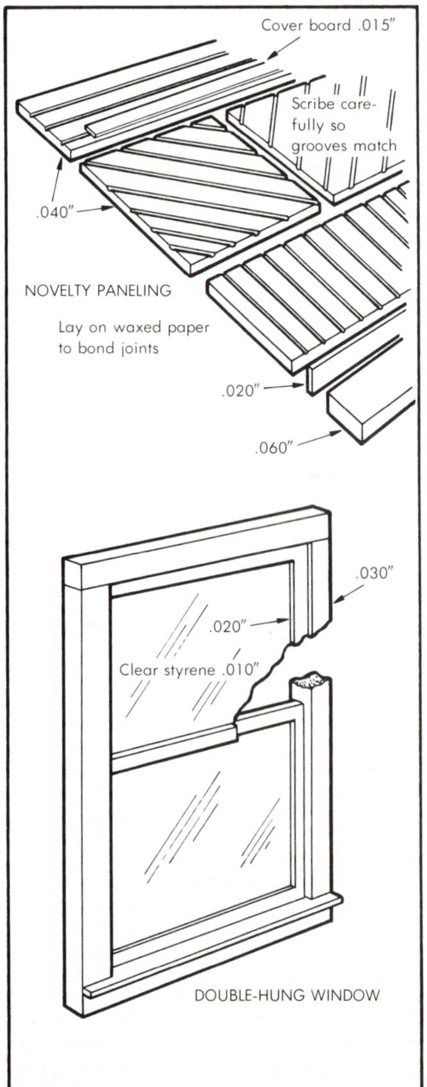

Fig. 3 WINDOW AND PANEL DETAIL

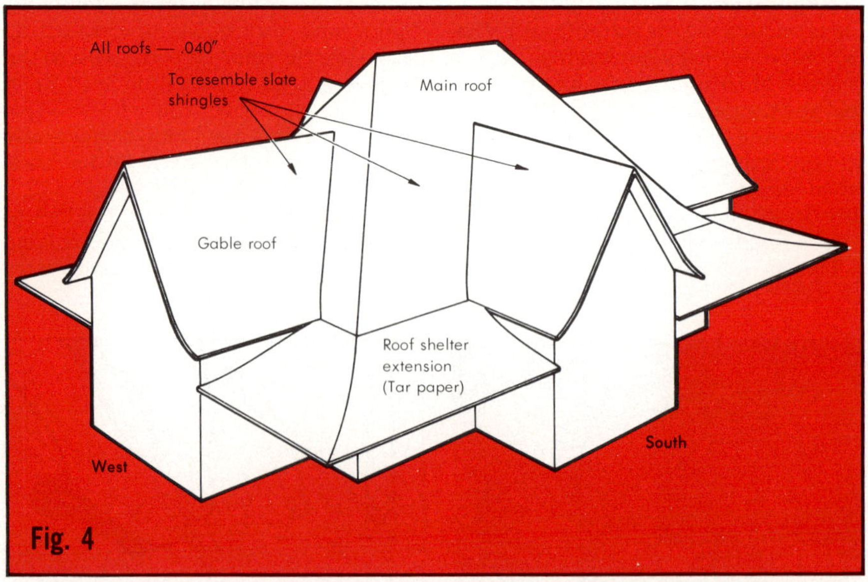

NOVELTY PANELING — Cover board .015", Scribe carefully so grooves match, .040", Lay on waxed paper to bond joints, .020", .060"

DOUBLE-HUNG WINDOW — .030", .020", Clear styrene .010"

Roof plan shows in color, above with room and outer walls indicated in black. Full size for N scale, .075" = 1 foot. Letters are keys to templates. See Fig. 8.

Outer edge of roof is 6'-6" from edge of track platform. Roof plan Extension roof ends here Slate shingles.

Tel. bay, Ticket windows, Lav., Bench, Shelf, Waiting room, Sliding door, Baggage room (optional), Step, Platform, Roof line

Fig. 4 — All roofs — .040", To resemble slate shingles, Main roof, Gable roof, Roof shelter extension (Tar paper), West, South

Studies in styrene

subassemblies and add backing pieces of styrene, fig. 1, to stiffen the walls.

Check against the floor plan as you assemble the wall units. A few accurately cut gussets placed in inside corners help ensure the building's squareness. This is important.

After the wall units have been assembled into a completed wall structure, it is a good idea to cut and fit the floor while you can still get at the inside of the model. Make the floor a snug fit, but removable from inside the walls, and it will hold the building in place without further fastening. It is easier to install or repair lighting if a structure is not permanently attached to its base.

If you want to include interior parti-

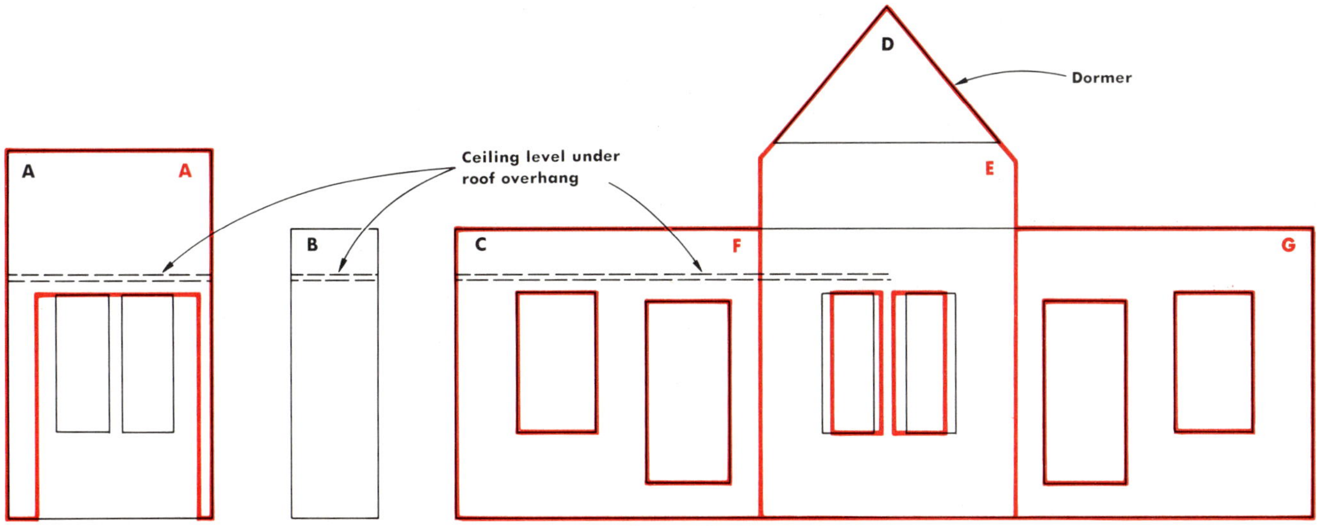

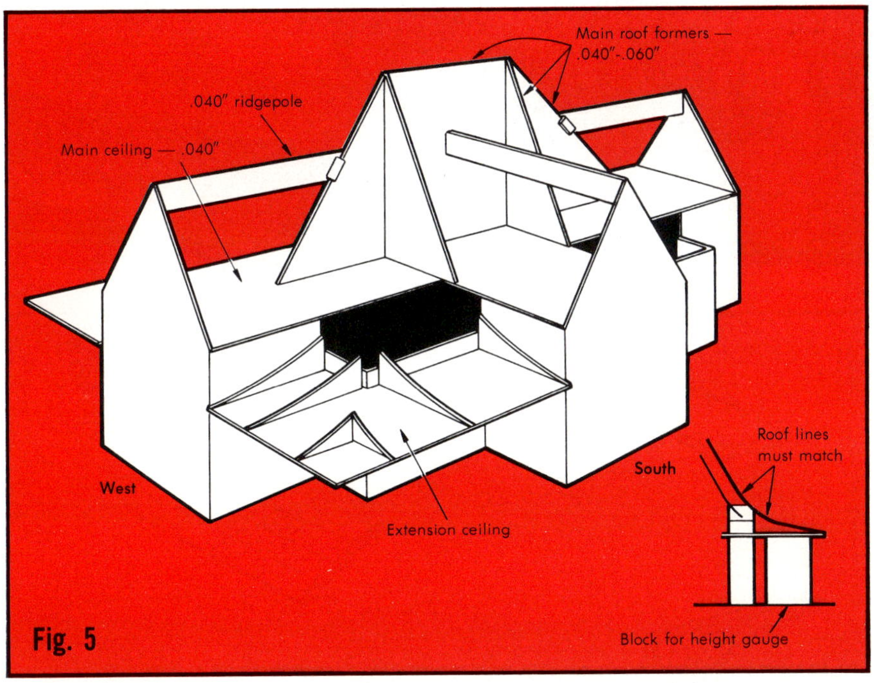

Fig. 5

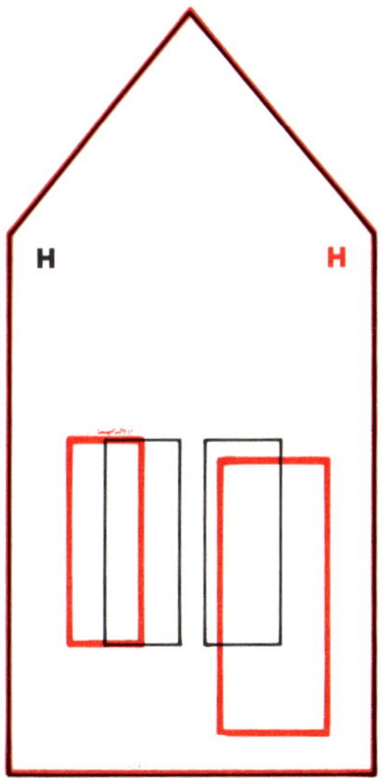

Full size for HO scale 3.5mm = 1 foot

One left, one right required of each

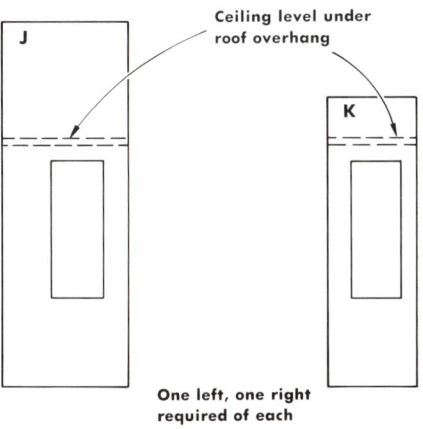

tions and other detail, now is the time. The general arrangement is shown in the floor plan; the fine points I will leave to you. Paint the completed floor and fasten it firmly in position in your scenery.

Roof and shingles

The next major project is the roof. Because of its numerous planes and joints it is a bit tricky to assemble. Note that the pagodalike curve of the roof shelter extensions carries up into the main roof. Figs. 4 and 5 show the general arrangement of the roof and its joints. Installation of the main ceiling is the initial step. This may be a single piece, though it is easier to make it of several pieces cut to fit. Accurately cut the main roof formers to the same angle, and see to it that the formers are properly aligned and spaced with respect to the walls or you will have a lopsided roof.

Add the roof shelter extension ceilings and formers with the same care. Though these ceilings under the shelter extensions are not on the prototype, they simplify construction considerably and add rigidity to the model. Adjust the height block until the main roof line matches that of the extensions; see the inset in fig. 5. Then bond parts in place. Once this assembly is true and square the remainder of the roof is relatively easy to construct.

I have shown ridgepoles, fig. 5, installed in a way that requires the roof parts to be slotted to fit around them. However, ridgepoles may be fitted to the main roof after it is assembled; just be sure they are centered properly. I don't recommend making the main roof and extension parts in one piece. This would only complicate the cutting and fitting problems. Build the gable roofs next. Use paper templates fitted by the cut-and-try method, then trace them onto the plastic. Joints need not be perfect in the roof assembly, as shingles will cover small inaccuracies.

Roof extension shelter parts are best made of light stock such as .020" for

27

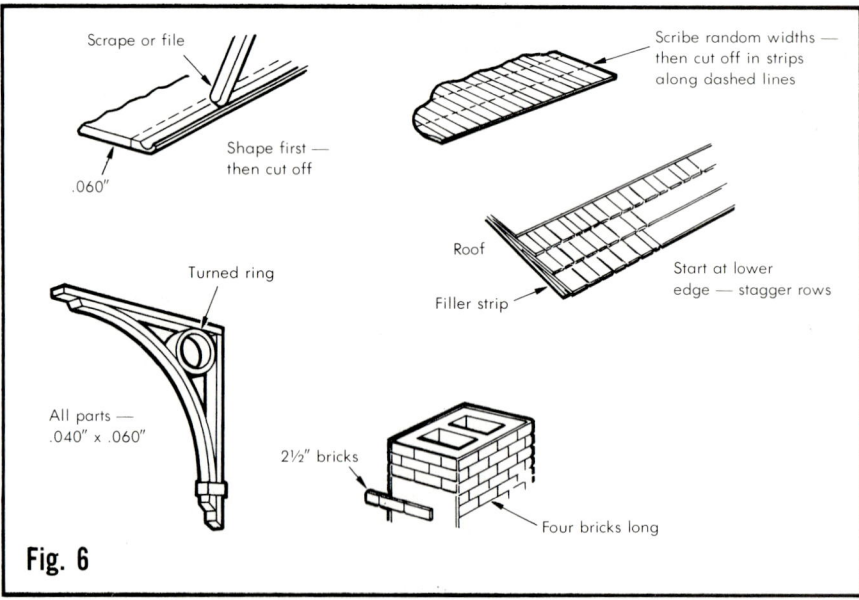

Fig. 6

Studies in styrene

easier shaping. Roll the parts around a cylindrical form before attaching them. Bond the small triangular gable wall on the north roof with a gusset for support, then add the roof parts.

To simulate the prototype's slate shingles I scribed, cut, and applied .010" plastic as shown in fig. 6. Be careful not to use an excess of solvent here; the styrene is so thin it will soften all the way through, causing distortion and sunken spots.

When shingling is completed, let the model stand for several hours to allow the shingles to harden, then trim the edges with a sharp blade or a razor. This method is neater than filing.

Add the cover strips on all ridgepoles and corners as shown on the elevations. Leave a slight "flat" on gable ridges to form a seat for the grillwork.

The roof extensions are covered with asphalt roll-type roofing material which can be simulated nicely with strips of fine-grit sandpaper. No. 400 wet-or-dry paper is excellent for our purposes. Use contact-type cement to attach the paper to plastic.

I simplified the chimney shape and made it as shown in fig. 6.

Because of the ceiling under the roof extensions, the roof support brackets do not exactly follow the original design. Two variations, one in the elevations and one in the sketches, are shown, plus a third style on my model. These supports, fig. 6, as well as the decorative framing in the gable ends can best be made from rings cut from sheet stock using the method shown in fig. 7. If your

28

model is absolutely square, both items can be preassembled in jigs, then attached to the building, but it is better to custom-fit each one.

Details and grillwork

This completes the depot except for details and finish. One detail is without a doubt the most difficult part of the whole job, the wrought iron grillwork topping the ridgepoles. It is one of the important elements in the building's intriguing character and thus a necessary item on the model. The prototype design is almost impossible to reproduce in HO, so I have simplified it to elemental patterns—but though it may look deceptively simple in the drawing, this ornamental tidbit is not the sort of thing you toss together in a few minutes. It is a project in itself.

The secret is to keep the design simple, using only straight lines and circles, or segments of circles, to create the desired effect without getting involved in the difficult job of making the irregular curlicues usually found in this type of ornamentation. Here is how the grillwork is made. The "rings" are turned from styrene rod and the "bar" stock cut from .010" sheet in strips .015" wide. If you can make them finer than this, so much the better, but don't enlarge the proportions or the grill will look more like a picket fence than the delicate, rococo decoration it is supposed to be. Start with the bottom strip and one end post; add rings and posts along the full length required. Then go back and add the intermediate horizontal bars. The gold balls are candy cake decorations, painted. Cementing them on top of a .010" x .020" post is no mean trick.

This is an extremely fragile assembly, so handle it with tweezers. Because the grill is in a particularly vulnerable spot on the model, paint it separately and do not install it on the roof until the depot is completed and ready to mount in the scenery. If you damage the finished ironwork it will be next to impossible to repair it successfully.

A typical platform outline appears on the floor plan, but the type of platform you choose will depend on "local" conditions on your layout. I followed the actual station platform in using asphalt material (fine-grit sandpaper) for the surface but elevated it slightly and added a curb. Planks or gravel would also be suitable.

Painting and aging

This brings us to the finishing stage, which to me is a critical part of modelbuilding. At this point you establish the age and condition of the structure. Also, you impart more actual realism to the model than you have at any other stage of construction. Choose a type of finish that will be consistent with the surrounding buildings, and use whatever

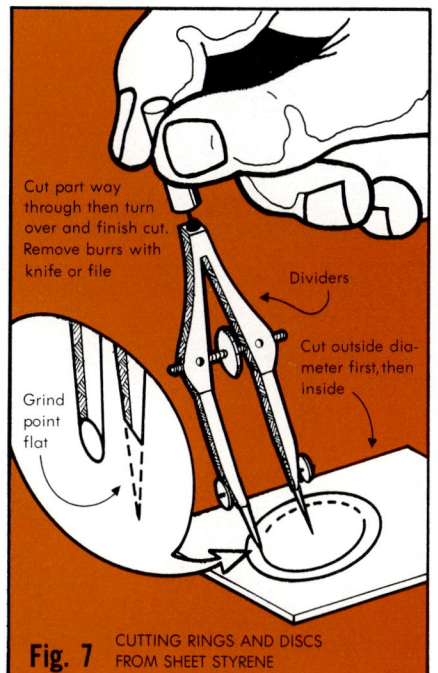

Fig. 7 CUTTING RINGS AND DISCS FROM SHEET STYRENE

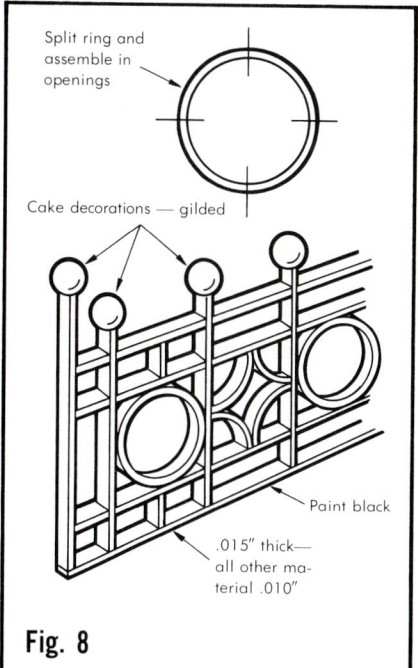

Fig. 8

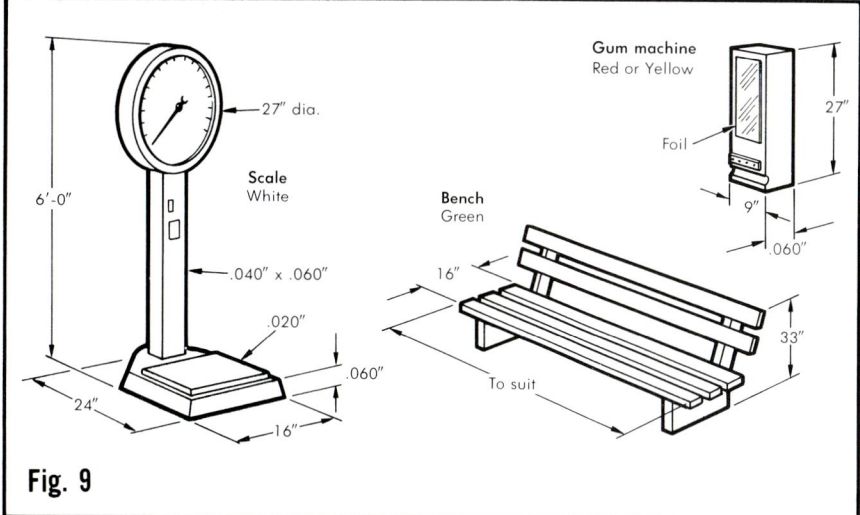

Fig. 9

colors suit your fancy. Styrene needs no sealer or primer coatings; they offer no advantage and would only be detrimental to fine detail.

If you have access to spray-painting equipment by all means use it, as it produces a thin, even coating which does not cover detail. Spray so that the paint will be nearly dry when it hits the model. You can accomplish this by holding the airbrush at a distance from the model or by using a large amount of air in proportion to the paint. Better yet, use one of the paints designed for use on plastics.

Once the basic color scheme has been applied, special effects like aging and weathering can be added with poster colors or casein, in the same way you would age a model made from other materials. One fact to remember is that you cannot use stains or washes on styrene without first applying an opaque coating of paint. If a building is to be white, for instance, paint it white even though you use white plastic in its construction. Washes will hold to the paint better and the general effect will be more realistic. I do not favor the wash method of aging a model; I prefer to put the highlights and tones on top of the base color rather than let the undercoat show through.

Now your station should be just about finished and ready to install on the layout. It's been fun, hasn't it? Use styrene for a few more projects, and I'll bet you'll never go back to wood and paper.

Studies in styrene

29

All photos, KALMBACH BOOKS: A. L. Schmidt.

Recombination station

Kitbashing: a hybrid modelbuilding technique that uses inexpensive, readily available plastic kits as "scratch"

by Bob Hayden

THE introduction of well-detailed mass-produced styrene models in the 1950's changed the model railroading hobby, and most admit the change was for the better. One consequence of this plastics revolution was the emergence of a new semi-scratchbuilding process based on altering and combining styrene kit parts. This method has become a favorite of experienced modelers, and has carried several names, among them crosskitting and kitlancing, but the one most often used is *kitbashing*.

Kitbashing can simply mean reworking or adding detail to a plastic kit or sawing a kit apart and putting the pieces together in a different configuration, or it can involve combining parts from two or more models. The key to this type of modelbuilding is the use of inexpensive injection-molded kit components to provide the basic shape, texture, and detail of the model. The technique finds widest application in structure building, where the limitations of standards and clearances are not as restrictive as with locomotives and rolling stock. The advantages of kitbashing are ease of construction and economy of time. Also, kitbashing enables you to assemble a model very different from your neighbor's unmodified kit (and with all the detail of a scratchbuilt model) in perhaps one third the time. Repeated use of one kit as the basis for several different models lends a family resemblance to your railroad's service structures, a prototypical feature that increases your layout's overall realism.

There is one other factor not to be overlooked: There are many superb European plastic kits on the hobby-shop shelf, but they are seldom considered by North American modelers because they have a distinctly continental look. Kitbashing opens the door to this bonanza; leave off certain trim parts, make a few simple changes, and these structures take on a typical American or Canadian flavor.

One process—two approaches

By far the most common—and easiest—approach to kitbashing starts

Studies in styrene

30

with a kit not quite suited to your layout but having features that you consider attractive—a particular siding type, roof texture, or window style, perhaps. You rearrange and modify the parts to approximate a prototype that includes similar features and at the same time meets your requirements. For example, you may have a kit that embodies all the features you want in a station for your pike, but is too small for your purposes. Look for a prototype station (one located in your area, or featured in a book or magazine) with similar lines that can be used as the basis for a larger model, and then use the parts from two or more of the "too small" kits to build a station that suits your needs. I call this the kit-to-prototype route.

The second approach begins with a prototype or free-lance design, and involves looking for the kits suited to building that design. Compromise is very important if you choose this avenue of attack, since strict adherence to your chosen prototype negates many of the advantages inherent in kitbashing. It's better, for example, to "give" a few scale feet one way or the other to keep the project rolling than to strive for perfection.

Kitbashing is especially useful for building a company look into your lineside structures. Many railroads had a common architectural style for all but their most important structures, and stations were often built to a standardized design. You can use the same kit to furnish identical siding, trim, and doors for several otherwise different models.

One note of caution regarding kitbashing: Use moderation. Have a plan before you start cutting and gluing, and stop now and then to consider whether the completed portion of your model looks presentable and believable. Said another way, although we are employing a patchwork process, we want to avoid a patchwork product.

This is an unmodified N scale Rico station. Three kits were used to kitbash the station shown on the opposite page. Kits for Rico station have been offered in HO and O scales.

Planning your project— "eyeballing"

Whether you choose the first or second approach to kitbashing, spread out the parts of each kit you are using to consider possible arrangements. While you are moving the parts around puzzle-style, keep in mind that joints between wall sections can be most easily disguised when they occur at door and window frames and along cast-in trim boards, that you lose at least the thickness of the razor-saw blade when you cut a wall apart, and that certain details can be left out without altering the impact of structure design. If you run into trouble visualizing how the parts will go together, spread the kit pieces out flat on the plate glass of a copy machine and make a photocopy to cut and paste. This allows you to make your mistakes with the scissors—not the saw—and to build simple three-dimensional mockups to see how the completed structure will fit on your layout. Take your time with this planning step; you should have a firm idea of the required cuts and ultimate arrangement of the parts before you start bashing in earnest.

Prototype first—Badwater Wells station in N scale

I needed a medium-size combination station for an N gauge layout. After some research I settled on Southern Pacific standard frame station design No. 22 from **Railroad Station Planbook** as a prototype. This "upstairs-downstairs" structure has an uncluttered, businesslike look that fits in well with the sparse, parched Western scene of the station I had in mind. Choosing the prototype committed me to the difficult path for kitbashing, but allowed

Studies in styrene

31

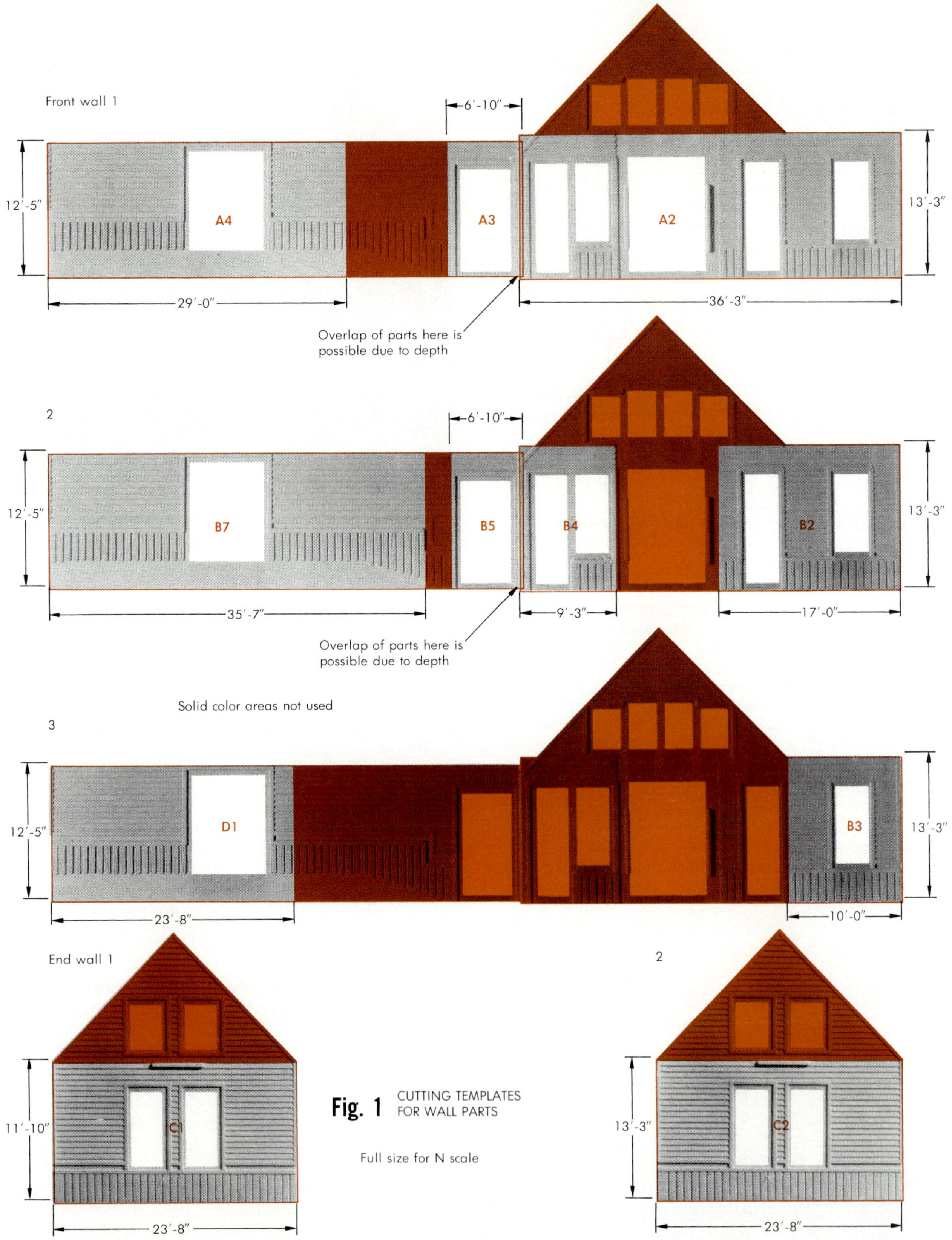

Front wall 1

Fig. 1 CUTTING TEMPLATES FOR WALL PARTS

Full size for N scale

End wall 1

Studies in styrene

complete exposition of the technique.

I spent several evenings paging through catalogs, and pawed over several kits at the hobby shop before settling on the Pola N scale Rico station kit as grist for the project. The prototype for the kit was built in 1891 for the 3-foot-gauge Rio Grande Southern Railroad in Colorado, and while it is an attractive structure, it includes a good deal of ornamentation and otherwise lacks the "typicality"—and that businesslike air I mentioned above—that I like in railroad structures. The N scale kit has been imported from its European manufacturer by several U.S. firms, and similar kits (with the same prototype) have been offered in HO and

32

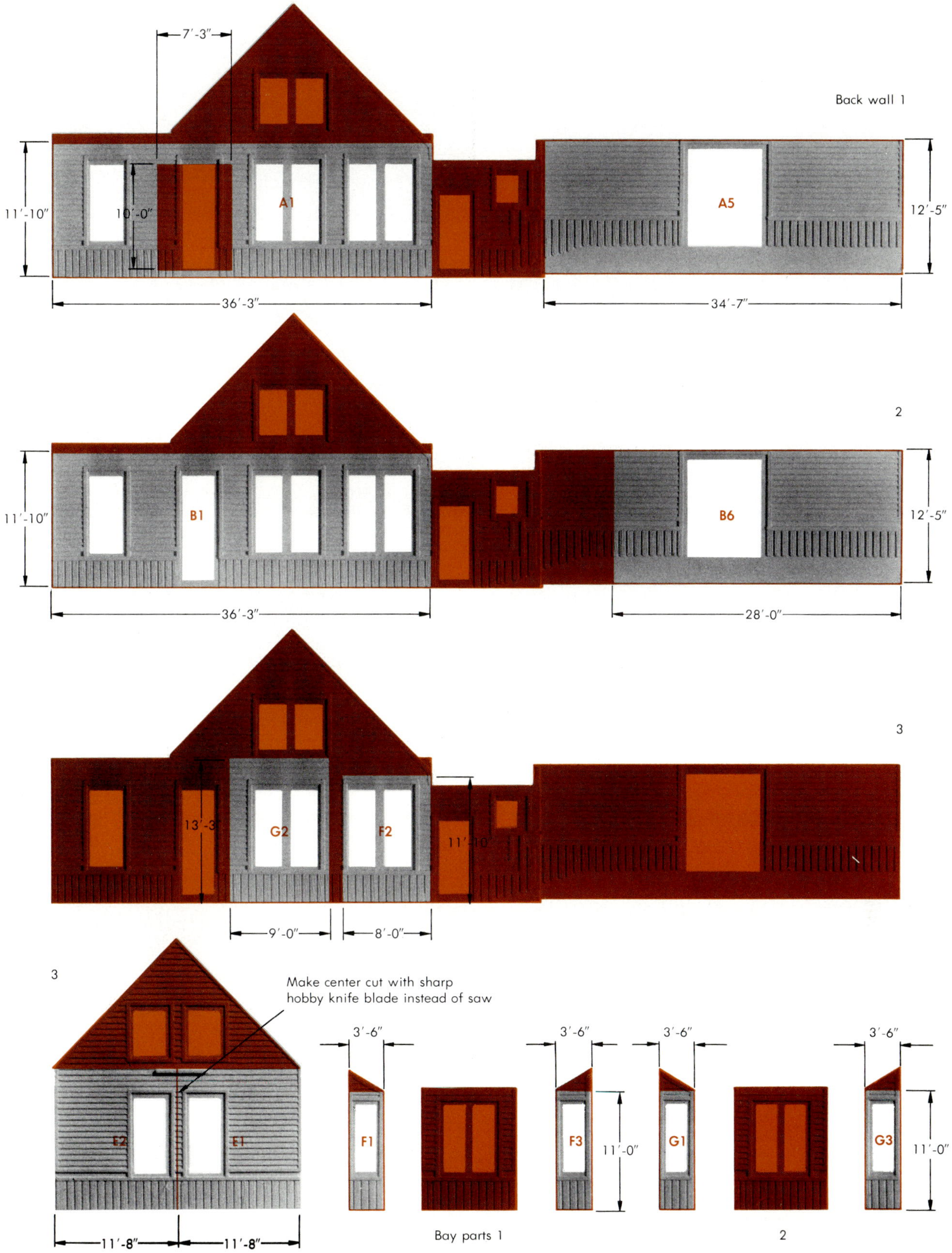

O scales. The kit comes cast in four colors and features excellent clapboard siding and shingle roof textures. The door and window frames, sashes, and mullions are cast on separate sprues, a construction feature that helps keep the kitbashing process simple and the work neat.

I elected to remain as close as possible to the Southern Pacific drawings, and my conversion required three Pola Rico kits. Be your own boss here (it's *your* station for *your* railroad!). After finishing the project I can see that a credible job could be done using only two of the kits by not widening the freighthouse section of the station and simply stacking the second story on top of the first

Studies in styrene

33

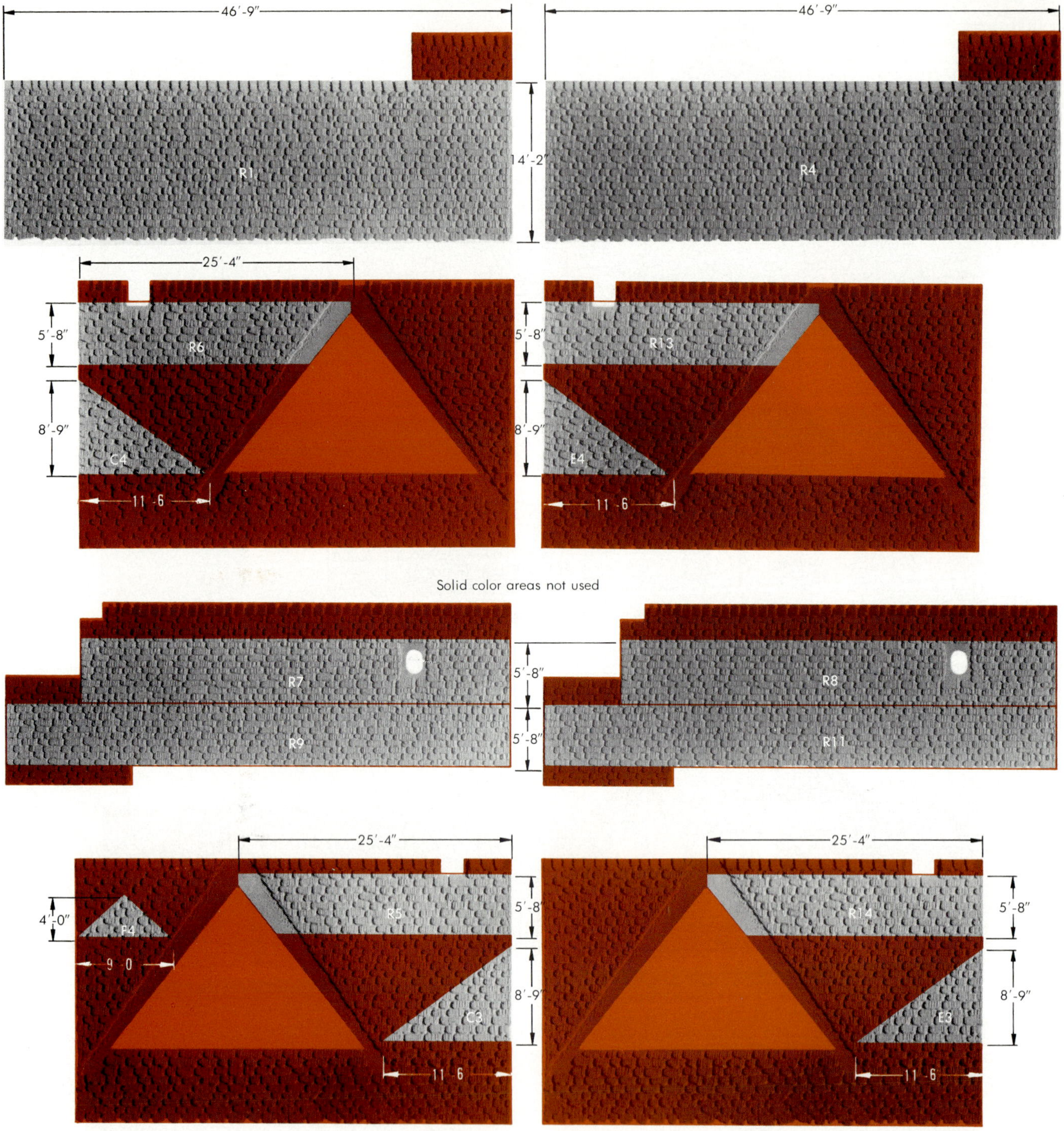

Fig. 2 CUTTING TEMPLATES FOR ROOF PARTS   Full size for N scale

without all the complex cutting and fitting. You may prefer to follow this simplified route, but let's delve into the more ambitious rearrangement—or recombination.

Studies in styrene

Materials

In addition to the three Rico station kits, you'll need styrene sheet stock in the following thicknesses: .010", .020", .040", and .060". You'll also need clear styrene for window glazing (.010" or .015" stock works best), some one-ply Strathmore paper, and a few scraps of colored bond paper for window shades. I substituted commercial HO scale chimney castings for those included with the kit, but you could make your own from scratch or even use something left over from another kitbashing project.

Go through the kits before you start to ensure that no pieces are missing, that all parts are formed correctly, and that nothing is broken. I say this because it is an awful lot easier to convince the hobby-shop manager to replace the kit at this stage than it is when you have already commenced bashing.

Getting started

Insofar as possible, I have used scale feet and inches throughout the text and in the figures. Decimal inch thicknesses are used to refer to material sizes for the N scale model.

Refer to the templates, fig. 1, and cut sections for the station walls. Remove all lugs and cast alignment aids on the

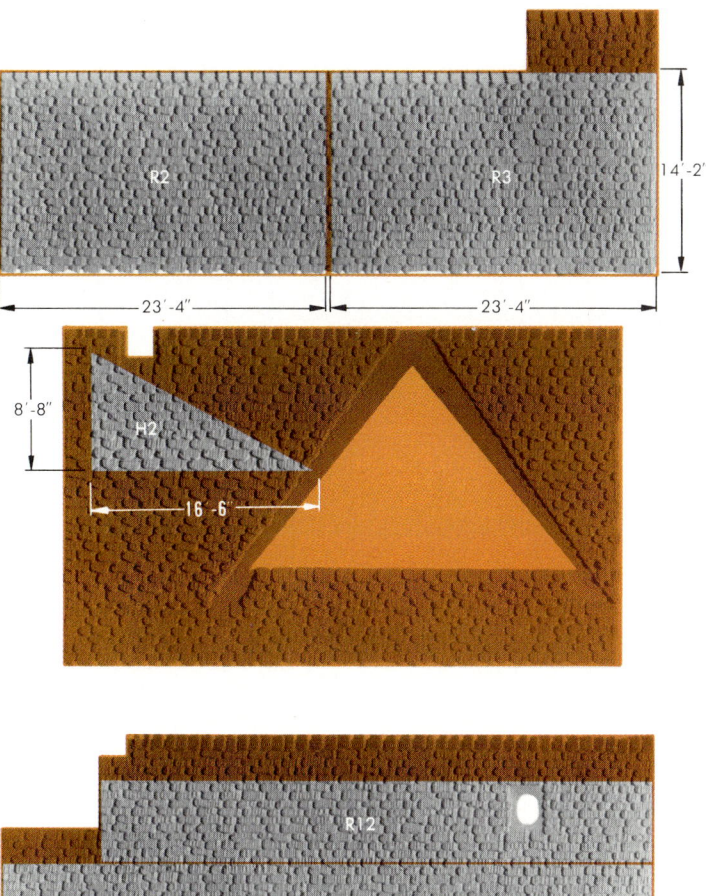
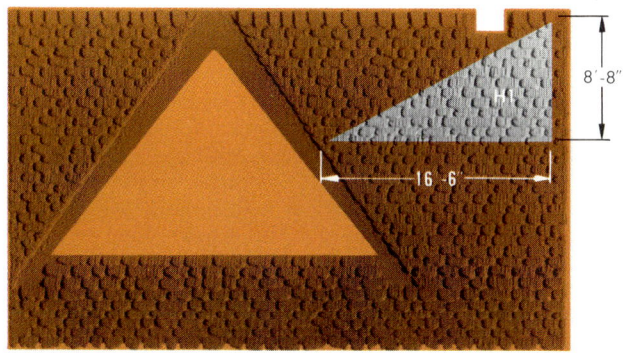
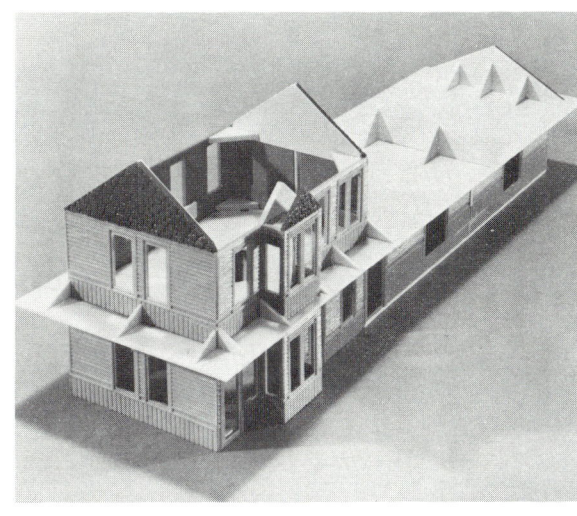

backs of the kit walls, file the edges true, and use a machinist's square to lay out the cuts. Cut out the panels and square up the corners and edges as you go. Do one wall at a time, trial fitting the parts and taking overall measurements to compare with the templates and the corresponding pieces. Don't assemble any of the wall parts until all are cut; you may wish to make minor adjustments in the length of several pieces to make the walls a uniform size and prevent a lopsided floor plan. The kit freighthouse walls are not as tall as the main station walls and require a spacer that also stiffens and aligns the assembly. Cut this from .060" styrene, full length for the long freighthouse walls. Take pains in this preliminary work, because it determines the overall neatness and accuracy of the model, and sloppy cuts and edges can't be undone or redone later without starting over.

After you've made all the wall pieces —it should take a couple of evenings— including the shingled gable sections, fig. 2 (C3, C4, E3, E4), dry fit each wall in accordance with the assembly key, fig. 3, and measure again to be sure the overall length of both sides is the same. I had to file one section of one wall for a proper fit. Do the same with the end sections.

The best way to assemble the walls is on a sheet of waxed paper placed over graph paper. I use a sheet of window

Studies in styrene

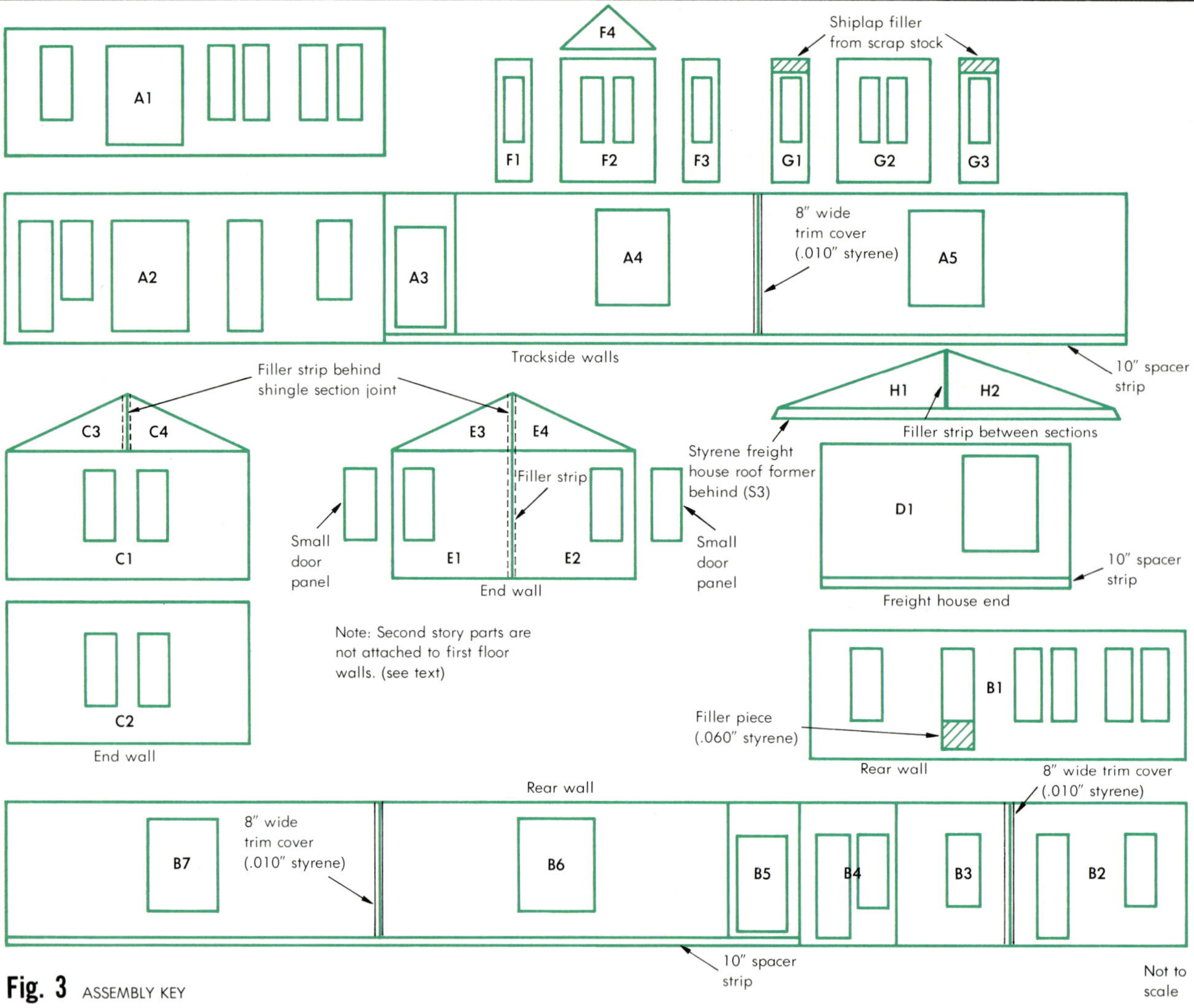

Fig. 3 ASSEMBLY KEY

Subassembly by floor units

glass as a flat surface, and while it isn't perfect, it works far better than the plywood top of my workbench. Use a steel straightedge—a scale rule works well—to align the wall sections, and touch a brush moistened with liquid styrene cement to the edge of the joints, allowing capillary action to distribute the solvent all along the edges to be bonded. Allow these joints to set for at least an hour and add stiffener strips of .060" stock to the inside top edge of each side wall. Finally, add the bay window to the track side of the structure. If you have the SP No. 22 station plans, you'll notice that I flipped the prototype floorplan to make it just a bit different—something the real roads did often.

When the joints of your first-floor walls have had an hour or so to solidify, assemble the walls into the rectangular first-floor unit. Do this on your flat surface, and use the straightedge, machinist's square, and weights to ensure that each wall is perpendicular and even. Note the .060" spacer, fig. 4 part S1, between the side walls. This not only stiffens the unit during handling, but prevents the walls from bowing in and keeps light from leaking into the freight portion of the structure. Make up a handful of .060" triangular gussets, fig. 5, and use them for reinforcement in all interior corners.

While the first-floor subassembly sets, use the waxed paper and flat-surface technique to assemble the second-floor walls. Add a .020" reinforcement to the back of each shingled gable end and trim to size. Let these joints set up, then assemble the second-story walls into a unit as you did the first-floor parts. Assemble the second-story bay window, but do not add it to the unit yet.

The major stiffening member in the model is the first-story ceiling and subroof, fig. 4. This sheet of comparatively thick material serves two purposes: First, and most important, it helps even out inconsistencies in the height of the first-floor wall panels, providing a flat base for the second-story unit. It also adds a great deal of strength to the building, making the model a lot easier to handle in the succeeding steps. Cut the subroof from .040" stock, set the first-floor unit upside down on it, align, and touch cement to the inside of the joints with a brush. This is an important bond, so weight the parts and let it harden overnight.

Fitting and adding the second-story unit is a critical operation. On the prototype, each wall is made of one piece, not two, so any misalignment between the upper and lower sections on the model will be obvious—and distracting. Check again to see that the walls are the same size. If there are differences, place the mismatch at the rear wall, where it will be least obvious. Add the second-story unit to the first floor, then carefully align the upper bay window with the one below, and cement in place.

Your model should be taking shape now, so keep up the momentum. Align

Studies in styrene

36

Fig. 4 SHEET STYRENE PARTS

- S1 Lower story spacer .060" styrene (22'-10" × 13'-1")
- S2 Bay gable former .040" styrene (9'-0" × 48")
- S4 Roof eave formers (13) .040" styrene (4'-8" × 2'-4")
- S3 Freight house roof formers (3) .040" styrene (33'-0" × 8'-8")
- S5 First floor ceiling and subroof .040" styrene (116'-9" × 33'-5") with 12' dia. hole for light and Holes for wires (lighting)

Fig. 5 MAKING RIGHT ANGLE GUSSETS

Make .060" styrene strip 3/8" wide. Divide into 3/8" squares. Connect corners of squares, then cut with razor saw.

Fig. 6 FIRST FLOOR ROOF EAVE BRACES

1'-3" × 1'-3", 6" hypotenuse. Cut here. Make 30 pieces. Draw small right angle template as shown in color, align 3" × 6" stock and cut at dashed lines.

Fig. 7 ASSEMBLING PRE-GLAZED WINDOW CASING UNITS

Tinted bond paper window shade (length variable). .015" clear styrene glazing. Back of window casting.

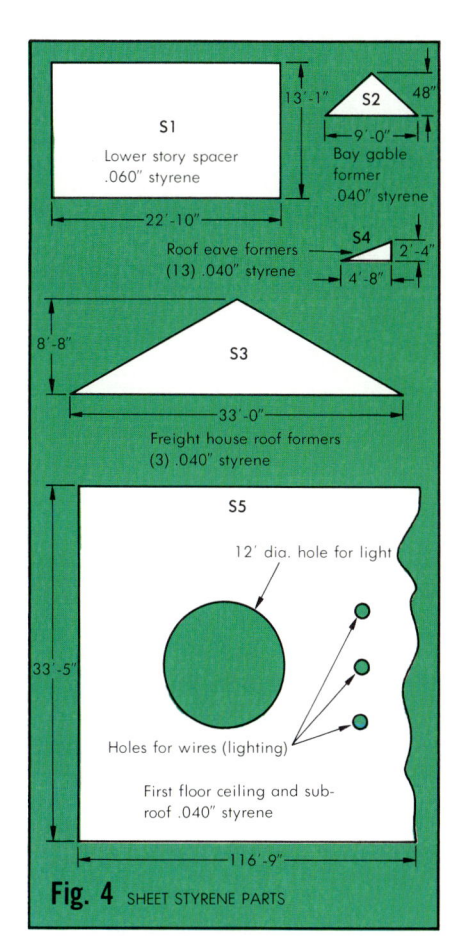

the shingled freighthouse gable end and glue it in place on the top surface of the first-floor subroof. Add the two plain styrene freighthouse roof formers, fig. 4 part S3, and gussets as shown in the photos. Cement the .060" styrene bay gable roof former in line with the shingled section of the second-story bay. Cut the eave roof formers and add them around the second-story base and at the freighthouse end. Install eave braces, fig. 6, and set the model aside for the joints to solidify.

I spray painted an initial coat of solid color on the station, but it could have been done just as easily with a brush and any one of the plastic-compatible model paints. I prepared a faded yellow color by mixing equal parts of flat white and yellow, and applied it inside and out. This overall coat helps seal the structure to prevent light leaks, and gives any colors you add later a kind of holding tooth. After painting, set the model aside for about a week while you fabricate the door and window units, roof sections, and station platforms.

Door and window work

Remove the required door and window castings from the kit sprues and dress the edges with your file. In my N scale kits the corners of these parts were quite rounded, and a few swipes from the file made them sharper and less clumsy looking. Use a sharp, new blade in your modeling knife to remove any flash, especially on the window muntins.

Build up the doors and windows as prefabricated units with clear glazing material and shades before they are added to the building, fig. 7. This step involves some extra cutting and fitting, but pays handsome dividends later in terms of neatness. Clean all the castings in denatured alcohol or a detergent solution. Dry and paint them the same color as your trim. I used a faded green made from equal parts of bright green, white, and tan. Let the paint dry thoroughly and cut clear styrene panes to fit the raised back of each window and door. The double windows require two panes, since they must clear a center strip in the corresponding wall opening. Add these panes using as little of the solvent cement as possible. Test-fit each glazed unit in its wall opening and trim the clear stock if it interferes with a proper fit. Finally, cut bits of colored bond paper—tan is a good choice—for window shades and glue them to the back of the glazing material with white glue. Do not install the completed units yet; it's best to wait until the walls have been colored and weathered.

Roof sections

The most demanding part of this project is assembling the shingle roof sections. Cut apart the kit roof sections, fig. 2, and trial fit the side and end roof pieces for the station, fig. 8. Refer frequently to the completed portion of the model to ensure your parts will fit, and leave extra stock on the first-floor roof pieces so you can cut the angles at installation. Note that the shingles at joints between sections should be undercut to help reduce visibility of the joints, and that the lower edge of the roof section (the edge that will show) should be shaved down to reduce the apparent thickness of the shingles, fig. 9.

Assemble and cement the shingle roof sections as you did the wall parts, and let the pieces remain on the flat assembly surface while the joints solidify. Add scraps of .020" stock for reinforcement behind the joints where they will not interfere with the roof formers. Paint the shingle sections a light color as a primer to accept staining later—white, buff, and tan are all accept-

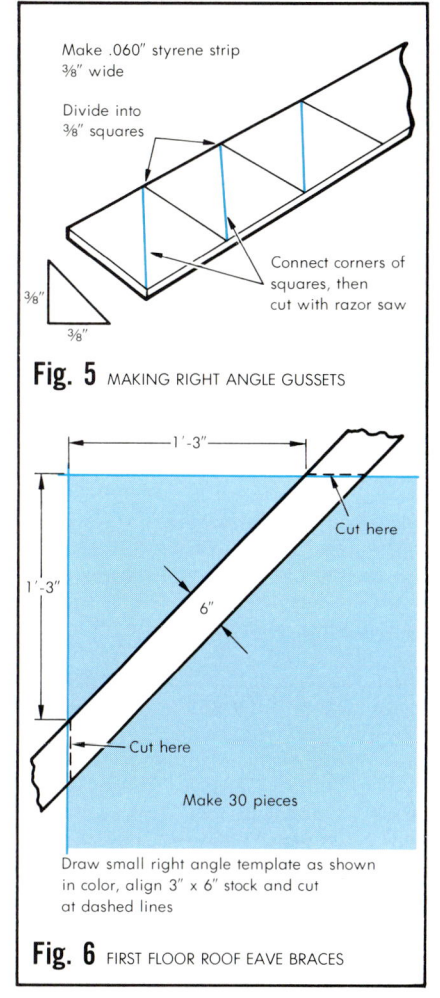

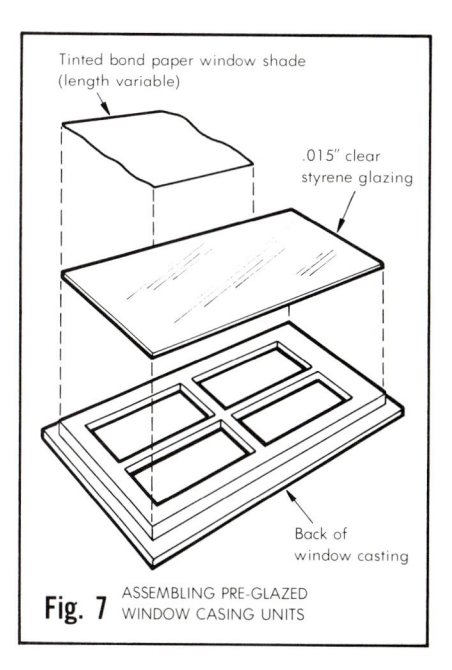

Studies in styrene

37

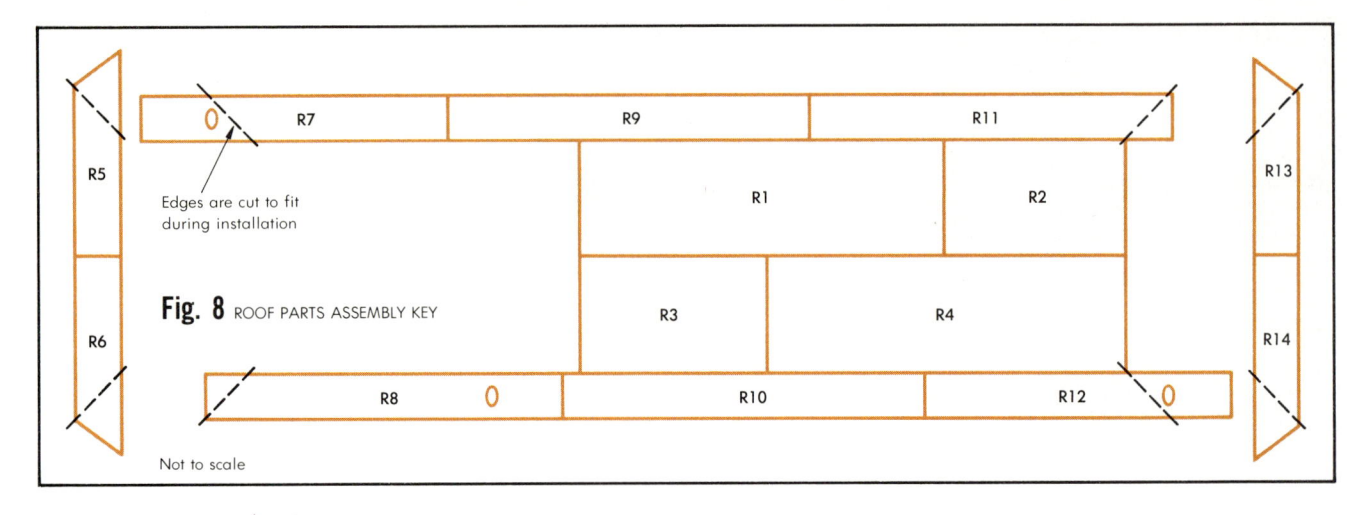

Fig. 8 ROOF PARTS ASSEMBLY KEY

Edges are cut to fit during installation

Not to scale

able—and put them aside for a while.

I had planned to construct the main station roof from a material simulating tarpaper because there isn't enough shingle area in three Rico kits to make the entire roof. I reconsidered in midstream, though, and decided to make a sheet metal roof with batten strips over flat galvanized material. Make a subroof assembly from .020" stock and a .060" inside former, fig. 10. While the joints are soft, test-fit the assembly on the structure. The figures show the final dimensions, reached after almost an hour of trial-and-error fitting. You may have to alter angles and sizes a bit to adjust them to your model.

Give the subroof assembly a half-hour to harden, and add roof batten strips of .010" material, 4" wide, spaced on 3' centers. Surprisingly, these thin strips add a great deal of stiffness to the .020" stock; the completed part is rigid enough to be used as a removable roof without additional inside formers.

Paint the simulated metal roof light gray-blue to achieve the color of unpainted weathered galvanized steel. Add some random streaks of silver, then blend the whole surface together with some rust colors—reds and oranges.

Note that we are keeping the main roof section separate from the structure so far; one of the basic tenets of good modelbuilding is to work with the smallest subassembly whenever possible.

Make the gable fascia trim boards from .010" stock, fig. 11, using the mass-production method shown. Cut out the parts for the eave trim and paint them the same yellow used for the structure walls. This done, cement the trim boards to the main station roof using a contact-type adhesive. Drill a small hole and add a finial made from a small roundheaded pin to each gable peak.

You are on your own for the chimneys. Mine are made from Grandt Line (No. HO-57) HO castings, but there are many other suitable types available. I made the larger chimney by trimming and stacking two castings. Carefully cut and file your chimney bases to match the roof angle, and paint them either a mottled red brick color or a color that complements your station color scheme. The two short vent pipes are simply bits of $1/16$" o. d. tubing painted black.

Final painting and assembly

Unless you plan to add interior detail, paint the inside walls of the structure a dark color. Dark paint cuts down on the amount of light bouncing around the interior (making it less evident that there's no detail), and it helps seal the corners and wall section joints against light leaks from inside. I decided to brush paint the shingled gable wall sections the green color used on the trim. I weathered all exterior wall surfaces with a thin wash of white water-base plastic-compatible paint for a dusty but well-maintained look.

Because the window castings and wall openings are already painted at this point, use a white glue like Elmer's to cement in the preglazed window and door assemblies. White glue has the advantage of not marring the clear window material should you misplace some of the adhesive.

By now the shingle roof sections

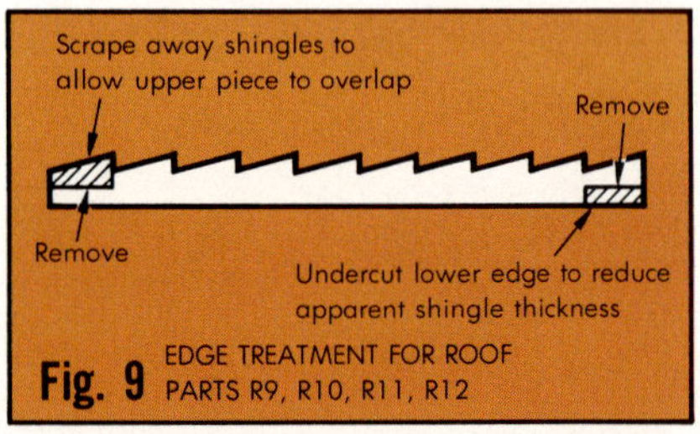

Fig. 9 EDGE TREATMENT FOR ROOF PARTS R9, R10, R11, R12

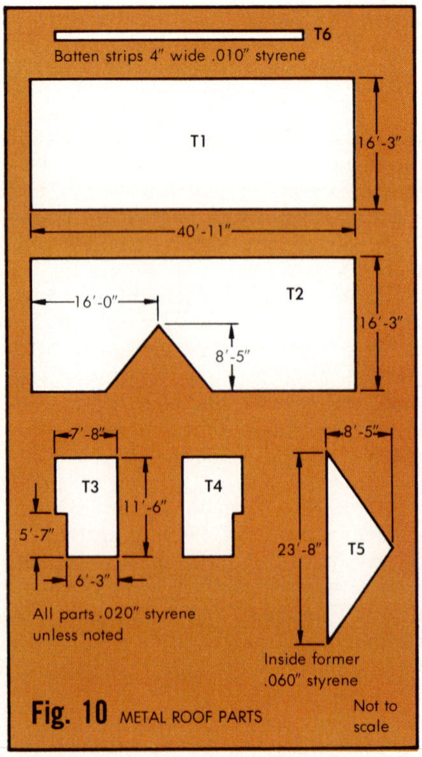

Scrape away shingles to allow upper piece to overlap
Remove
Undercut lower edge to reduce apparent shingle thickness

Studies in styrene

Fig. 10 METAL ROOF PARTS

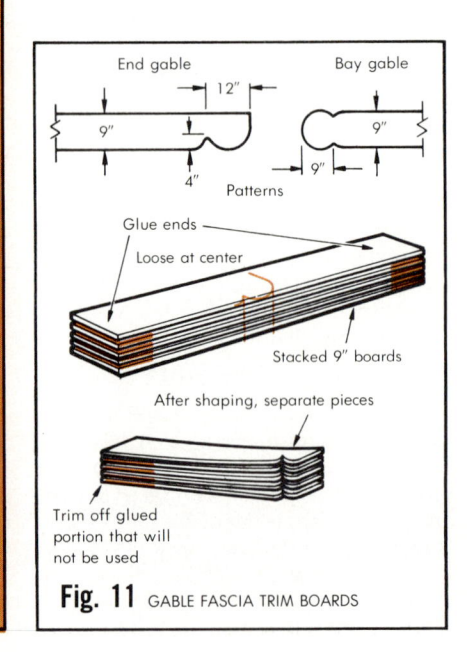

Batten strips 4" wide .010" styrene
T6
T1 16'-3"
40'-11"
T2 16'-3"
16'-0"
8'-5"
T3 T4
5'-7" 11'-6"
6'-3" 7'-8"
T5 23'-8" 8'-5"
All parts .020" styrene unless noted
Inside former .060" styrene
Not to scale

Fig. 11 GABLE FASCIA TRIM BOARDS

End gable — 12" — Bay gable
9" 9"
4"
Patterns
Glue ends
Loose at center
Stacked 9" boards
After shaping, separate pieces
Trim off glued portion that will not be used

38

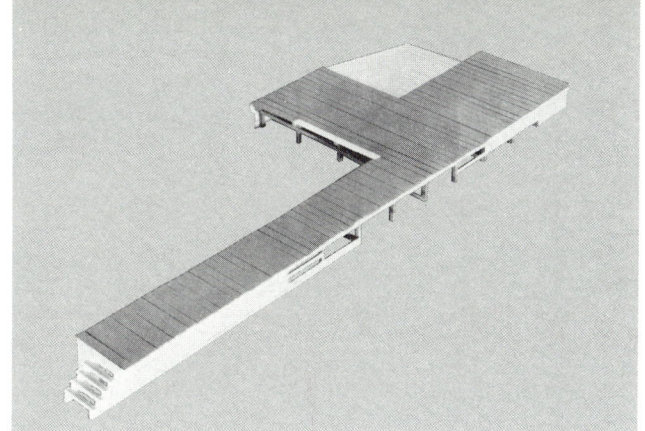

should be ready for staining. I simulated old, weathered wood by streaking on four shades of very thin brown paint and one shade of silvery gray. Do not mix the colors to a uniform shade, but apply each to different parts of the same section; the blending that takes place when they run together does the mixing for you. Don't let the roof get too dark or the fine shingle detail will be hidden.

Add the two large shingle roof sections to the model after carefully cutting their ends to mate with the smaller sections that will be placed across the ends. Then trim and add these smaller pieces, filing them to make a neat joint at each corner.

Cut the roof ridgepole flashing and the flashing material that joins the roof and walls from one-ply Strathmore paper. Fold and crease the paper, and then cut through both thicknesses to get the same width of material on each side of the crease. Paint the flashing pieces with the blue-gray galvanized metal color you used on the main station roof, and attach them to the roof joints using a contact-type adhesive. The elliptical hole beside the second-story bay window is covered with a small rectangle of one-ply stock on my model, but could accommodate the standard for a train-order signal if you need one. Weather the shingle and flashing surfaces with washes of tan, gray, and white. As you paint, extend your coloration across the joints to de-emphasize the joints between roof sections. Don't bring one color up to the separation line and begin another.

Station platforms from scratch

The main station platform is built up on a slab of .060" styrene for strength and dimensional stability, fig. 12. Cut out the platform base, place the model on it, and scribe a line around the bottom of the walls. Use this scribed line as a guide for adding strips of .010" planking so that the structure will nestle down *inside* the planking. Plank with scale 10"-wide styrene boards; use .015" stock for the planks around the rear baggage door, and .040" stock for the long platform timbers that will be sunk into the terrain around the rear freight doors so that wagons and trucks can back up to load and unload.

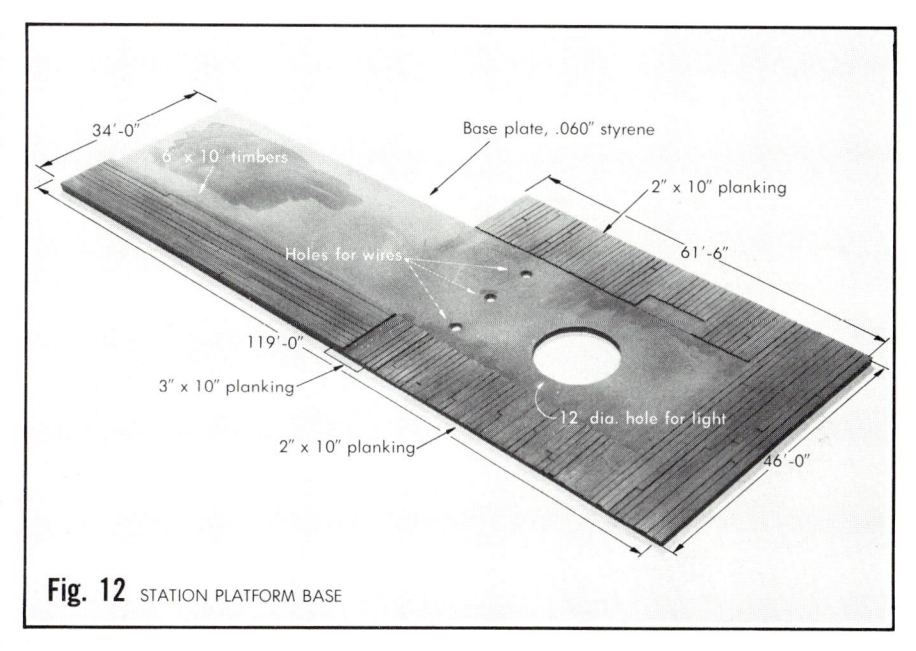

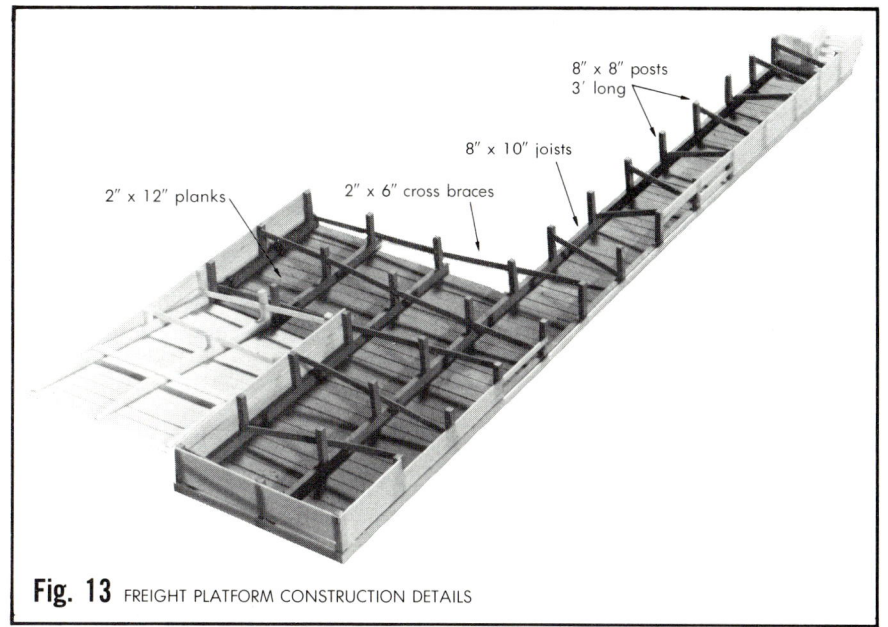

Fig. 12 STATION PLATFORM BASE

Fig. 13 FREIGHT PLATFORM CONSTRUCTION DETAILS

The freight platform is a spindly affair built from individual styrene timbers and boards. The dimensions are not critical; fig. 13 shows the construction details. Start by drawing the platform deck full size on graph paper. Cover this with waxed paper, and put down two strips of double-coated transparent tape as positioning aids for the 2 x 12 planks.

Studies in styrene

39

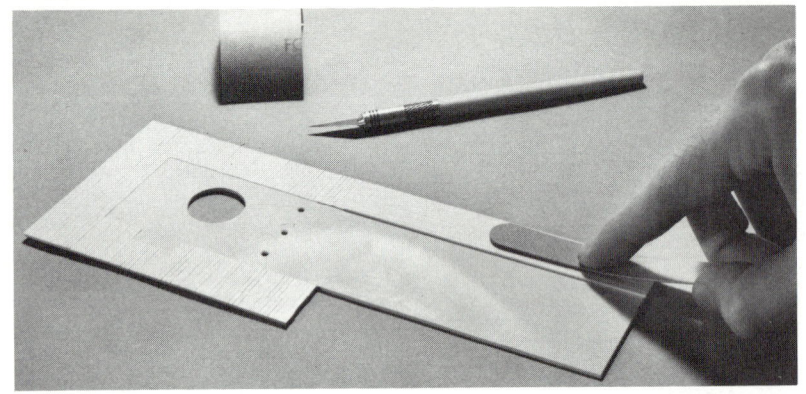

Dust the tape lightly with talc so it will release the platform later and place the precut planking pieces over the template outline. Then build the platform framework upside down on top of the planking with 8 x 10 joists, 8 x 8 posts, and 2 x 6 cross braces. Give this assembly some time to dry while you build up a sloping ramp and short stair section.

The photos of the prototype Southern Pacific stations show fully sheathed platform sides, and I added all but a short section of this boarding. I did not model the raised sheathing trim which divides the side surfaces into panels, because I had no styrene stock thinner than .010". I would rather leave a detail off than model it clumsily. You could leave off the side sheathing entirely, but this would sacrifice the blocky look of the prototype.

Before painting the platforms give the planking a suggestion of wood grain by lightly rubbing it with the coarse side of an emery board. Move the abrasive board over the planks in the direction of the supposed grain, reminding yourself that you are roughening rather than smoothing; it takes only a couple of minutes to get the hang of it.

Clean both platforms and paint them with a light tan primer. Give the paint adequate time to cure (most paints can be considered cured when you can hold the model close to your nose without smelling the thinner—usually three-eight days) and overstain with very thinned gray, black, and white washes to develop the driftwood look of unpainted sunbaked boards.

Detailing and installation

If you choose to permanently affix the main station roof to the structure, cement it in place now. I used only a few dabs of white glue on my model to allow disassembly should I change my mind and opt for interior detail.

I made station signs using .015" opaque white styrene sheet. I painted a hand-sized sheet of this material with my background color—in this case a strong blue—and applied Railroad Gothic style dry-transfer letters from an alphabet set. After spraying the lettering with clear flat finish and letting this set up hard (about five days), I cut the signs down to size and used the edge of a hobby knife to scrape away a thin band of the paint layer, leaving a neat white border. This technique is easy and effective, but I strongly suggest practicing on some painted scrap stock before attacking your lettered signs. I added a sign to each station end roof using an ultra-fast, ultra-strong ACC "super glue" adhesive.

The protective sheathing along the bottom of the freighthouse wall on the rear of the building and to the right of the baggage door on the track side was often used to prevent wear on the station siding from carelessly handled crates and boxes. I made mine from strips of .010" styrene, and painted them boxcar red for additional color.

Assembling the station structure and the platform completes the project. I in-

Studies in styrene

BASIC TOOLS—BASIC TECHNIQUES

Only a few inexpensive tools and easy-to-master skills are required for kitbashing. The overall list of tools is short, but a few of the items are truly indispensable keys to the technique: a sharp razor saw, a small machinist's square, one 10- or 12-inch medium-cut mill file, a file card, and the familiar hobby knife.

The large file, fig. A, will come as a surprise to some modelers who think that because our parts are small, we must use little tools. In this case, you'll find that if you use a small file to smooth and square the edges of the plastic parts, you won't achieve a long, accurate surface, but rather a series of short stretches that, overall, constitute a bumpy border. The large file is just as well balanced as a smaller one, and is easier to control. Its length allows it to be in contact with the entire surface to be smoothed, ensuring a clean fit all along the joint later on. The file card—an inexpensive stiff wire brush used to dislodge material from between the teeth of your files—is an item you should have on your bench. Use it often and your filing will require less effort.

The first step in kitbashing is parts layout using the machinist's square, fig. B. After you have determined where a cut must be made, use the file to true up the edge of the piece where you will rest the square. Position the square, and use the back of the point of your hobby knife to scribe the layout line. Then move the edge of the blade so that it overlaps the layout line, and use the square as an aid for cutting with the razor saw, fig. C. It is particularly important that you use the square when sawing into the finished or detailed side of the plastic part, since the square blade protects the surface against unintentional marring. Always leave between $1/32''$ and $1/64''$ of material to be removed with the file when you make a sawcut.

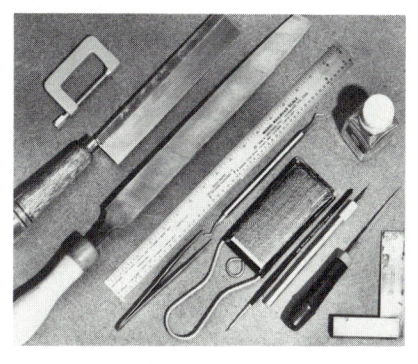

Plastic structure kits usually have tabs or lugs cast into the back of the parts as alignment aids. Remove these. They often prevent exact fitting, and they do not allow the parts to lay flat on the assembly surface. See fig. D. Work with a new blade in the knife and remember to always move the cutting edge of the tool away from you.

The hobby knife is used for more than cutting. A scraping technique is used to remove excess material and cutting burrs. Hold the blade at a right angle to the stock and scrape it along the edge. It will remove a chip much like a machine tool does, fig. E. This technique is extremely handy for rapidly shaping a thick plastic section, such as a wall-panel corner joint where you must remove material to achieve a 45-degree angle.

The final photo in the series, fig. F, shows a method of holding small parts or narrow strips of material for accurate cutting. Place the C-clamp at the edge of the cutting surface—a Masonite pressed board rectangle in this case—and use it as a third set of fingers. This simple wrinkle saves a lot of wear and tear on your hands, and also allows better control of the sawing action.

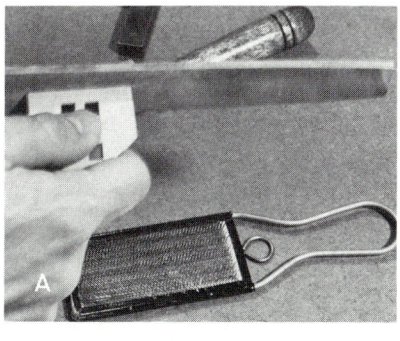

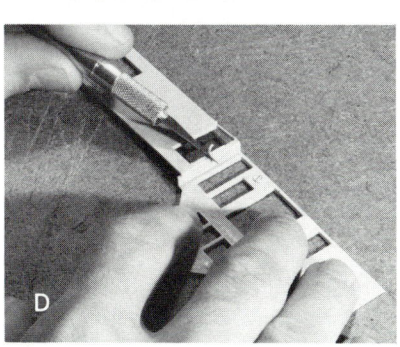

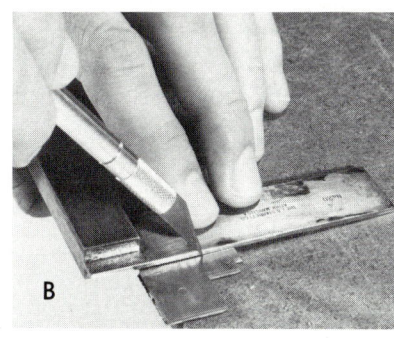

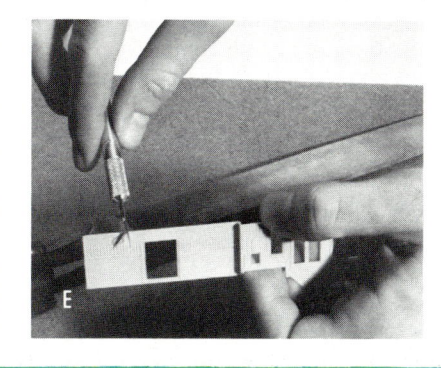

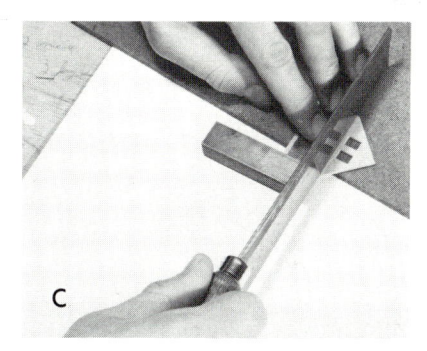

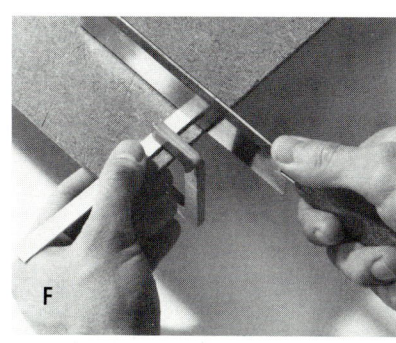

---

stalled the .060" platform base at trackside and worked my scenic material up to and around it, and then added the freight platform and the structure. There is plenty of room on the platforms, and you'll need lots of baggage, barrels, boxes, and scale people to make the station look busy. You may even be able to make several small outbuildings from the leftover plastic parts in the three Rico kits.

As a parting observation, the model is a far-from-perfect replica of the Espee prototype. It is, nonetheless, easily recognized as a derivative of the original. I feel it is an attractive model station in its own right, all in all, and an enjoyable and successful kitbashing project.

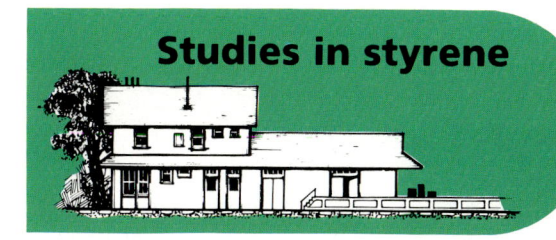

Studies in styrene

A small brick station

Modeling in brick presents some interesting construction problems. Jim Findley solves some of them with mass production

by Jim Findley

THIS small brick station once stood at Spreckels, Calif. It was torn down several years ago, but well-known model railroader John Allen had passed it many times and had recognized its attractive possibilities. He presented me with a set of photographs of the structure, and I built the model from them.

I have almost no information on the history of this little building. The style of construction and the ornamental brickwork date it around the turn of the century, and the bay window leads me to believe the station started life as a passenger facility and was later "demoted" to a freight station. Because it is quite small it could serve as a scale house or power substation if your pike needs such a building.

A close inspection of the prototype photos disclosed that the little brick station could be a deceptively tricky modeling project. My first thoughts were that justice could only be done to the brickwork by the application of one heck of a lot of individual bricks, and that no commercial shingling materials would be adequate for the roof. Fortunately, those first impressions were, for the most part, wrong, but keep them in mind as we proceed. I built my model in HO, but all dimensions are given in prototype sizes so that you can easily adapt them to other modeling scales.

Getting started

To begin, cut the sides and ends from 9"-thick hard balsa sheet to the dimensions shown in fig. 1. Save the pieces removed from the openings. Cover the sides and ends with your favorite commercial brick paper. I used a casein adhesive. Fold the brick paper into the door and window openings, fig. 2. Crease the fold lines with the back of a knife to form a sharp 90-degree angle at the corners. The tabs that fold in and cover the sides of the opening are trimmed flush with the inner surface of the walls to give the appearance of depth. Those pieces saved from cutting the openings serve admirably as plugs to hold the tabs flat against the sides of the openings while the adhesive is drying. Once the brick paper is in place the sides can be made perfectly square by using the vertical and horizontal mortar lines as a guide in trimming to size.

It is worthwhile to do paint touchup work as you go. Mix flat red, black, and brown model railroad paints until you have matched the color of the bricks on the commercial paper you are using. As each strip, individual brick, and piece of arch material is cut to the required shape, paint the exposed white edges of the cardstock. Later, aging will also help make the edges less obvious.

All of the material for the brick sills can be made in one operation. Cover one side and one end of a 4 x 13 x 25'-0" strip of stock with brick paper, fig. 3. Fold the paper before cementing the strip in place for a sharp corner running along a mortar line. When this strip has dried and has been neatly trimmed, cut individual sills from it, notching them 2" at the ends and fitting them snugly in each window. We'll add the door sills later.

To brick the tops of the arches over the openings cut a strip of brick paper one brick wide and long enough to pro-

Stations built to last

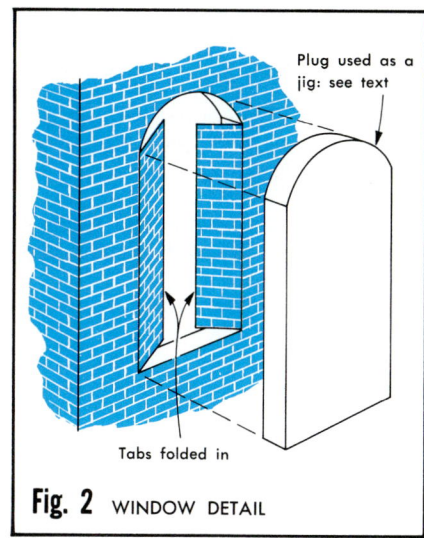

Fig. 2 WINDOW DETAIL

Fig. 1

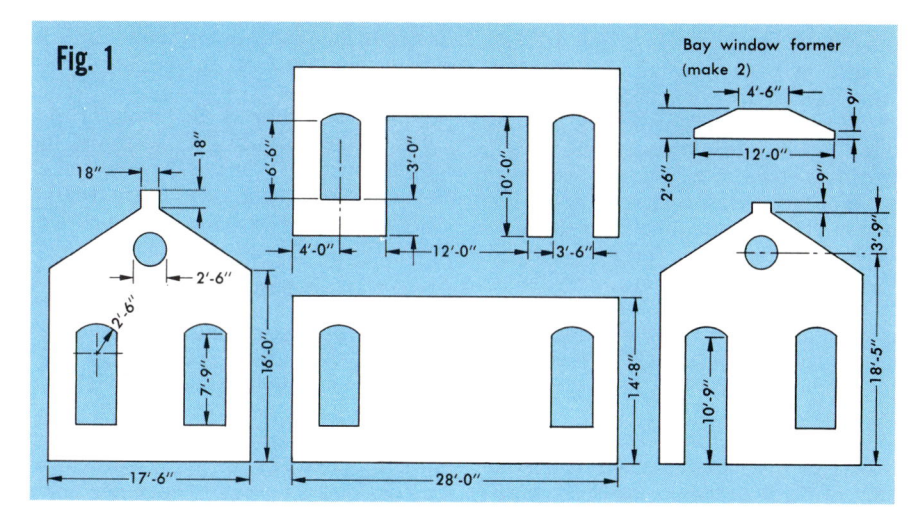

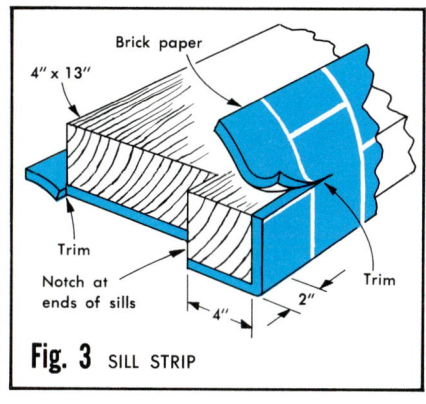

Bay window former (make 2)

Fig. 3 SILL STRIP

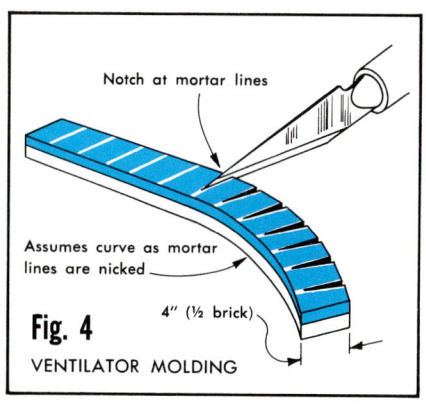

Fig. 4 VENTILATOR MOLDING

vide the pieces needed for the eight window and door openings and the two attic ventilators. About 40 running feet will do it.

Use 1½ x 5 material for the wood framing. I used scale lumber, supplemented with filecard (or Strathmore paper). Before cementing in the material, paint it. I painted mine light gray. Remember in modeling that lighter colors will always make details stand out.

Before tackling the projecting brick arches over the openings, lay out and rule all of the window glazing, including that for the bay window and the door transoms. Use a pen from a drawing set, filled with the same paint used for the framing, and a small compass with a nib for the curved line at the tops of windows and transoms. You can work directly over the plans if you have them enlarged or reduced to your scale, or you can make a pattern for the outside frames and tape your clear plastic stock directly to it. Go over the area of the transom windows with very fine sandpaper to simulate frosted glass.

Lay the windows aside for the time being. If they are installed now they are likely to pick up unsightly scratches when the brickwork is added.

Since the top inside surfaces of the brick end walls are partially visible in this style of structure, they must be covered with brick paper. Start about 15 feet from the bottom edge and extend brick paper all the way to the top and trim it to the configuration of the walls. This will cover the back of the round ventilator openings and ensure the ventilator is flush with the inner surface of the wall when it is added.

The decorative brick arches over doors and windows project half a brick length, or 4", from the openings. Therefore, this area must be covered with brick paper in the conventional arch pattern before adding the projecting arch. This pattern need not be made of individual bricks, but can be made using the method to be described for fabricating the protruding arch and attic vent molding.

Cement brick paper to a piece of cardstock 15 x 30 feet, 2" thick. This will be sufficient for all the stripping and individual bricks. Cover this material with waxed paper and dry it under pressure—a stack of magazines for instance—to prevent warping.

The height of the bricks in the projecting arch should be uniform. Cut a strip of brick paper and cardstock material vertically along the mortar lines of one brick, making it as wide as the length (8") of one brick and 35 feet long. The arch consists of a whole brick alternating with two brick ends; using a very sharp blade, make cuts at each mortar line along one side of the strip, extending the cut 6" to 7" in from the edge, fig. 4. These cuts will cause the strip to

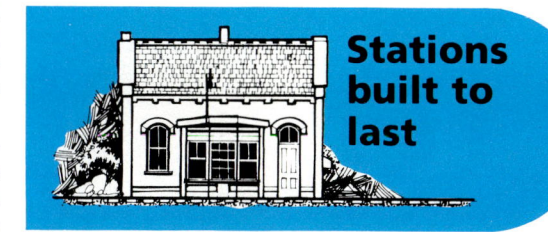

Stations built to last

43

curve, making it simple to form and cement each arch in a single piece, rather than brick by brick. The dog-ears under the ends of the arches drop a short distance at each side and are also located 4" from the opening. These pieces are made from the strip of brick-on-cardstock, cut to fit as shown in the drawings. A single brick on 1"-thick backing is added at the bottom of these ears.

Once you have completed the arches, add the circular brick molding around the attic vents. The system used for the door and window arches also works well here, except that the strip is half a brick (4") wide, and the cuts at the mortar lines are 3" deep. Total length needed is 20 feet.

Using a dowel wrapped with waxed paper and inserted in the vent hole as a guide—a knife handle worked nicely for me—cement the molding strip in place with the inside edge touching the guide all the way around. When the cement has dried remove the guide. You will be surprised and pleased with the result.

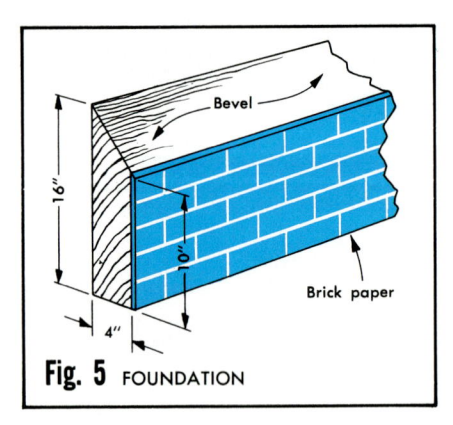

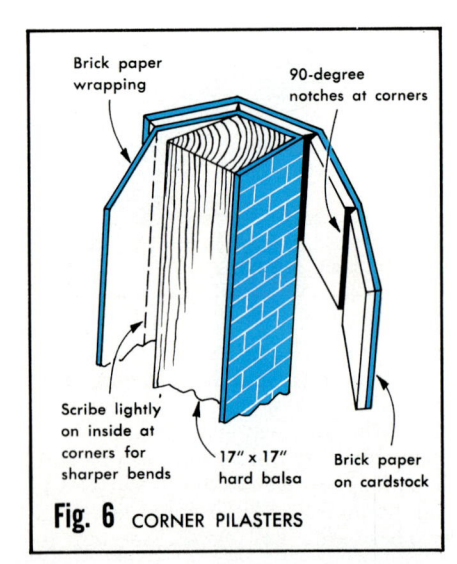

Next add the strips that build thickness around the foot of the walls. Start with a 4 x 16 strip of basswood about 100 feet long. Add a strip of brick paper five bricks wide to one side of the strip, fig. 5. Bevel the strip from the top of the bricks to the top of the back. Sand the bevel and paint it a concrete gray. Cement this strip to the ends and bay window side flush with the bottom. Trim the ends even with the ends of the sides. Add the back wall foundation when the chimney is in place for an exact fit. Shape a small piece of brick paper to fit the end of the beveled base strip and add it to the exposed ends at either side of the two doors.

End wall finishing

Now proceed with the four corner pilasters. Apply brick paper to four lengths of hard balsa 17 x 17 x 17'-0" long, fig. 6. This is longer than required to allow for trimming at the bottom later. Scribe each corner crease lightly (with a needle in a pin vise) for sharp corners. One inside corner of each pilaster won't be visible, and it's not necessary to match this corner perfectly. However, the same corner is not hidden on every pilaster, so use care when adding the projecting brick sections at the tops of these pilasters. Careful study of the drawing will show which corners are exposed.

The projecting section, or crown, of the corner pilasters is made from a wrapping of brick paper on cardstock material cut approximately 18" wide. The widths of bricks on brick paper vary from one make to another; the make you are using will determine the exact width of this wrapping. Cut it to the mortar line nearest the 18" dimension. Fig. 6 shows how to notch each corner for a sharp 90-degree angle. Be careful here that the open edge of the lapped joint is hidden on the back inside corner of the pilaster where it is cemented in place to the walls. But wait! . . .

Before affixing the corner pilasters to the end walls, cement 4 x 12 x 12'-0" lengths of basswood to the inside corners of all walls, flush with and parallel to the ends, fig. 14. These allow walls and corner pilasters to be pinned flat to your working surface during assembly. The crowns of the pilasters should extend past the edge of your working area to allow for the added 2" depth. The spacers added to the inner surface will cause the pilasters to project 4" from the surface of the wall. These strips serve a dual purpose. They take any warp—inherent where unlike materials are cemented together—out of the walls and provide a surface for adding an inside corner brace when the walls are assembled.

Having determined the height of the crowns, make notches 2" deep and as long as necessary in the top corners of the end walls to accommodate them. Carefully remove any cement squeezed out on the brick paper during assembly.

Doors—and more brickwork

While the end wall assemblies dry, make the doors. These consist of two thicknesses of cardstock with the paneling cut out of the outer piece, fig. 7. Both doors are trimmed square, 7'-6" high and 6'-0" wide. The extra width provides for cementing them to the inner surfaces of the walls. Paint the doors the same color as the framing and lay them aside with the windows.

The brick strip running between the crowns of the pilasters is made in the same manner as the foundation strip.

Fig. 5 FOUNDATION

Fig. 6 CORNER PILASTERS

Stations built to last

The front surface is made of three bricks that together are approximately 8" wide. The strip is 6" thick. The total width at the back of the strip is 10"; again we will bevel, sand, and paint the beveled surface a concrete gray. A little judicious sanding will lend the thickness needed to bring the bricked side flush with the pilaster crowns. Cut the length so the strip fits snugly between the crowns with the lower edge even with the bottoms and cement in place. Rolling a large dowel across the joints at the end of the piece will make them less noticeable.

Add the brickwork from the pilasters up to the roof peak next, fig. 8. Again, cement brick paper to cardstock. The bottom strip should be four bricks wide, the top strips three and two bricks wide respectively. Place the tops of all three strips flush with the tops of the end walls, and cut them vertically at the peak and bottom ends to match at the top center. Then fit them against the pilaster crowns. The bottom should be trimmed and beveled horizontally to fit snugly against the crossmember. See the end elevation drawing. Add two strips of brickpaper/cardstock material directly below the crossmember. The bottom strip is three bricks wide; the top strip, two bricks wide. Fit these between the pilasters, the top strip flush with the outer surfaces.

The gingerbread bricks added to these strips are shown in fig. 9. On 4'-3" centers, add two individual bricks-on-cardstock on the face of the bottom strip and against the lower edge of the top strip. Center a single brick below these two bricks and cement it to the wall. At the ends these additions should be cut down to one brick in place of two and half a brick instead of one.

To make the end peak trim, cut a 6"- thick piece of basswood 18" wide. Notch at the bottom to fit against the brickwork at the peak, cover with brick paper, and cement it in place against the vertical projections at the top of the ends. Leave the brick paper longer than necessary and it will cover the sides of these projections.

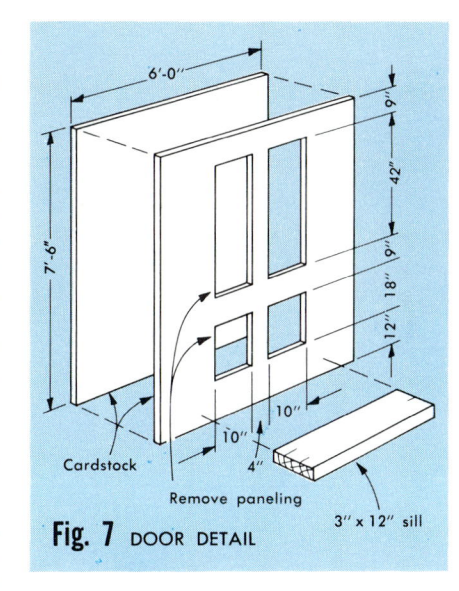

With all of the brickwork detail in place on the outer face of the ends, add a single brick-on-cardstock strip to the inside surface, parallel to and flush with the angles at the top (just as the strips were added to the outside).

Bay window

Before starting the bay window, study the plans and fig. 10. Prepaint the material required for construction with your trim color. Cut formers from 9"- thick balsa and cement them in place, fig. 1. Place the top former flush with the top of the bay window; the lower former flush with the bottom of the wall.

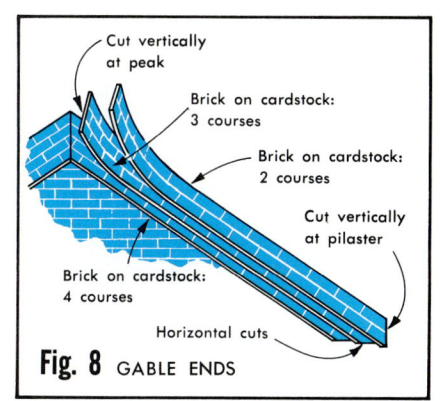

Now cut and fit the 6 x 6 framing at either side of the center window, and across the top and bottom of the three windows that constitute the sides of the bay. Apply 3"- thick basswood siding scribed 3" above and below the windows. It extends 2 feet up from the base, with an opening 18" wide at the center and 2 feet down from the top of the upper former. Bevel the siding pieces at the ends to match the wall and the adjoining scribed siding.

Install the 1½ x 3 framing piece that runs across the top of the bay window. Bevel the ends to fit flat against the wall. Next add the 1½ x 10 vertical framing at the far ends of the bay window; these too are beveled along the edge to fit against the brick wall. Remove a section from the bottom of this strip to allow a neat fit over the foundation. Fig. 10 shows the bay-window construction in detail, with a minimum of dimensions. Best results are achieved here by cutting each piece to fit as it is added. This allows for any slight variations.

Add the 1½ x 5 framing around the

Fig. 7 DOOR DETAIL

Fig. 8 GABLE ENDS

Full size for HO scale 3.5mm = 1 foot

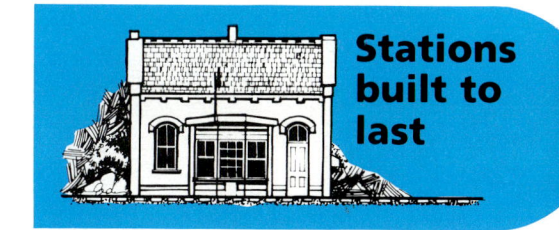

Stations built to last

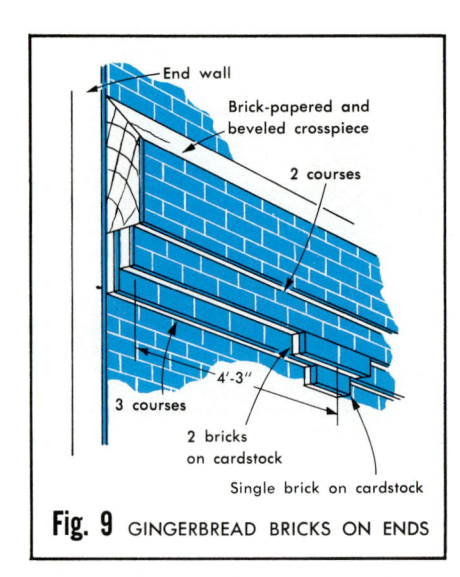

Fig. 9 GINGERBREAD BRICKS ON ENDS

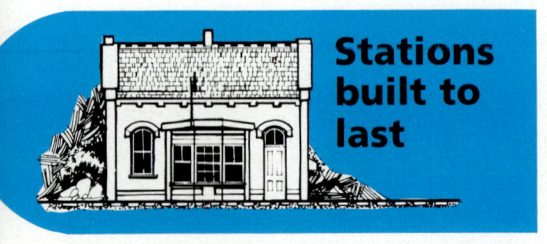

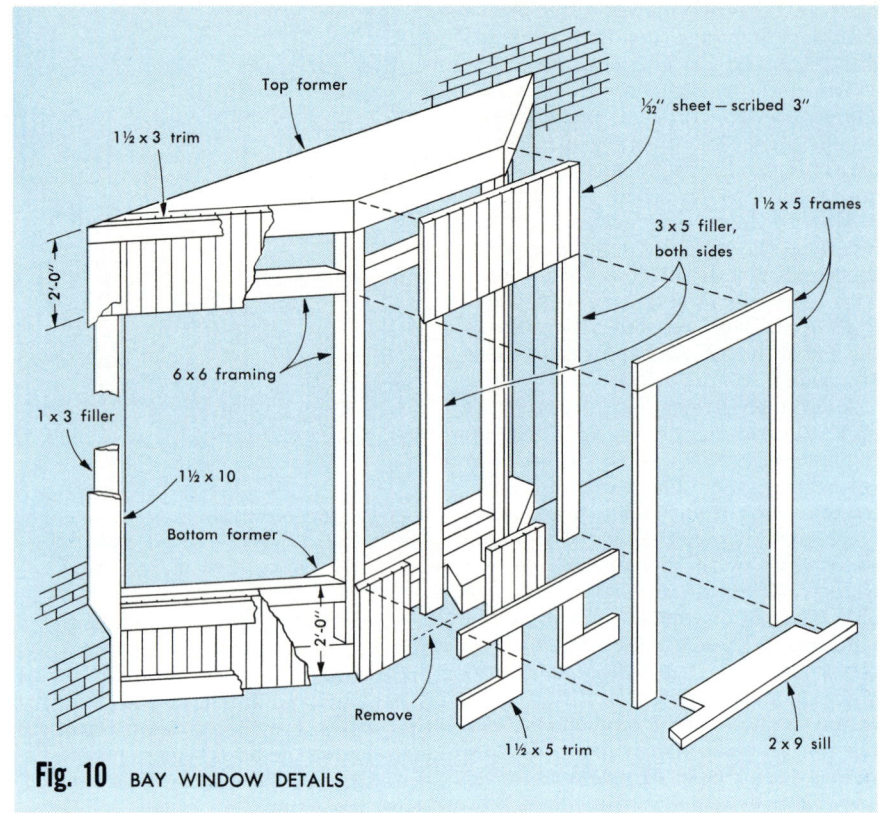

Fig. 10 BAY WINDOW DETAILS

Fig. 11 BAY WINDOW ROOF

wainscoting at the bottom of the bay window next. Note that the horizontal piece below the sill runs across the center opening. Before the window framing is added, filler pieces must be installed at either side of the windows. These are made of 3 x 5 stock, cut to fit between the scribed sections at top and bottom. These fillers give the framing a uniform thickness. Also, clear window material is cemented to them later.

The window framing is 1½ x 5 and fits exactly around the openings we have formed. There will be a 1½" to 2" crack at each angle. Basswood 2 x 9 stripping is used for the sills. Cut these a little longer than required and notch the three sills at either end to a depth of 6" so they fit neatly into the window openings. Cut the ends of the sills at a slight angle to make a smooth joint where they join, and trim the sills square where they touch the vertical framing.

The lined "glass" prepared for the bay window must be installed carefully. After cutting it to the proper size, fit the glass to the window sides and glue it in place, being careful not to get glue on the visible part of the pane. Now touch up any areas exposed by cutting and trimming. Window shades are made of ordinary brown envelope paper, cut and installed at random heights.

The bay window roof is built directly on the top bay window former. Prepaint the material with flat silver, including the 1½" cardstock for the actual roof (I used a calling card). Also, paint a piece of bond paper 3 feet wide and 15 feet long for flashing. Start by cutting two pieces of 6 x 6 stock 2'-3" long. Taper them to a point, fig. 11, and cement them in place at right angles to the brick wall, centered over the angles at the front of the former. The center section of the roof is a rectangle of painted cardstock 2'-6" x 4'-10", which allows for a 6" overhang at the front. It may be necessary to trim the cardstock to make it fit over the center of the two "rafters," but the point where the roof meets the wall will be covered by flashing, allowing for a small error. The triangular roof ends are 2'-6" wide, and come to a point 5'-0" from the 90-degree angle. This also allows a 6" overhang.

Next cut a strip 3" wide and long enough to make two ribs each 2'-6" long from the cardstock. Now make a crease in the center of the prepainted bond paper; measure 8" on one side of the crease and 3" on the other. Cut along these lines and use the creased piece for flashing material. The center flashing strip is 4'-10" long and the two end strips are 5'-0". When these are in place, trim the ends flush with the roof edge where it comes to a point, using the mortar lines as a guide. Install the ribs, centered over the two joints.

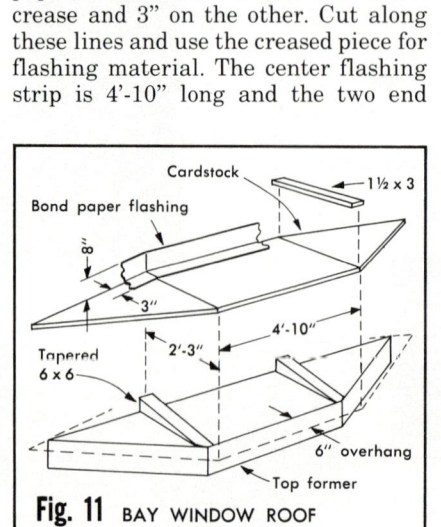

Touch up the edges of the eaves and wide sides of the ribs. Next remove the section of the bottom former below the center window, fig. 10.

Side walls

Decorative brickwork along the top of the wall is next. It is identical to the brickwork below the crossmember on the ends. Before starting, check the height of the sides with the corner pilasters already in place on the ends. The top of the sides should fit exactly against the bottom edge of the pilaster crowns. If either doesn't, now is the time to trim, or to add a shim strip at the top since the brickwork applied next will hide any adjustment.

Cement a strip of brick/cardstock three bricks wide flush with the top of the wall, then a strip two bricks wide. Add the one- and two-brick pieces as on the ends, but mount them on 3'-6" centers. As before, cut to a single brick and a half brick where the walls join the corner pilasters.

Before installing doors and windows, cement 4 x 12 filler strips at the ends of both walls to eliminate any warping.

When installing the windows be sure that they are centered and that the lined framing is uniform on all sides. Also, take care to keep the adhesive from squeezing out onto visible areas of the "glass." The cardstock doors should

Stations built to last

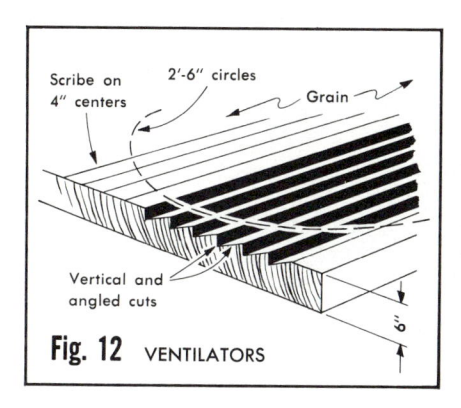

Fig. 12 VENTILATORS

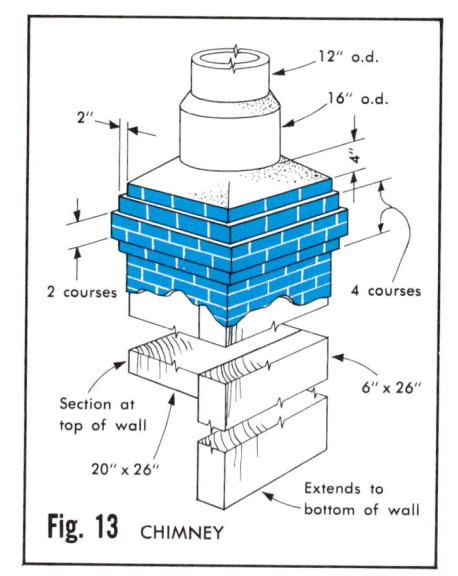

Fig. 13 CHIMNEY

be cemented in place with the bottoms matching the lower edge of the wall. Hold the transom window in place and scribe lightly across the doortop. Cut along this line and cement in position with the window touching the door. Cover this with a 1½ x 3 transom strip cut to fit snugly between the side framing. Add a sill of prepainted 3 x 12 basswood to complete the operation.

Slats in the ventilators

Add the ventilators next. Cut a rectangle of basswood 3 x 6 feet with the grain running the long way. Line this piece with the grain, on 4" centers. Fig. 12 shows the vertical and angled cuts made along the guidelines which will, in effect, give a 4" shiplap siding. Use a triangular jeweler's file to clean up these cuts. Stain the finished material by applying flat brown paint with a piece of cloth. The color will be darker where it gathers at the bottom of the cuts; this helps emphasize depth. Draw two circles on the material slightly over 2'-6" in diameter. Cut them out and sand to fit the openings. Use the mortar lines of the bricks to align the "slats" horizontally.

Chimney

The body of the chimney is made of two pieces. The longer, outside piece that extends down the back wall is 6 x 26 x 21'-0". Cement the second piece to this, even with the top end. The second piece measures 20" x 26" x 7'-0", giving a 26" x 26" section at the top. Cover this assembly with brick paper except where the inside surface of the 6 x 26 section will fit against the rear wall. This section will be three bricks square at the top and three bricks by three quarters of a brick at the bottom. Match the mortar lines at the corners. Bevel the top square section on all four sides to a point 4" above the top brick line; see fig. 13.

Just below this top brick line and by the width of one brick, add the first of the two wrappings. Cut the first wrapping four bricks wide and approximately 8 feet long. Use mortar lines as guides, and make 90-degree notches to ensure sharp outside corners—the same as in the pilaster crowns. Add this fancy brickwork to the chimney. Center a second wrapping, two bricks wide, on the first one. Paint the exposed beveled top a weathered, soot-tinged concrete gray.

Next, make and install the pipe at the top of the chimney assembly. Select a piece of aluminum or brass tubing of 12" outside diameter. Ream one end to bring the tubing wall to 1" or 2" thickness. Cut 3 feet off this reamed end and apply a wrapping of bond paper 15" wide to bring the outside diameter of the pipe to 16" at the lower end; cut a 3" bevel at the top of the wrapping. To make a solid joint between the pipe and the chimney, force-fit a dowel in this lower end and cut it off so it extends 6" to 8" from the

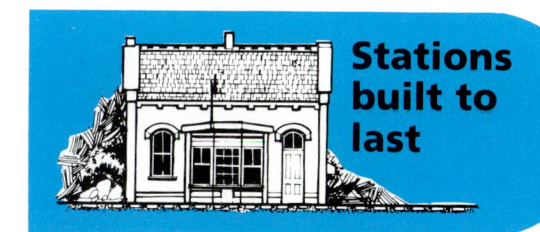

Stations built to last

47

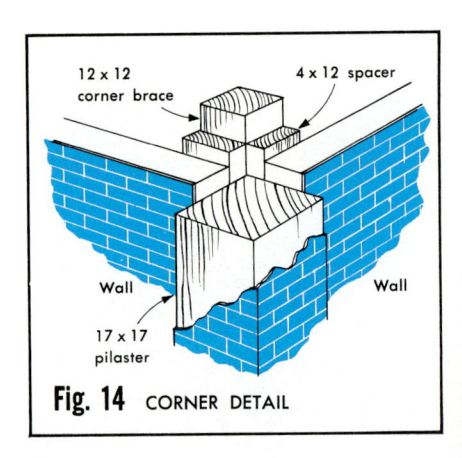

Fig. 14 CORNER DETAIL

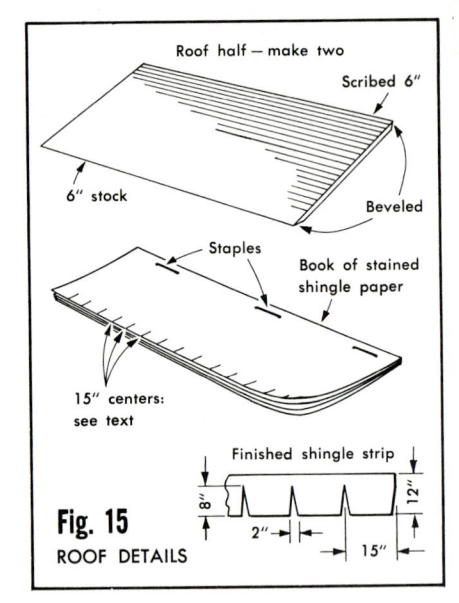

Fig. 15 ROOF DETAILS

bottom. Drill a hole in the center of the chimney so this plug will fit snugly, and cement the plug in place. Paint the bond paper bevel wrapping concrete gray, the upper portion of the pipe, sooty black.

Carefully locate the chimney assembly on the back wall. The chimney step should rest on the top of the wall. After the joint has dried, trim the bottom of the chimney even with the wall.

Add the two remaining sections of prepared brick foundation strip on either side of the chimney. They run out to the end of the wall. The fancy brickwork at the top of the wall can be added with two-brick strip and individual bricks. Space them as you did the decorative bricks on the front wall, eliminating the center pieces.

Interior detailing and assembly

Before assembling the sides, consider whether you want to detail the interior. Bear in mind that if the interior is detailed, the corner braces should be eliminated in favor of a floor; the structure will not lose rigidity. Even without interior lighting, the bare minimum for a station that will be under close scrutiny by visitors is a small desk with a blotter, some papers, and a lamp in the bay window. I chose this middle ground for my building. I installed the desk in the bay window and a few additional details, then illuminated only the front section—leaving it to the observer's imagination to assume the rest.

Once the interior is completed, proceed with the assembly of the walls. Fig. 14 gives a cross section of the corners with the bracing strips in place. These strips lend strength and help to obtain absolutely square corners. Don't stint on the cement (but be careful it doesn't go where you don't want it). Let the assembly dry overnight before starting the roof.

Shingling the roof

The roof is made by applying consecutive strips of prepared shingles. If you want to save time you can use those sold by various firms; I made mine the hard way. Take two sheets of bond paper and apply the selected roof color to them. I used dark green clothing dye, a tablespoon to about a half pint of water. I applied the color in vertical strokes, with no attempt to obtain a uniform shade; in fact, I made sure that there were subtle changes from stroke to stroke. Lay the sheets aside to dry.

Cut the two roof halves from a 6"-thick basswood sheet. These measure 12'-6" x 29'-0". They should be about 3 scale inches oversize to allow for trimming after they are installed. Rule these two pieces lengthwise with lines 6" apart to provide guidelines for applying the shingle strips. Bevel these pieces on the eave edge, to lie flat on the wall top, and on the upper edge, to fit against the ridgepole.

When the sheets of shingle paper are dry, cut them into sections about 20 feet wide and staple them into a book, fig. 15. Using a sheet of fine-line graph paper as a top sheet to the book makes cutting the shingles a lot easier, and gives considerably more accuracy. With the book stapled and squared, cut into the edge across the bottom on 15" centers to make individual shingle tongues. Each of these cuts is actually a small V about 2" across at the opening and at least 6" deep. I cut one layer at a time. As each strip is finished I cut it off to a 12" depth. Continue until you have enough material, about 2000 linear feet, to cover the roof halves. (That's around 1600 individual separations, or 3200 strokes of the knife!)

Apply the shingle strips starting at the eaves and working to the top, using the guidelines. The bottom strip should extend 3" past the edge of the roof base sheet. Apply the strips so that each is a half-shingle off the preceding strip. In other words, every other strip has the shingles aligned vertically; alternate strips have the shingles aligned vertically but half a shingle off center. Apply the shingles all the way to the top. Later a small piece of shingle material will be used for flashing between the roof and the ridgepole.

With shingling completed, carefully cut and fit the roof halves between the ends. Two notches are required on the front for the pilaster crowns; two similar notches plus a rectangle to accommodate the chimney are needed on the rear half. Exact dimensions are impossible to give for this step; it's just a matter of cut and fit, taking a little more with each cut until you have a snug fit. I waited until this point to make the bevel at the peak of each half, in order to keep the opening between the halves 3" wide for fitting the ridgepole.

When both roof halves are fitted to your satisfaction, cement four braces inside the end walls, one under each end of the two halves, to ensure a firm foundation for seating the roof sections. Cement both of them in place, using a

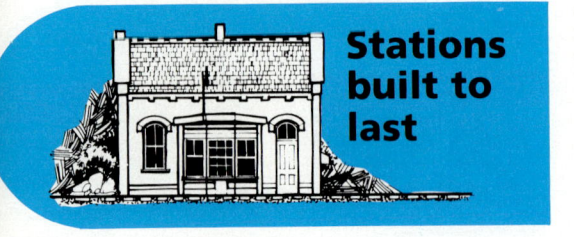

Stations built to last

Fig. 16 ROOF TRIM

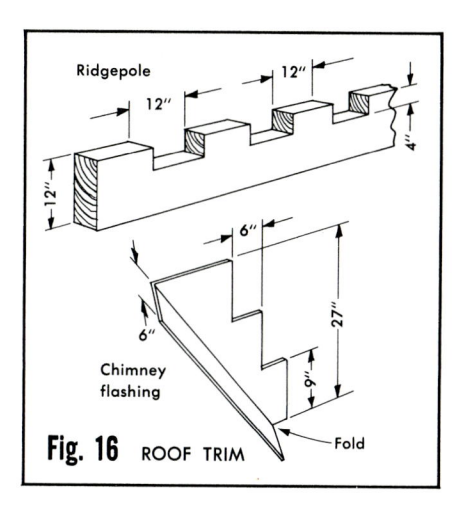

small strip of 3" material to hold the ridgepole opening to the right spacing. The overhang at the eaves is about 6" on the real building.

Make the ridgepole from a 3 x 12 strip 29 feet long. Tick-mark the entire length at 12" intervals and make cuts 4" deep. Connect these cuts with a straightedge, and remove every other section to form crenellations, fig. 16. Clean the notches with a jeweler's file and paint the ridgepole dark gray before cementing it between the roof halves.

The chimney flashing is bond paper painted flat silver to simulate sheet metal. The shape and dimensions of the side flashing are shown in fig. 16. Don't forget that one of the sides is a reverse of the pattern. The chimney has flashing on only three sides. The flashing on the third side will be determined by the height of the side flashing—it must match. It must also match the width of the 6" section of side flashing that extends out from the chimney.

The capping on the end walls can now be added. Start by cutting a strip of basswood 60 feet long from 3 x 26 material. Paint the strip concrete gray. First cut the capping for the four pilasters. This projects 2½" over the three outer sides and is even with the inside edge of the pilaster crown, where it adjoins the capping running up the angle at the top of the end wall. Cut four pieces for this angle capping. Bevel these at the bottom to fit against the pilaster caps, and notch them at the top to fit the projections at the peaks of the end as shown in the front elevation drawing. The pieces meet at the center of the top on the inside of the wall and should be cut to fit neatly. When they are matched with the pilaster caps they will project the same 2½" from the brickwork at the top of the wall on the outside.

Final details

The overall dimensions of the order box hung near the door are shown in fig. 17. Make it from scrap balsa or basswood, with a cardstock top cut to project 2" on the front and sides. Paint it brown and cement in place.

The support for the signal flag and the flagstaff are made of 2" wire. The shape is shown in the drawing. Drill holes in the main and bay roof for mounting the frame. Make the flag from bond paper and add it to the staff before mounting. Fasten the flagstaff to the frame with a touch of solder and install the assembly. According to an old-time railroader, a red flag meant "Stop for orders," and a green flag meant "No orders."

Use your favorite method and materials for aging the structure. Remember that years' accumulation of soot would have washed vertically down the sides, and gathered in corners of the gingerbread brickwork. My station was aged with a fine chalk powder rubbed vertically with a soft cloth. If you use a wash, be sparing with it—there is no way I know to erase mistakes on brickpaper surfaces!

The station is now finished, and you should be able to pick up a card as a journeyman bricklayer at the local union office.

I will leave construction of the platform to you. You know the shape and size of the area on your layout available for the station; whether it is on curved or tangent track; and how far the station will stand from the track. I suggest a cinder platform with 6 x 15 timbers holding the fill. The platform detail should be the usual clutter of boxes, barrels, crates, and similar items found in l.c.l. (less-than-carload-lot) freight shipments. If your platform is long, there might be a baggage truck or two.

One thing is certain: If you locate the station on a main line, be sure to include a train-order stand. By the very size of the station we can assume that the fast blue-ribbon varnish and hotshot freights will go storming past with no more than a whistle blast to acknowledge our way station. In our mind's eye we see the station as the hub of activity for the small community it serves. On a balmy summer evening the daily mixed local drifts to a stop about 8:15. All of the local inhabitants have strolled down to the station to see if any of the town's citizens are making the 40-mile trip to the big city, and to stare curiously at any drummers arriving to spend a day or so at the local boardinghouse. The conductor has a casual, friendly chat with the agent, then calls "All aboard!" and waves a highball to the waiting engineer. The mixed moves out with considerably more noise than speed. The townspeople exchange small talk for a while, then gradually make their ways home—leaving the little station to doze in the bright moonlight until aroused in the morning by the rattle of the milk train.

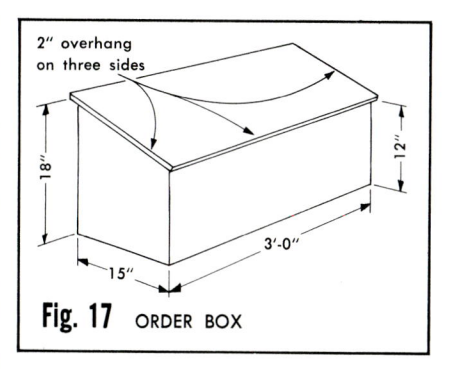

Fig. 17 ORDER BOX

Stations built to last

49

All photos, KALMBACH BOOKS: A. L. Schmidt unless otherwise credited.

Mail-order station

Choose parts and materials from a wide range of available components and assemble your own "kits" from a catalog. The result: Unique stations for your railroad.

by Bob Hayden

NOT a great many years ago the mail-order catalog was more than a way of finding odd items not stocked at your local shopping center—it was virtually the *only* means of obtaining anything but the staples carried in your town's trade district. The first step in home additions, automotive repairs, farm improvements, or even a new wardrobe was perusal of thick and thin catalogs. After much soul-searching, off went the letter with a postal money order, and for several weeks the daily visit from the postman was an event of great importance and suspense. Railroads also purchase many hardware items mail-order, ordering everything from nuts, bolts, and rail joiners to locomotives from manufacturers' catalogs of stock items.

More firms than ever before now stock and sell parts for model railroad structures, and the extensive variety of these commercial materials (see box) makes catalog shopping possible in miniature. The resulting "technique" falls between scratchbuilding and building from kits, because while you use many of the time- and work-saving parts featured in kit models, you still do the designing and planning associated with the scratchbuilding process.

Choose the station first— then the parts

To mail order a station of your own, start by selecting a design. This can be a model that someone else has built, a prototype building for which you have drawings, or your own free-lance pattern. Once you have chosen a structure, browse through a stack of catalogs from hobby shops and model railroad supply houses. With photos or sketches of the structure in hand, decide what parts and materials to use. Determine which doors, windows, and detail items offered suit the design you've selected, and make a list of such items, along with their part numbers, on scratch paper. Have a scale ruler handy to "scale out" pieces that are not shown full size in the catalogs. Look for siding material and roofing stock, and add notes to your list as you progress. Make sure you consider such things as substructures and bracing material. Try to generate as complete a list of required items as you can, including quantities of materials based on your estimated measurements of the building.

When your note pad is crammed full of numbers, decide what materials you'll use, and mail off your order. Improvements in postal and private parcel delivery have shortened many mail-order transactions to only two or three weeks, and this wait is often justified by your savings in transportation alone. Anyway, there's plenty to do while we await arrival of the goods.

Scaling your own drawings

I had no drawing for the station I chose to model via mail order, a small stone lakefront structure called Marbles, built in 1906 to serve a sprawling resort hotel in Rangeley, Maine. The station was at the end of the 2-foot-gauge Phillips & Rangeley Railroad, just 2 minutes by rail from Rangeley station. It looks—and is—sturdy, and outlasted both the railroad and the massive frame hotel by several decades. Quite austere, it lacks the difficult-to-model curlicues and gimcracks that often characterized resort stations.

Because I had no plans or dimensions of the prototype, I based my model on

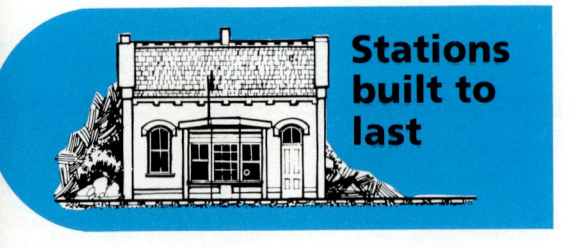

Stations built to last

50

Hayden collection.

Hayden collection.

USING COMMERCIAL PARTS

Many modelers substantially reduce the time, effort, and tedium involved in constructing structures by using commercial door, window, and detail castings. These parts eliminate the repetitive operations required to make frames, sashes, and trim parts, and allow you to move quickly through the basic construction steps.

Cast structure parts are either soft metal or plastic, with the metal items sporting the higher price tags. While styles change as manufacturers change their lines, there are always plenty of types to choose from; the best way to determine what is available is to consult a large mail-order hobby catalog. Your local hobby shop may carry several brands of castings, but chances are he can't keep all lines and styles in stock.

Because cast parts offer advantages in time and ease of construction, it's worth expending extra effort to use them properly. Use a hobby knife, files, and a sanding block to eliminate excess material or mold separation lines from the castings. To remove mold release chemicals and finger oils, wash the parts in denatured alcohol or a detergent solution, rinse with water, and air dry. Handle the parts with tweezers after cleaning, since your hands exude oils that can prevent paint from adhering.

Paint the parts before assembling your structure; spraying saves time, but careful brushing produces excellent results. Use plastic-compatible paints that won't attack the finished surfaces of plastic parts. After painting, let the parts cure for two or three days. This drying period is important to ensure that the paint will not rub or chip off during handling.

When you prepare your structure walls to accept the parts, cut openings undersize and sand or file for a snug fit. This ensures that you won't have to discard a wall section because an opening is a shade too large.

photos. I used the sizes of the parts I had chosen and some common-sense reasoning to scale my working drawings of Marbles station. I began by assembling all the photos I could find of the building. I scaled the diameter of the cylindrical turret portion using the width of the first floor Grandt Line windows I had chosen from the catalog as an assumed dimension, and made the distance between windows proportional to the width. The process—applicable to any structure you want to model—went something like this: Reasoning that I could see precisely half of the cylinder in a photo, I noted all three window-casing openings were in one half of the turret, with the distance between window casings being greater than the width of the windows. I measured the Grandt Line window width (3', including trim) and used 1½ times the width (4½') as the distance between windows. The circumference of *half* the turret, then, is equal to the width of three windows (3' x 3 = 9'), plus twice the distance between windows (4½' x 2 = 9'), or 18'. That makes the circumference of the whole turret section about 36'. To determine the diameter of the cylinder, I divided the circumference by the factor *pi* (3.14 is close enough for our purposes) and came up with a figure for the diameter of 11½'. A trip to my local stationery store produced a standard 1½" inside diameter (i.d.) mailing tube which scales 11'-8" outside diameter (o.d.) in

Stations built to last

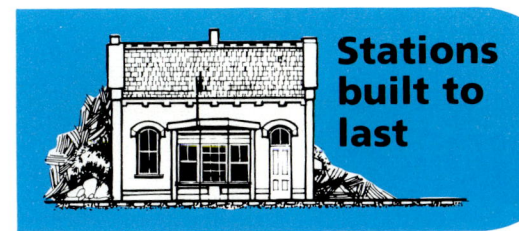

51

Full size for N scale .075" = 1 foot

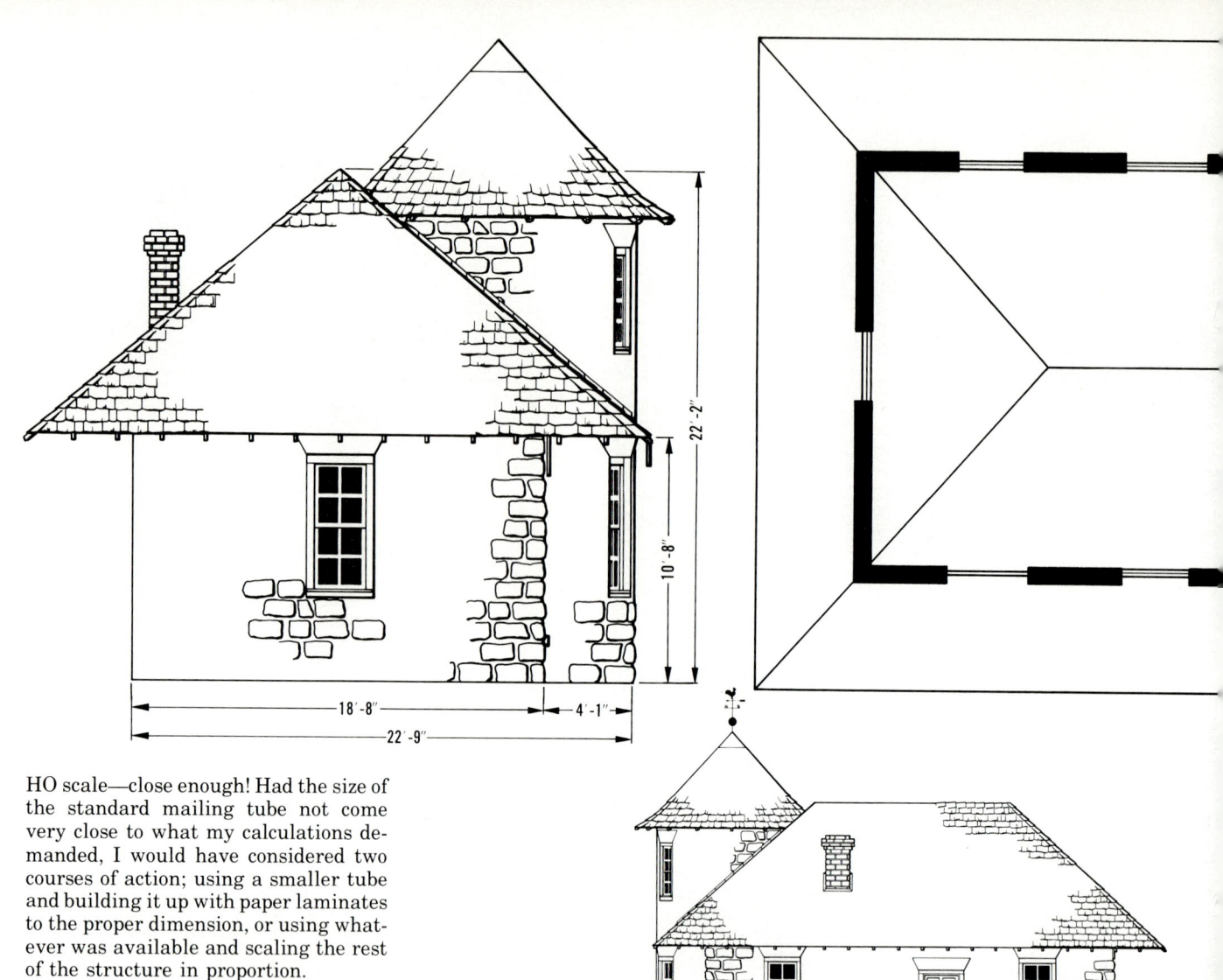

HO scale—close enough! Had the size of the standard mailing tube not come very close to what my calculations demanded, I would have considered two courses of action; using a smaller tube and building it up with paper laminates to the proper dimension, or using whatever was available and scaling the rest of the structure in proportion.

I used the diameter of the turret as a basis to roughly determine the other measurements of the structure. Referring to a photo that showed the station from the greatest distance (to minimize distortion caused by the camera in a closeup shot), I used dividers to develop a ratio between the height of the turret section and its diameter. I arrived at a "guesstimate" of just under 2:1—the height of the little tower is not quite twice its width. I settled on a height to the eaves of 21'-3".

Armed with the above information, I started my rough construction drawings. Make your initial "sketch" drawings on tracing paper. Place a sheet of graph paper under the top sheet of a tracing paper pad to provide a guide for right angles and parallel lines. The tracing paper allows you to check your drawing by placing it over plans of a similar structure. This will reveal discrepancies and inconsistencies such as windows placed too high or low or insufficient ceiling clearances in a multi-story building. After drawing the turret section, I used a similar approach to estimate wall lengths and heights.

To determine the size of the hip roof profiles, I simply chose several ridgepole heights and lengths and experimented to find which ones looked best. This type of roof is perhaps the most difficult to scale in this manner. The hip corners must fall over the structure corners, making the shape of the roof dependent on the proportions of the wall structure.

One note on designing your station and drawing your own plans: Don't consider your plans final or begin construction until you have your door and window pieces in hand. Place them over your drawings and re-evaluate your planning; you may want to change something for a better effect, and it is much easier to make changes *before* you've bitten into the materials.

Construction

Begin work on the station model by altering the door and window castings, fig. 1. Note the short length of HO 4 x 4 stock added to the bottom trim of each part to represent the heavy wood sill of the prototype. I built my doors without the diagonal novelty muntins shown in the plans and prototype photos, because I did not feel I could do the job neatly and to scale. When the modifications are complete, clean and prime for painting all but one of each type casting (door, large window, small window); you'll need these as guides for cutting and fitting the wall openings.

Lay out the main subwalls on a sheet of heavy cardstock, fig. 2. I used an inexpensive multi-ply material, .055" thick, called mounting board. Mine was white on one side and gray-green on the other, with a light gray middle. In this application it works particularly well because it provides rigidity, a good gluing surface, and a ready-made dark interior. Use a new single-edge razor

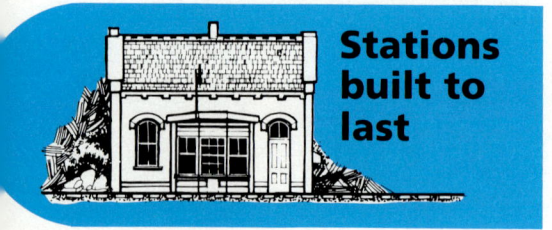

Stations built to last

Full size for HO scale 3.5mm = 1 foot

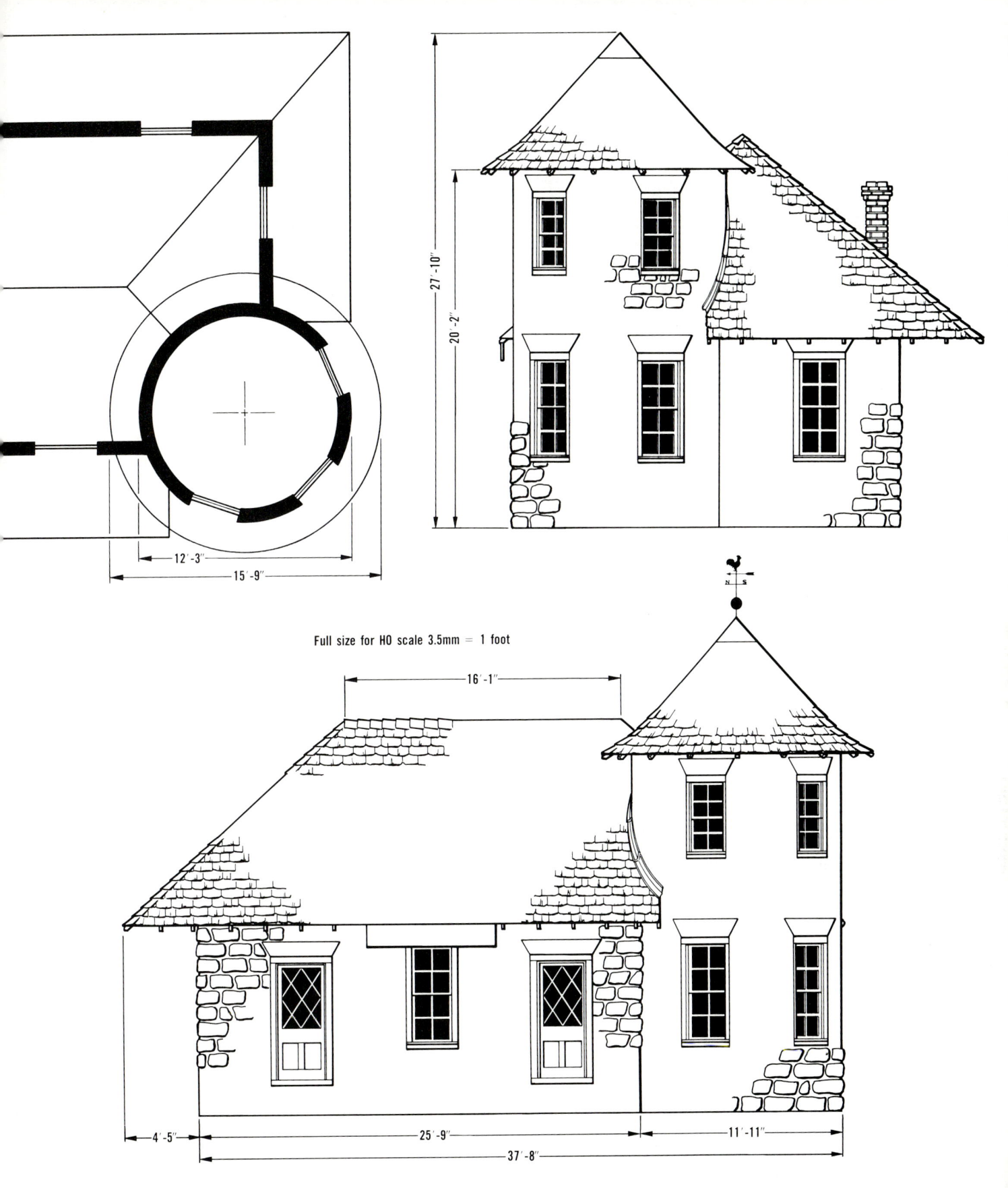

blade or modeling knife to cut the window and door openings slightly undersize, then cut the subwall section from the sheet. Cut the three corners halfway through and bend to form a rectangle, leaving room for the turret. Add stripwood or styrene bracing and corner blocks to the interior, including some thick corner gussets. Make sure this assembly is sturdy (see photos), because it will be handled a lot in subsequent steps.

The subformer for the turret on my HO model is made from a 1½" i.d. mailing tube. The turret will be 21'-3" tall, but cut your stock about 6 inches longer to allow for sanding at both ends. Sand the ends by rubbing them over a sheet of

Stations built to last

53

A Typical Mail-Order Shopping List
BILL OF MATERIALS: HO SCALE

Commercial parts

1 pkg.	Campbell Scale Model Profile shingles No. 800
1 sheet	Campbell stone No. 810
1 pkg.	Campbell pigeons No. 1401
1 set	Concept Classic Detail etched brass weather-vane kit No. 400
2 pkgs.	Grandt Line Products HO eight-pane double hung window No. 5029 (27" x 64")
1 pkg.	Grandt double hung window No. 5030 (27" x 48")
1	Grandt baggage wagon No. 5033
1 pkg.	Grandt station door, No. 5058
1 set	Jordan Products spare baggage No. W-10
1 pkg.	Kemtron Corporation nut-bolt-washer castings; medium, hex nut, No. 575
1	Structure Company Station chimney No. 1504
1 set	Union Line dry transfer alphabets — white, Railroad Gothic (sign)

Wood, card, and styrene stock

1 pkg.	Camino "Handy Pack" HO scale 10 x 10 (platform)
1 sheet	Strathmore two-ply bristol board (dunce cap roof)
1 sheet	mounting board, approx. .055" thick
1	mailing tube, 1½" inside diameter (turret)
1 pkg.	Evergreen Scale Models styrene strips, HO sizes: No. 8112 - 1 x 12 (lintels) No. 8204 - 2 x 4 (rafter ends) No. 8404 - 4 x 4 (sills) No. 8612 - 6 x 12 (bracing)
1 pkg.	Evergreen .020" styrene sheet No. 9020 (sign)
1 pkg.	Evergreen .060" styrene sheet No. 9060 (gussets, platform base)
1 pkg.	Walthers .015" clear styrene sheet No. 949-599 (glazing)

Miscellaneous

1 scrap	.010" straight wire (weather-vane staff)
1	roundhead plastic map pin (weather-vane ball)
1 scrap	gummed brown paper kraft tape (cap shingles, flashing)
1 pkg.	cinder or crushed stone fill

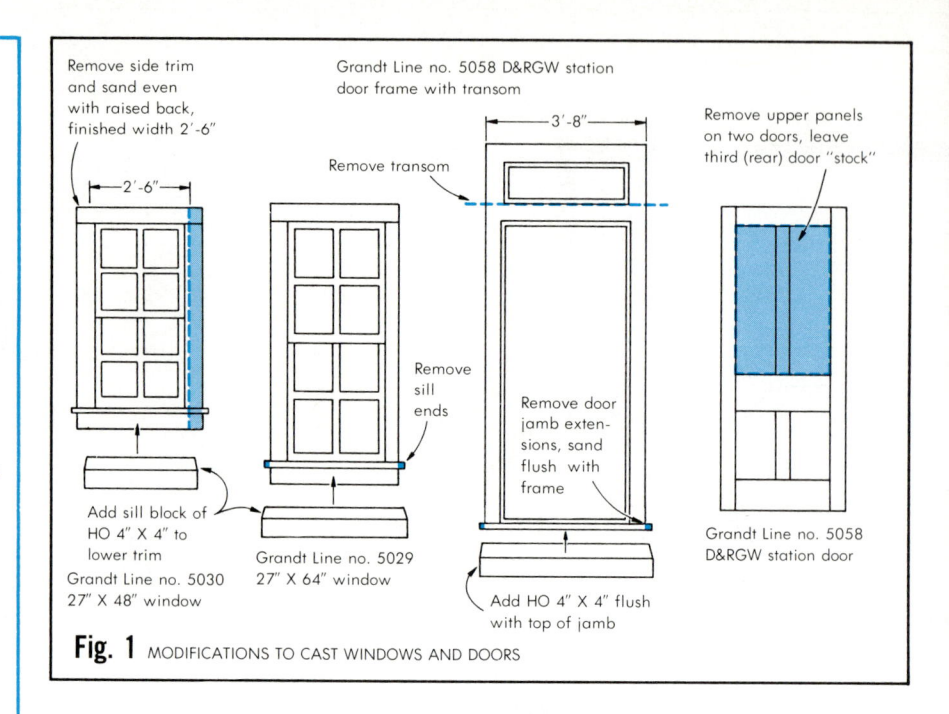

Fig. 1 MODIFICATIONS TO CAST WINDOWS AND DOORS

- Remove side trim and sand even with raised back, finished width 2'-6"
- Add sill block of HO 4" X 4" to lower trim
- Grandt Line no. 5030 27" X 48" window
- Remove sill ends
- Grandt Line no. 5029 27" X 64" window
- Grandt Line no. 5058 D&RGW station door frame with transom
- Remove transom
- Remove door jamb extensions, sand flush with frame
- Add HO 4" X 4" flush with top of jamb
- Remove upper panels on two doors, leave third (rear) door "stock"
- Grandt Line no. 5058 D&RGW station door

sandpaper taped to your work surface until the former is correct. Use a flat surface and a small square to check that the cylinder stands up straight all around.

Lay out the window openings on the turret former as shown in the drawings. Cut a 6'-square opening in the rear of the former to allow light to show through the rear windows and into the bay area. Again, cut the window openings undersize.

Now, using an emery board, carefully sand out the window openings in the turret and the main structure wall former to a press fit for your window and door castings. Because they are expendable, the emery boards can be cut down the middle to make small sanders for the narrow windows and odd corners. Do not attach the turret former to the main substructure yet.

Stone texture— and some special adhesives

The molded stone material that I selected to represent the granite blocks of the prototype Marbles station is one of several such products available. All have a 3-D texture embossed or molded (vacuum-formed in some cases, injection-molded in others) into one side. Used properly, each provides a good simulation of a masonry surface. They do, however, present problems in two areas: adhesives, and edge finishing. Most adhesives did not adhere well to the Campbell material I used, and some with good holding power made the stone sheet shrink after application. The edge problem stems from the fact that stone or brick buildings do not have convenient corner trim boards as do frame structures, and require treatment to make the wall texture look as if it continues around the corners. Since the 3-D textures are often hollow on the back, simply butting them together at joints or corners leaves unsightly gaps that require some kind of filler, and sometimes even a little sculpting.

I made sample sections of both the mailing tube and mounting board sub-base materials, and set out to find acceptable gluing methods, and ways to handle corners, edges, window openings, and shrinkage. After some noteworthy failures, I hit upon the method described here. While it involves some extra work, it minimizes sculpting, eliminates the corner problem, and defeats any shrinking tendencies.

The stone material is first cut to wall height, formed into a wrapper, washed in detergent and water, and glued to the cardboard formers with a 5-minute setting two-part epoxy glue. This adhesive has a thick, syrupy consistency, and flows into the pockets in the back of the plastic stone material, providing a cast duplicate of the hollow back side that serves to lock the stone in place and prevent shrinking. After about half an hour of setting, though, the stone material can be loosened and pulled away from the epoxy—the bond is not 100 per cent sound. I therefore recommend this two-step gluing process: (1) Glue the stone sheet in place with epoxy, wait 30 minutes, and loosen, and (2) cement the stone back to the epoxy surface with an ACC (cyanoacrylate) adhesive, one of the modern "super glues." It sounds tricky, but it isn't. The key to success and neatness lies in taking time to carefully align the stone texture sheet during both stages.

The round turret form requires some special preparation, so let's start with the main section of the structure. Cut a horizontal strip of the stone material

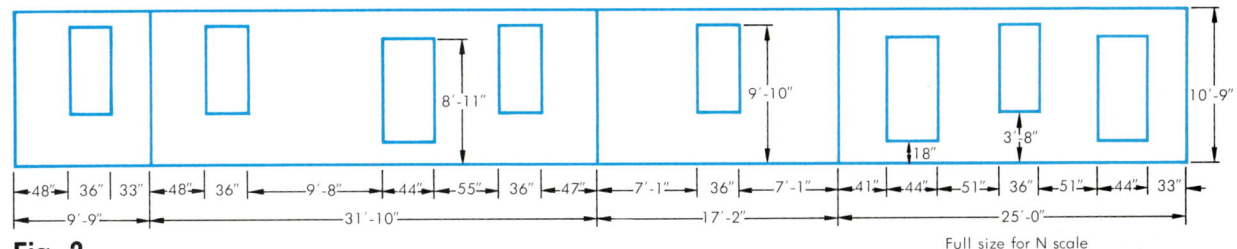

Fig. 2 MAIN WALL FORMER

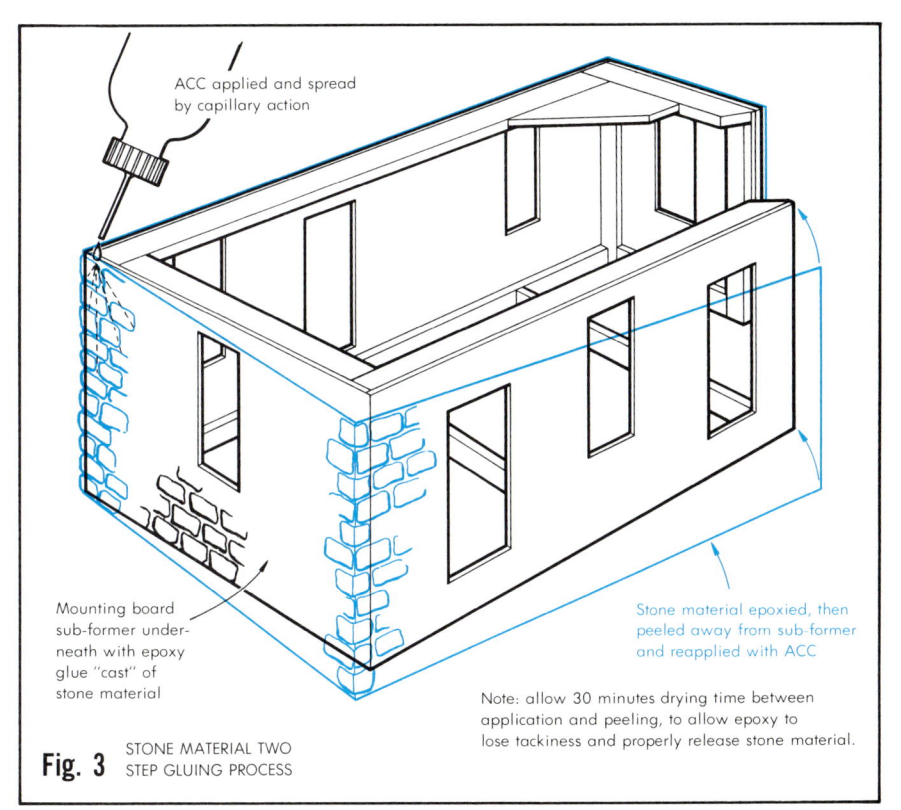

Full size for N scale

Fig. 3 STONE MATERIAL TWO STEP GLUING PROCESS

ACC applied and spread by capillary action

Mounting board sub-former underneath with epoxy glue "cast" of stone material

Stone material epoxied, then peeled away from sub-former and reapplied with ACC

Note: allow 30 minutes drying time between application and peeling, to allow epoxy to lose tackiness and properly release stone material.

12'-6" wide, or 14 stone courses high, and the full length of the stock. We will sidestep the corner problem by carefully folding and creasing the stone sheet to fit around the form; sculpting will be required only where the main part of the building intersects the turret—two easy-to-disguise inside joints. Make a right-angle bend in the strip of stone material by folding it over a straightedge. Check to see that the bend is perpendicular to the horizontal stone courses before you fold. Then hold the once-folded sheet in place over the form and mark the location for the second right-angle bend. Fold again, check the results, and continue until your stone material is a slip-fit wrapper for the mounting-board former. I made a couple of 1/32" mistakes here and found it possible to gently flatten the stone sheet and refold it, although more than two refoldings started to produce stress cracks in the stone. If your folded stone wrapper is too small to fit the form, try rounding the corners of the form, or even lightly sanding the face of the mounting board to achieve a workable fit.

When you've completed bending the wrapper, clean it in detergent and rinse, dry, and start epoxying it to the rear wall. Align the bottom edge of the stone material with the base of the former. Mix epoxy in manageable batches and apply it in 1" vertical bands as you move along the wall. When the rear wall is done, wait 30 minutes, peel it away from the former, and re-cement with ACC, fig. 3. Continue working, one wall at a time, until the main structure section is complete.

Preforming the turret wrapper

The wrapper for the turret cylinder must be preformed to the contour of the mailing tube former in order for the two-step cementing technique to work well. After considering several forming methods, I used hot water to heat the stone material while holding it around a cylindrical form. Cut a strip of stone sheet 21'-3" high and long enough to fit around the mailing tube with no more than a ¼" (actual) overlap. Wrap the stone sheet around a 1½" o.d. metal pipe, wood dowel, or other material that will withstand both heat and moisture, and wrap about three layers of shirt cardboard, poster board, or other dense cardstock material around this, secur-

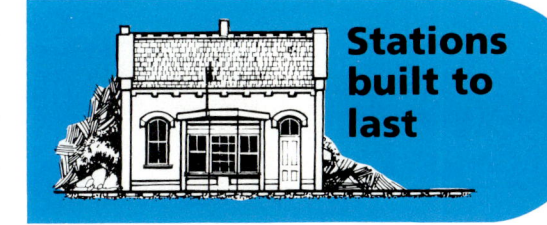

Stations built to last

55

Fig. 4 PRE-FORMING STONE TURRET

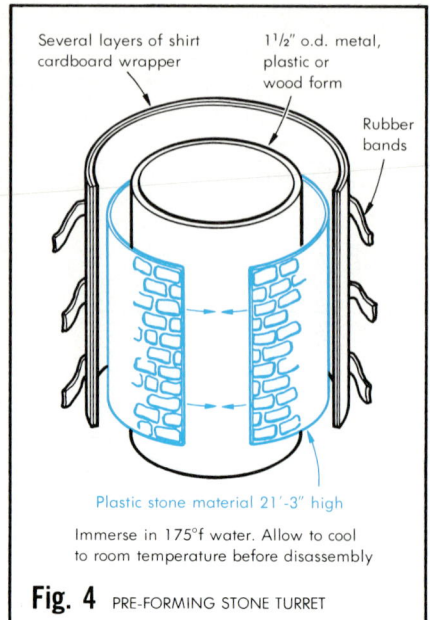

- Several layers of shirt cardboard wrapper
- 1½" o.d. metal, plastic or wood form
- Rubber bands
- Plastic stone material 21'-3" high
- Immerse in 175°f water. Allow to cool to room temperature before disassembly

ing the entire multi-layer roll with several heavy rubber bands, fig. 4.

Place your rolled mandrel, plastic, and cardstock into a heatproof vessel such as a Pyrex or metal container, and pour in enough hot water to cover the whole works. The water should be below boiling temperature when you pour it in—mine was about 175 degrees F.—and should be allowed to cool slowly to room temperature. When you remove the soggy cardboard the plastic stone stock will have assumed a permanent cylindrical set. Align the bottom edges and glue the wrapper to the turret former using the same two-step gluing method employed on the main wall section. I found I had to work slowly here, first placing epoxy on a ¾"-wide vertical band in the center of the wrapper, and working in ½"-wide bands on either side of the first until I reached the joints opposite the center set of turret windows. Unlike the method used for the flat walls, each application of epoxy is peeled away and cemented back with ACC as you progress around the turret.

Use a modeling knife with several sharp blades to cut out all window and door holes in the stone sheet. Do not cut all the way to the edges with the knife, but leave about 1/32" to be removed with emery boards, again making press fits for the window and door castings. Fill in the edges of the window and door openings with dabs of epoxy to hide the "hollow" backing of the material, and once more sand to accept windows and doors.

Door and window lintels

Contrasting solid stone lintels were worked into the walls of the prototype station above each opening flush with the surrounding stonework. I substituted protruding lintel stones, as flush construction is too difficult to model neatly. Use templates, fig. 5, to cut the lintels from scale 1 x 12 styrene. Preform the lintels for the turret by bending them with your fingers, and glue all lintels in place with epoxy, lower edge flush with the upper edge of the opening. Test adhesion after 30 minutes setting time; if a lintel comes loose, glue it back with ACC. Then lightly coat each lintel with epoxy. As the adhesive sets, manipulate it so the surface becomes rippled and uneven; simply dip your knife blade into the glue and lift a small portion of it. The glue will set with gentle waves on the face of the lintel—just the effect we want. Spread epoxy over the lintel edges, and while it is still soft—but no longer fluid or tacky—trim it even with the edges of the lintel to simulate a cut stone piece that extends back *into* the wall. Check fit the doors and windows again, and remove any projections that interfere.

At this point you can join the inside corners where the turret and main wall sections meet. On a flat surface, place a sheet of waxed paper over the plan view of the structure and use epoxy to glue the wall and turret sections together. When this assembly has set, fill the joints with epoxy and sculpt them with the knife (while the epoxy is soft) to represent mortar lines continuing through the corners. This step completes the stone walls of the structure. You'll find that the model, like the prototype, is quite sturdy.

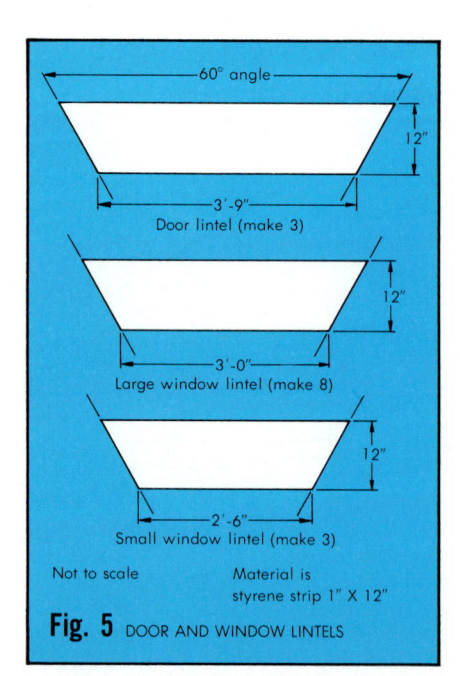

Fig. 5 DOOR AND WINDOW LINTELS

- 60° angle
- 12"
- 3'-9"
- Door lintel (make 3)
- 12"
- 3'-0"
- Large window lintel (make 8)
- 12"
- 2'-6"
- Small window lintel (make 3)
- Not to scale
- Material is styrene strip 1" X 12"

Construction break: painting time

Before we move on to roof construction, let's get some paint on the wall parts. To maintain a resort flavor in my model, I selected colors to enhance the whimsical, vacation atmosphere of the design. The walls are a warm blue-gray concocted from 1 part light blue, 3 parts earth tan, and 10 parts medium gray. The blue is the strongest color of the three, so mix the paint by adding blue to the gray, not vice versa. I used earth color to give the rock warmth; we want a warm gray color with a blue cast. The mortar treatment will tone down whatever colors you use, so apply a color that is somewhat stronger than the color you want. The Campbell stone is compatible with all types of paint, and you can use

Stations built to last

56

full size for N scale   Material: mounting board .055" thick

Fig. 6 HIP ROOF FORMER LAYOUT

Layout on .055" (actual) thickness mounting board as follows: Draw line A-B, length 15'-9". Set compass to 15'-9", put the point on B, and draw a short arc from A above line A-B. Set compass to 21'-9" and draw semicircles outward from points A and B. Set compass at 33'-6" and draw arcs from points A and B to intersect the 21'-9" semicircles at points C and D. We'll label these two points of intersection C and D. Draw a third 33'-6" arc segment from B to define point G. Draw lines A-C, B-D, and C-D. Set compass at 27'-3" and draw arcs from C and D to intersect the 21'-9" semicircles at points we'll call E and F. Draw lines A-E, B-F, C-E, and D-F. Set compass to length of C-D, and draw an arc from F to intersect the 33'-6" arc drawn earlier from B. This intersection becomes G. Set compass at 21'-9" and draw arc from G to intersect the 15'-9" arc from B. This is H. Draw B-H, F-G, and G-H. Erase construction lines and draw in cutouts for turret freehand for trial and error fitting on the structure.

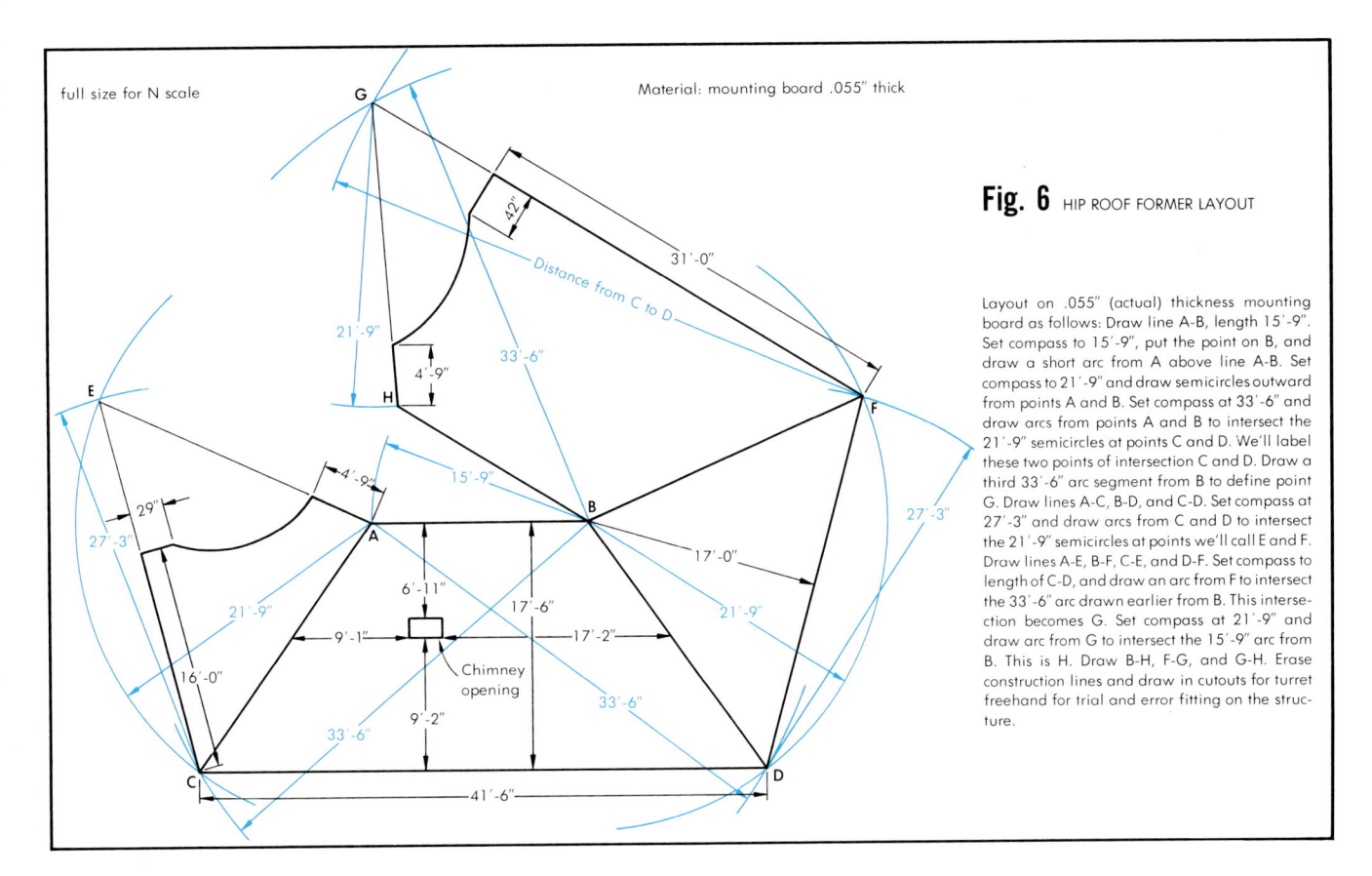

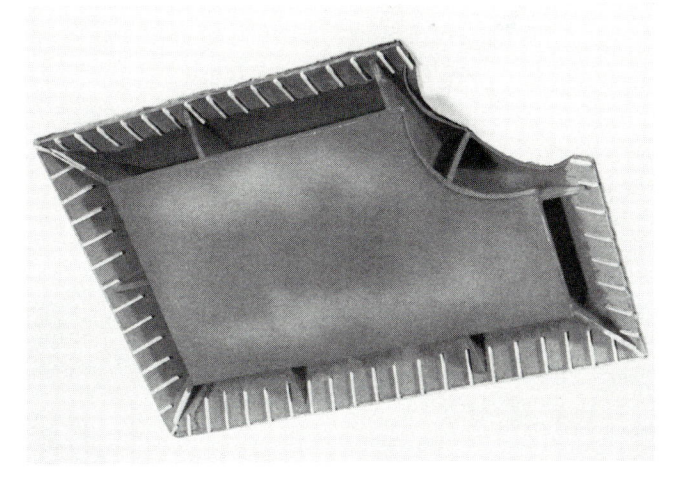

either brush- or spray-painting techniques.

I settled on chalky earth pink for the window and door color, a combination of bright pink with earth tan and light gray thrown in. Clean the cast parts—including the chimney—with denatured alcohol and apply the paint. Be sure to use a plastic-compatible paint if you are brush painting. Do the chimney in dark red. Put all the parts aside to dry thoroughly while we prepare the roof sections.

Hip roof

To determine the shapes for the hip roof formers, just use the templates shown in figs. 6-9. You must first decide whether you will have interior detail in the structure. If you decide you will, make the entire building so that it can lift off its base rather than building a liftoff roof. With this approach little or no finishing of the interior walls is required. I did not detail the inside of my model, so let's begin the roofing work.

Lay out the hip roof panels on .055"-thick mounting board, as shown in fig. 6. You'll need a compass with a hard, sharp pencil point and a scale ruler. For my roof I used Campbell shingles, which came supplied with ruled cardstock. Individual roof panels could be cut from the ruled cardstock, but the resulting operation would be more complex and more prone to inaccuracies than that shown in the figure. After you have cut the multipaneled roof from the board, draw horizontal shingle guidelines at 8" intervals. The cutouts where the corner of the roof intersects the turret are segments of true ellipses, but it is not worth the trouble to construct them geometrically. Sketch in an approximation of the contours shown on fig. 6, and leave an extra 1/32" of stock when you cut. The final fitting will be done by trial and error; even if there is a slight gap, it will be hidden entirely by shingle overlap and flashing strips later.

Proceed with roof construction by cutting the base, end, and side-to-side for-

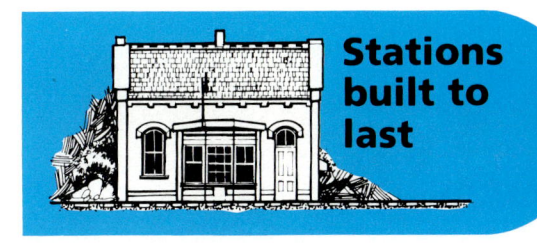

Stations built to last

57

mers (again from .055" mounting board), fig. 7. Assemble these parts, and add the panel section, fig. 6. Position the roof on the structure and carefully trim the roof cutouts for a good fit around the turret. Apply shingles according to the directions packaged with them. Note: If you are simulating a slate shingle roof in good repair (like the one on my model) do not shorten or remove any shingles. Tweezers help immeasurably for handling the shingle strips after their gummed adhesive has been moistened, and they are also handy for tugging and coaxing the strips into proper alignment before the adhesive sets. Although the joints will be covered by cap pieces, try to align the shingle courses at the corners.

To make cap shingles, sharply crease a length of brown gummed kraft tape, adhesive side inside the crease. Leaving the tape folded, cut a strip 10" wide from the creased edge to produce a length of gummed tape that is the same width (10") on either side of the crease. Cut this into foot-long pieces, and apply to the roof joints. Start at the four bottom corners of the roof and overlap the cap shingles as you work up.

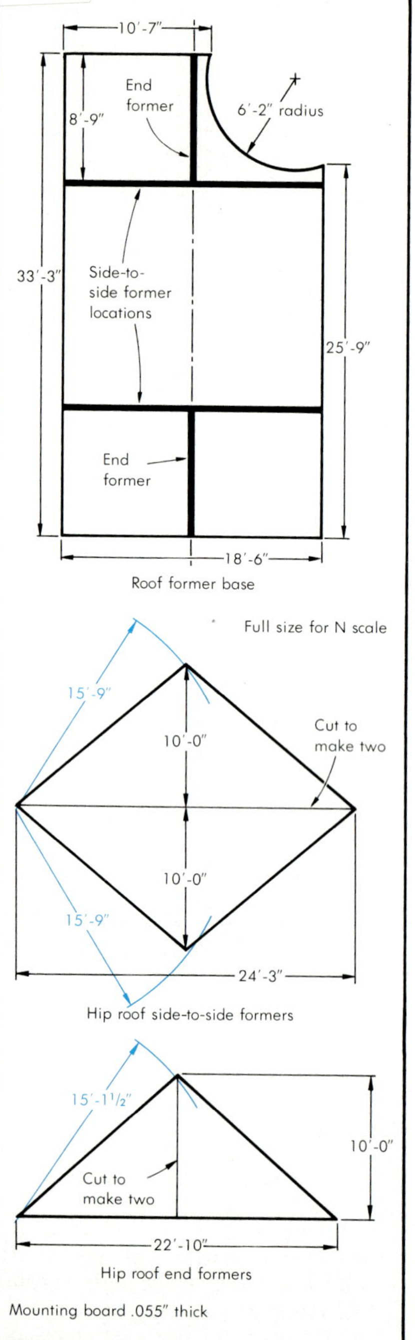

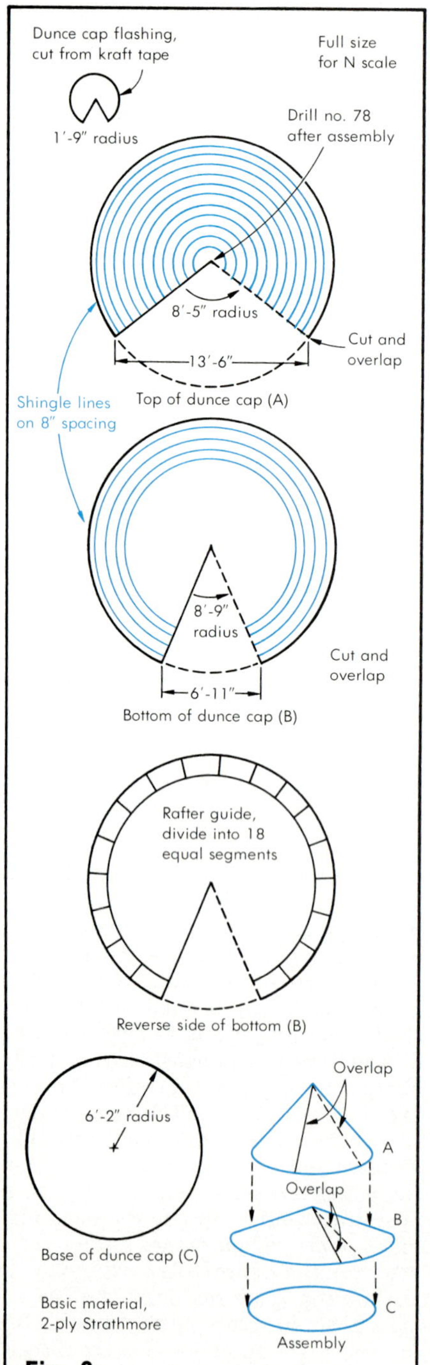

Dunce cap

The flared conical roof on the turret is one of the appealing parts of the structure, and it's quite easy to construct. Lay out and cut the parts from two-ply Strathmore, fig. 8, and assemble them with fast-setting epoxy. Also, apply heavy fillets of epoxy inside the cones as stiffening material. The epoxy gives the cardstock surprising rigidity, and allows sanding and filing to smooth the overlap joints.

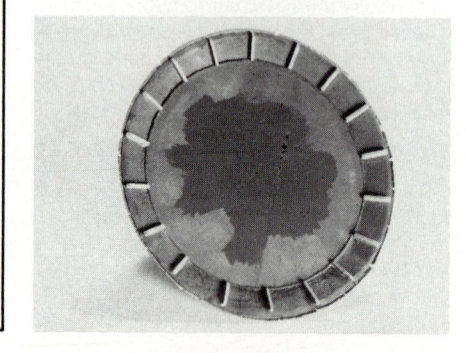

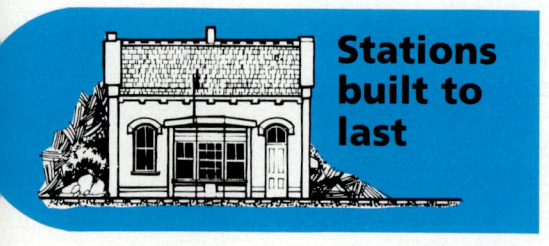

Brush paint the bottom of the dunce cap skirt dark brown or gray, taking care to color the edges and eaves without obliterating any shingle- or rafter-end guidelines. Shingling is not difficult here, but proceed slowly. Twist the shingle strips before applying them to make them more flexible; moisten only a few shingles at a time, and hold them in place until they adhere. Both roofs are painted dark green to represent an ornamental slate surface. I mixed some of the blue-gray wall color into a stock dark green to provide a slate-blue tinge, and finished by lightly drybrushing the completed shingle surfaces with the blue-gray mix. The light streaks in the photos are drybrushed white paint to represent pigeon droppings.

Back to the walls

The paint on the wall unit should have cured quite thoroughly while we worked on the roof parts, so let's continue with the coloring. Mix thin white or gray paint to use as a mortar color in the lines between the siding stones. Use paint that will not attack or lift the gray color. Test a few drops on the back of the turret—where it won't show—to ensure this new coloring is compatible with the earlier one. Brush the thinned paint liberally over the walls, then pat it off the surface of the stones with a scrap of soft cloth or paper towel. Do not *rub* the excess color away—that risks wiping off the gray stone color and leaving bits of lint on the wall surface. Continue adding and removing thinned color until you have built up a realistic-looking mortar effect in the grooves, then put the wall section aside to dry. Brush paint the lintels with either light or dark gray to contrast with the wall color, and lightly drybrush some of the stone with lighter grays and earth tones to vary the individual stone colors.

Windows and doors

The Grandt Line window castings have recesses on the back to accept clear panes of window glazing material, and they allow a layered double hung look. To construct the windows, cut a 24"-wide strip of clear styrene, and then cut pieces from the strip to fit in the window casting recesses. Cut clear glazing for the windows on the two front doors, and apply all the glazing using a very fine (5/0 or 3/0) brush and liquid styrene cement. Cut and add small rectangles of colored bond paper for window shades, and install the completed door and window assemblies, recessed about 2" from the face of the stone in the wall openings. Adjust each casting until it is straight and even in the opening, then touch a drop of ACC to the rear of the opening to cement the casting in place. If there are noticeable gaps between the window frames and the openings, fill them with dabs of epoxy—again applied from behind—and dab on black paint to prevent light leaks.

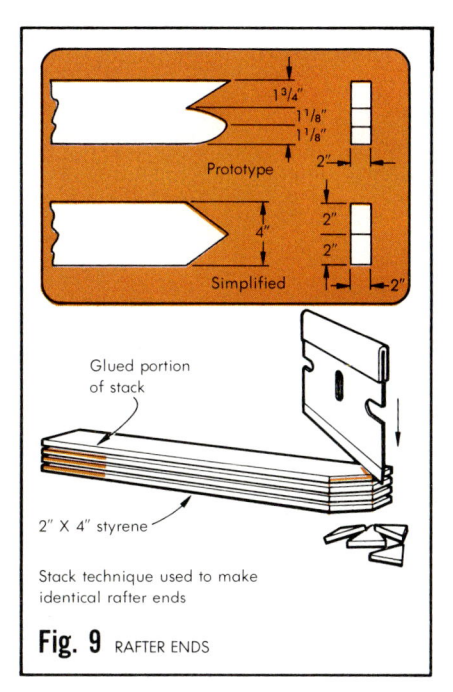

Make up several multilayer stacks of scale 2 x 4 styrene stock, and prepare the rafter ends, fig. 9. The prototype was more complex in design than the one I chose; see inset fig. 9. I painted the rafters on my model the same pink color as the windows and doors. Cut the rafter ends to length and glue them over the positioning lines on the underside of the dunce cap skirt and around the perimeter of the hip roof eaves at 24" intervals. The rafters for the hip roof should be about 36" long, except for a few short ones needed to clear the roof formers.

Assembling major components

Glue the hip roof to the wall structure with epoxy. Crease a piece of kraft tape just as you did for the cap shingles, and this time cut a folded strip 3" wide from the creased edge with the stickum on the *outside* to make the 6"-wide flashing between the hip roof and the stone turret. Paint the flashing a chalky light silver-blue, and install it around the turret in 24" sections. Cut a 42"-diameter disk of kraft tape, notch (fig. 8), paint it the same light blue, and install as the dunce cap flashing. Glue the dunce cap to the structure.

Treat the chimney with the same thinned mortar color used on the walls. For extra ornamentation apply bright red and white paint to the two protruding brick courses on the chimney using a 3/0 spotting brush. Install the chimney in its opening, fig. 6, using epoxy, and add flashing.

A crushed rock platform

Marbles station sported a planked platform, but I wanted something just a bit different, in keeping with the resort atmosphere. I settled on a heavy timber coping lined with crushed stone fill. I chose a buff yellow stone with flecks of dark red to add color.

If you've settled on a location for the station on your layout, and if the scenery is prepared, you can build this type of platform right in place as the prototype did. If your model, like mine, is destined for a spell on the shelf, start with a slab of .060" styrene sheet and cut a hole in the center to accept the station. Allow a 1/64" gap all around the base of the structure for the stone fill, to be added later.

Epoxy scale 10 x 10 or 12 x 12 timbers to the edges of the .060" styrene subbase; fig. 10. Prepaint about 30 nut-bolt-washer castings (N-B-W's) a rusty black, drill the timber facings to accept

Fig. 9 RAFTER ENDS

Stack technique used to make identical rafter ends

Stations built to last

59

them, and install the N-B-W's to represent anchor and tie-rod ends.

On a flat surface covered with waxed paper, set up the platform you have built thus far, wrap the base of the station with plastic food wrap, and insert the station in the platform opening. Then pour fine crushed stone material into the trough formed by the timber coping and structure walls. I used commercial ballast material and worked it into the corners of the trough with a small brush before smoothing it with a table knife. For adhesive, mix one part acrylic matte medium (available at art-supply stores) to 3 parts water, add a drop or two of detergent, and use an eyedropper to flow this solution into the crushed stone. Add the liquid to the trough from one or two locations only— the opposite corners are good choices— and allow capillary action to distribute it throughout the loose particles. When the platform surface is dry to the touch, in about 2 hours, gently lift off the station building and remove the plastic food wrap. Replace the structure, and use the tip of a small screwdriver to manipulate some of the crushed material into the space between the bonded particles and the building. Then add small amounts of matte medium solution. When this dries the structure will be bonded into the platform, but the crushed material will still *look* loose within the timber forms.

Final detailing

The weathercock listed in the shopping list is a bit of sheer whimsy, but it adds a great deal to the finished model. Significantly, it is the sort of detail that most of us would not add were it not available by mail order. I assembled the photo-etched parts with ACC on a staff of .010" wire, and added a ball made from the head of a plastic map pin. The weather vane is delicate and liable to damage, so you may want to simply drill a hole in the dunce cap flashing to make the vane removable and use it only on visitors' nights and for photo sessions.

The station sign is made from thin styrene sheet painted blue. The lettering is from a dry transfer alphabet set. The baggage wagon and suitcases are all mail order, as are the pigeons!

These details complete the station as I built it, although there is plenty of room for more send-away details, or a longer platform, or some fancy trim. I've used this same pick-and-choose method for several structures, and I have yet to be disappointed in the results. Neither will you if you just give it a try.

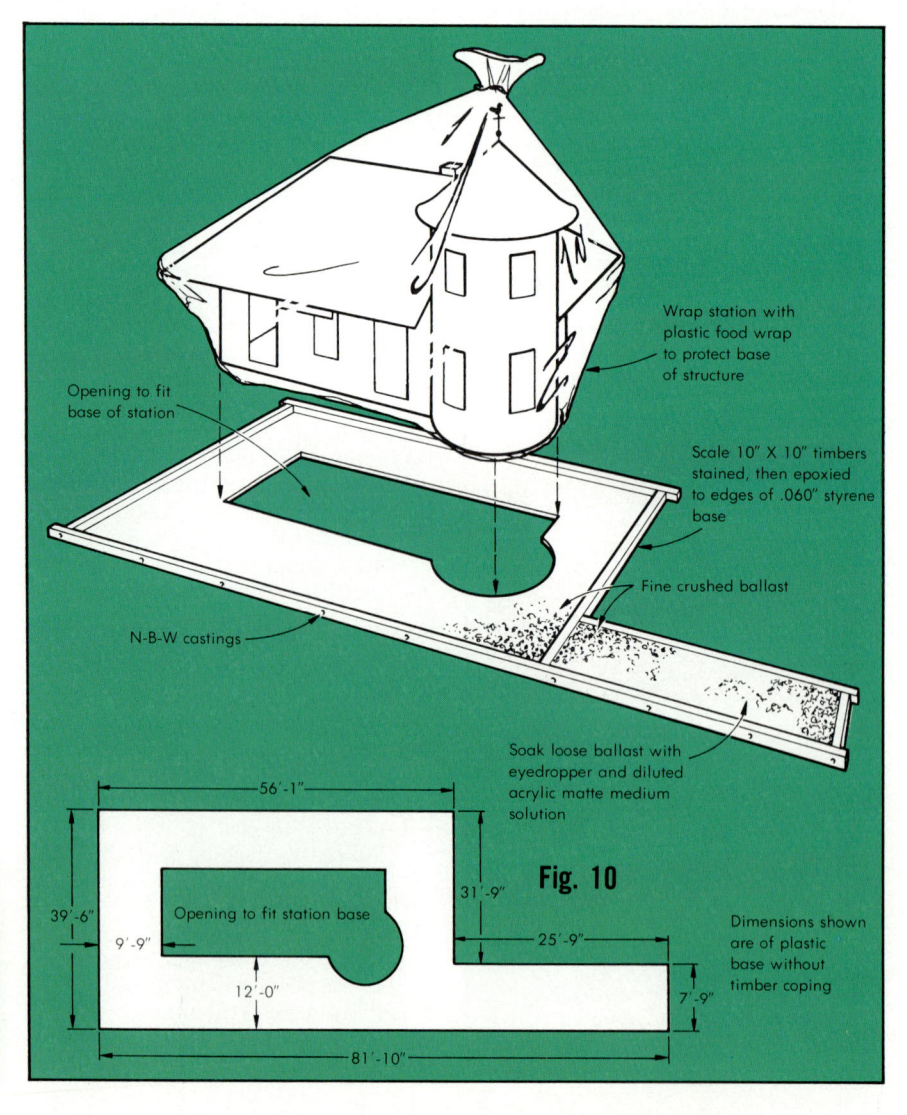

Stations built to last

Fig. 10

Hermosa Beach freight station

A small project that involves an unusual technique for simulating concrete and stucco surfaces

by Donald Sims

SANTA FE'S freight station at Hermosa Beach, Calif., a quiet suburban town, is just a few blocks away from the Pacific Ocean. The structure is small, and its strictly Western style is in contrast to the mid-Victorian look of many older frame stations.

The little building is quite easy to model because it has smooth sides and no complex wood or brick textures. The slightly rough concrete and stucco textures are easily duplicated with inexpensive materials, and my model was built largely from scraps left over from other projects. All dimensions on the drawings are given in scale feet and inches, and if your scrap box doesn't have the precise sizes of stock called for, improvise—it's that sort of model.

Walls

The prototype structure is built on a slight embankment, but my model and the drawings are designed for a level ground installation. This design is suited to a variety of track layouts, including an arrangement where the tracks are on both sides of the long platform.

Although I used plywood for my building's walls, you could substitute cardstock. Offhand, I'd say plywood is the better choice, since cardstock would require extensive bracing to accept the plaster stucco coating without warping, and would also need a right angle cover strip at each corner to hide the joints.

Transfer the exterior dimensions of sides and ends of the building to a piece of ⅛" (actual) plywood. Any piece of scrap plywood will do, just so it is free from warpage. On my model the sides were made to overlap the ends, though either way is all right since the final finish will hide the joints.

As you lay out the overall dimensions of the walls, draw in the correct outlines for windows and doors. Using a saw, trim the outlines of the walls, then proceed to the windows and doorways. In cutting out the windows allow about ¹⁄₃₂" (actual) excess stock all the way around so they can be filed to the exact dimensions. The double window set openings are 7'-9" square, the single windows 3'-9" x 7'-9".

Because a thick-sided construction method is used a frame is not necessary,

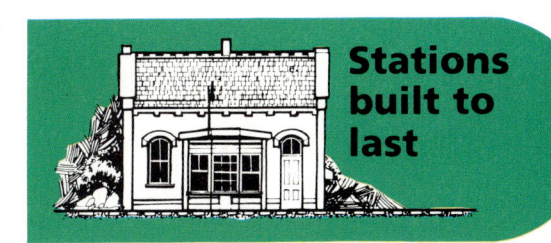

Stations built to last

61

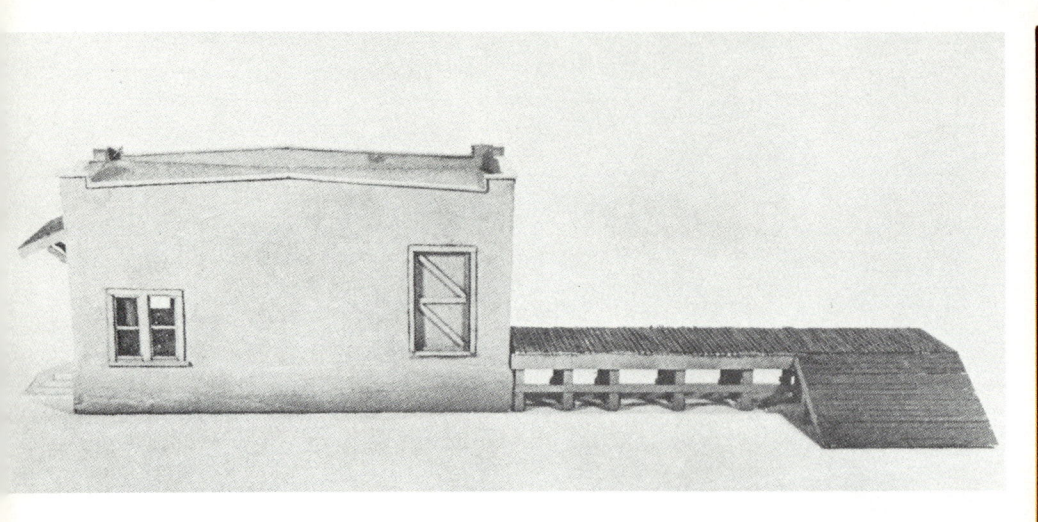

but I found a simple frame made from ¼" (actual) scraps came in handy as a guide to erect the four main pieces of the body section. It takes only a few minutes to assemble the frame pieces on a flat surface, thus ensuring sides and ends will stand perpendicular. If you use any cardboard siding, a frame is necessary.

The lower portion of the structure is slightly thicker and has a smoother cement finish. This extra thickness is achieved by cementing some 3" sheet material to the plywood sides and beveling the upper edge to conform to the drawings.

Before adding window or door detail, put the exterior finish on the model. This task may get slightly messy, so have a supply of old newspapers on hand. To obtain the slightly roughened surface on the model follow this simple procedure: Mix up a small batch of inexpensive patching plaster. Follow the directions on the package, and add water till you get the proper consistency. Mix in a small amount of whatever color suits you. The prototype is a well-weathered brown which once was a very deep hue. It is not absolutely necessary to add color at the mixing stage, since painting can be done after construction is complete. The advantage in introducing color during the mixing process is that you achieve a solid tone throughout, and if any plaster is knocked off, you don't have to touch up white spots. The only requirement is a color base that will mix with the water and plaster. Mortar colors or the dry pigments used for "zip texturing" scenery will work fine.

Before spreading the plaster on the walls, use a paintbrush to daub the wood with a sticky varnish. (I used spar varnish.) Let the varnish become tacky before applying the plaster mix. This varnish coat helps hold the plaster to the wood surface.

Apply plaster with your fingers. Don't worry about obtaining a smooth surface at first; just make sure the plaster covers the exposed wood. After approximately 1 hour, at which time the plaster will be firm-bodied, you can level the wall surface. The roughened surface on my model was achieved by making swirl marks with my fingers. Keep your fingers wet while smoothing out the plaster; otherwise it will stick and break away from the wood.

As a final touch, spray the entire plastered surface with a dull lacquer coat to seal the surface and reduce the possibilities of cracking or peeling.

Windows, doors, and roof

Now add details to the windows and doors. The two freight-door frames are lined with 5"-square basswood stock. The freight doors were made from odds and ends of material with outside bracing made from 3 x 5's.

Window frames are made from 3"-square wood or plastic material, laid over a piece of clear Plexiglas. This window assembly is then fitted to the opening in the wall.

The roof slants slightly from the front of the building toward the rear to allow

Brush spar varnish onto raw plywood walls

While varnish is still tacky, add thick paste-like plaster with fingers

STUCCO WALL TECHNIQUE

Stations built to last

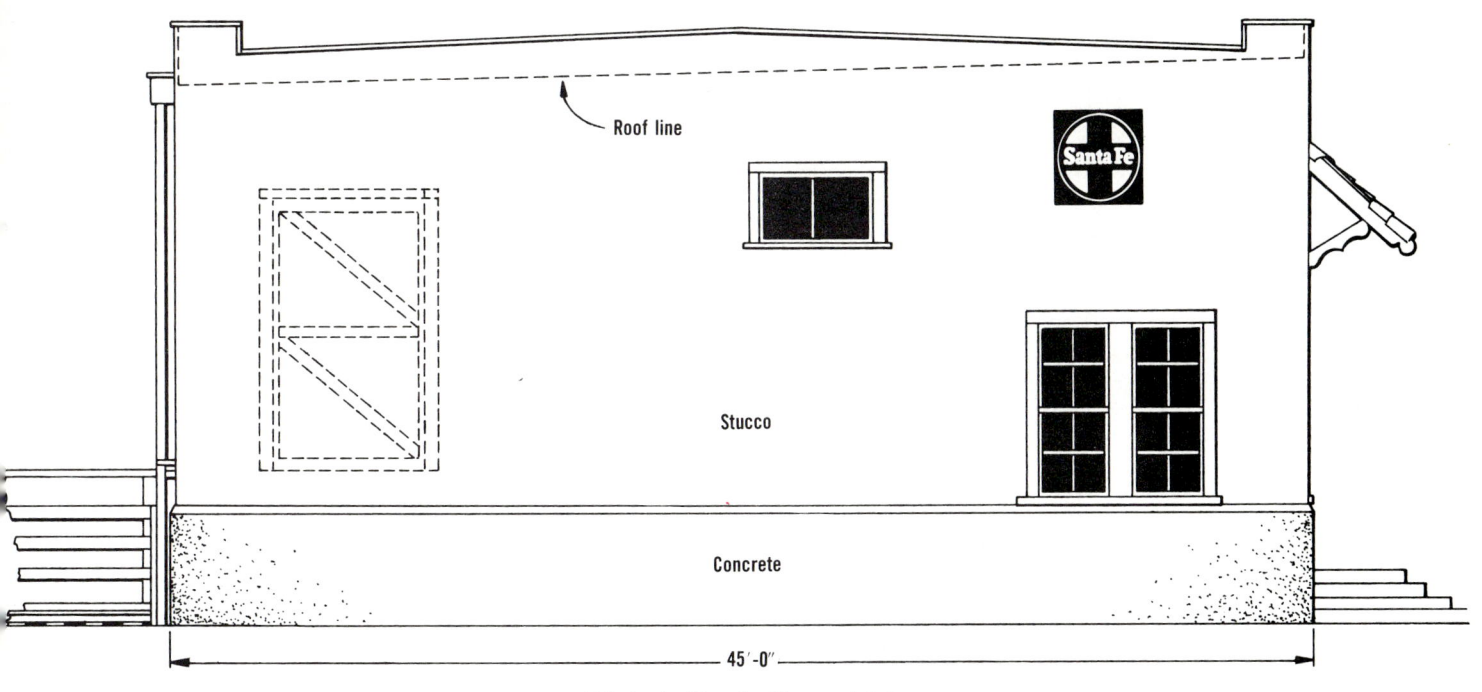

Roof line

Stucco

Concrete

45'-0"

Full size for HO scale: 3.5mm = 1 foot

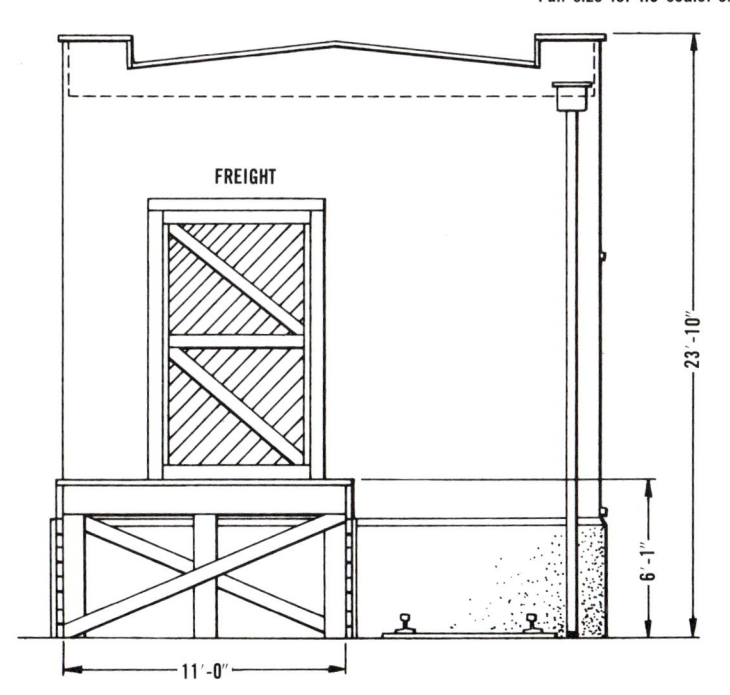

FREIGHT

23'-10"

6'-1"

11'-0"

HERMOSA BEACH

21'-6"

for drainage. To support the roof, cement sections of 14" square wood along the two sides at the roof line. I used a sheet of medium-grade sandpaper cemented to a sheet of 6" wood for the roof covering, but stiff cardboard could also be used.

Loading dock platform and ramp

I shortened the length of the loading dock to 48 feet. The prototype is several feet longer, but I felt that room enough to handle one box car was all that was necessary. By moving the car stop closer to the building, you gain space and cut down on the work needed for a longer platform.

The loading dock is made from 12"- square beams laid crosswise on vertical uprights of the same stock. Add a 2 x 6 X-frame at each pair of uprights. Next glue a 3 x 14 strip across the ends of the crossbeams, then add your platform deck, which is made from 3 x 8 basswood planking, allowing a slight overhang at each end. Paint the platform dull black to match the creosoted wood of the prototype.

It seems a shame to go to a lot of work to build up the under-platform area and then cover most of it with side strips, so I used only a single board extending along each side of the platform. This strip is of 2 x 6 stock. Add a ramp so that trucks can run along the dock, and you are almost finished with the freighthouse.

Final details

Front-end details for the building include four steps formed from 6" stock. The small overhanging porch roof was slightly altered from the prototype; a small piece of sandpaper was used to simulate roofing paper in lieu of the

Stations built to last

63

3" X 8" planking

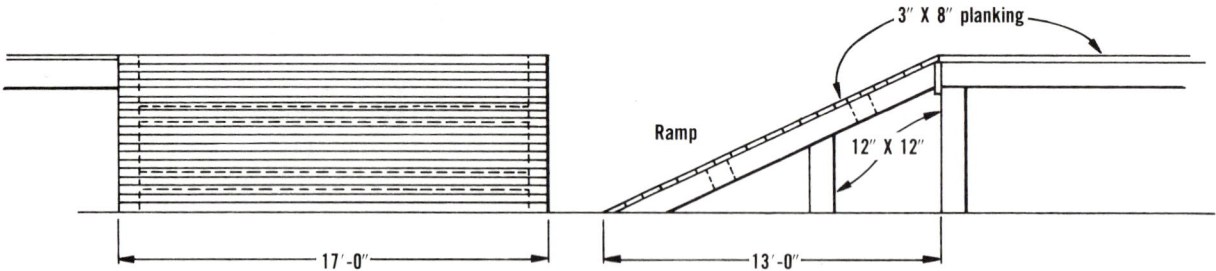

Ramp

12" X 12"

17'-0"

13'-0"

Full size for HO scale: 3.5mm = 1 foot

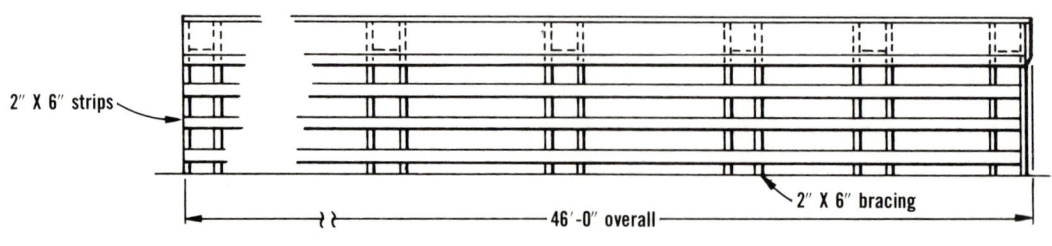

2" X 6" strips

2" X 6" bracing

46'-0" overall

Platform

Stations built to last

tiled roof. The curves on the roof support pieces were made uniform by holding the pieces together with tape and filing them all to shape at the same time. In order to glue the porch overhang to the building front, chip away a slight amount of the plaster so that the wood surface is exposed. Since the brown color is mixed into the plaster, you won't have to touch up this area afterward.

My loading dock was not attached to the model building but was left as a separate unit so it can be spotted in various positions to vary the use of the station with different track patterns. For that matter, if you tire of the station, the dock can be adapted to another railroad structure.

All photos by the author.

Alturas depot

An excellent example of a station building built to fit both a location and a purpose

by Whit Towers

LIKE most model railroaders I faithfully placed depots at the towns on my Alturas & Lone Pine Railroad, but I kept putting off installing a station at Alturas. Visitors and fellow operators often chided me on the lack of proper station facilities at my headquarters town, and a friend went so far as to slip a commercial kitbuilt station into place while my attention was diverted. He lettered and weathered it — even detailed it with a sign which read FOR SALE — TO BE MOVED.

Designing the station

The kit station technically solved the problem of providing a depot at Alturas, but I had quite a different building — of my own design — in mind. I wanted something imposing, and big enough to include space for the railroad's general offices. I endured the good-natured gibes of my operating groups over the puny size of the Alturas depot when compared to those at Lone Pine, Sonora, and Auburn. Meanwhile, all that time I was searching through back issues of magazines for ideas and a suitable design. While Alturas is the largest town served by the ALP, its under-5000 population hardly justified an imposing granite structure or even a brick one. Logically the building would be constructed of wood, the material favored by westerners in the 1870's and 1880's.

I came across a photo in MODEL RAILROADER which showed the three-story wood station at Canaan, Conn. It seemed logical to build a three-story wood structure for Alturas; the lower floor could contain the waiting room, ticket office, and baggage and express facilities, and the upper floors could house the railroad's general offices.

From this information, thoughts and ideas of others, and a copy of Walter C. Berg's *Buildings and Structures of American Railroads,* published by John Wiley & Sons in 1893 (and reprinted by Newton K. Gregg), I began to design a plan.

Most of us face space limitations when building our railroads, so conserving real estate is one of the most important considerations in planning a building. Two questions I always ask myself before constructing a building are "Will it fit the space I have available?" and "Will it interfere with track or scenery?" I decided to make the Alturas station floor plan long but narrow; roughly 21 x 131 feet. This provides an imposing structure in a minimum ground area.

I noticed that builders and architects of the 1870's and 1880's often used several types of siding in a single structure, combining them in pleasing patterns for a varied surface texture. Shiplap siding (clapboard), board-and-batten (capped), and even tongue-and-groove (scribed) were found in the same wall. Drawing is not one of my long suits, but I sat down and laboriously drew a portion of a two-story building, using combinations of different materials in different sections to study the effect, fig. 1. I showed this sketch to the members of my operating groups. After hearing their opinions I made my decision — a combination of board-and-batten and shiplap siding,

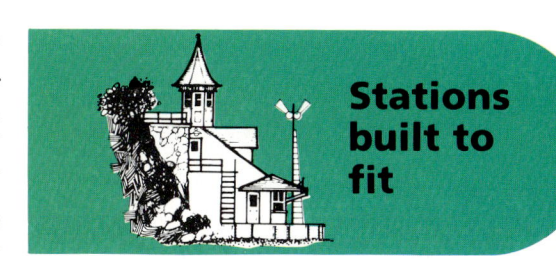

Stations built to fit

style A. Each would be separated by a strip of different-colored wood trim to emphasize the contrasting textures.

Each railroad has its own color standards for structures, and the ALP is no exception. Service structures are dark gray with dark green trim for windows, door frames, and the like. In the case of the Alturas depot, the boards separating the different types of siding are painted dark green.

I've included the dimensions for my Alturas depot on the drawings. I'm not going to bore you with step-by-step details on how the station was constructed. If you've assembled a few kits and have scratchbuilt a couple of buildings, you have your own favorite construction techniques.

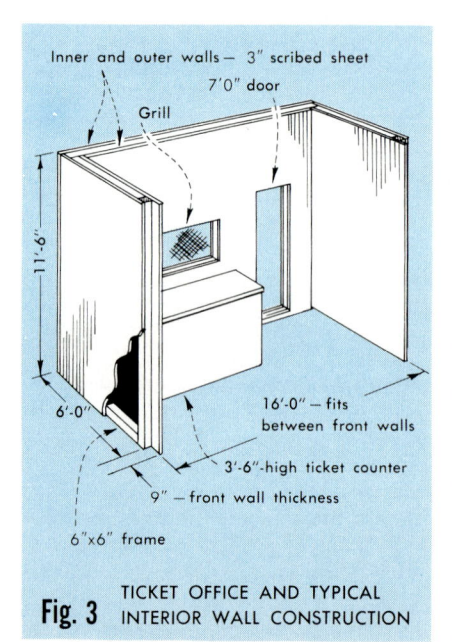

Sandwich-style wall construction

The construction methods I used and the materials involved are shown in fig. 2. The exterior walls are built as a sandwich, using prepainted 3"-thick siding run vertically for the interior walls, and prepainted 6"-thick siding for the exterior walls. All parts were painted prior to assembly, leaving only minor touchup to be done.

The first- and second-floor plans show the outline of the building with the locations of all windows, doors, partitions, stairways, and interior walls. Note on the elevation drawings that the overall dimensions are given as 21'-0" x 130'-6". These are the dimensions *inside* the exterior walls; they show the net size of the floors and ceilings. The actual structure is larger by two wall thicknesses each way.

Fig. 2 shows the wall construction. To ease fabrication, I strongly advise the use of a flat drawing board covered with waxed paper. To keep walls square and in correct alignment, fasten a strip of brass along the bottom edge and another strip along the left-hand edge. This makes a square against which parts can be held to ensure tight joints, and more important, square and flat wall sections. The type of brass material isn't important; any sheet metal approximately $1/16$" thick (actual) will do. Use white glue, so it's easy to get parts away from the metal where excess glue oozes out.

To continue with wall construction, note that the interior wall is cut to exact size. The corner members of the building are 9 x 9. The interior wall is butted against the left-hand corner, and the exterior wall parts are cut and glued to the interior wall. Leave openings in the exterior wall where you want doors or windows. I again used patterns made from scrap brass sheet, cutting pieces the exact size for the commercial door and window castings. The brass pieces are used to ensure proper clearance fits for the cast parts, and can easily be dislodged after the glue has set. They allow you to fit and hold the various pieces of the exterior wall together tightly while gluing, and eliminate the task of cutting out each door and window opening after the walls are assembled. You do have to cut out the interior wall openings, but this is a simple task with a sharp modeler's knife.

There are five exterior walls, not

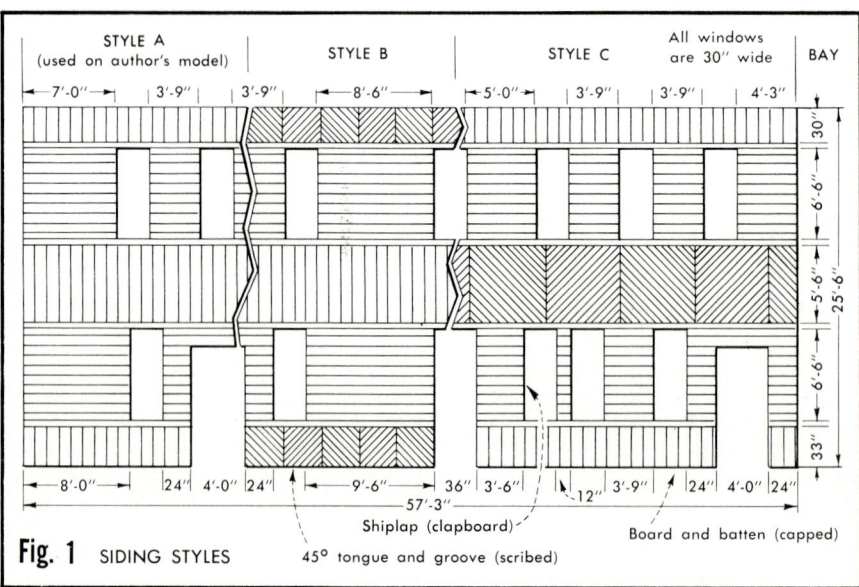

Fig. 3 TICKET OFFICE AND TYPICAL INTERIOR WALL CONSTRUCTION

Stations built to fit

Fig. 1 SIDING STYLES

Fig. 2 GENERAL CONSTRUCTION

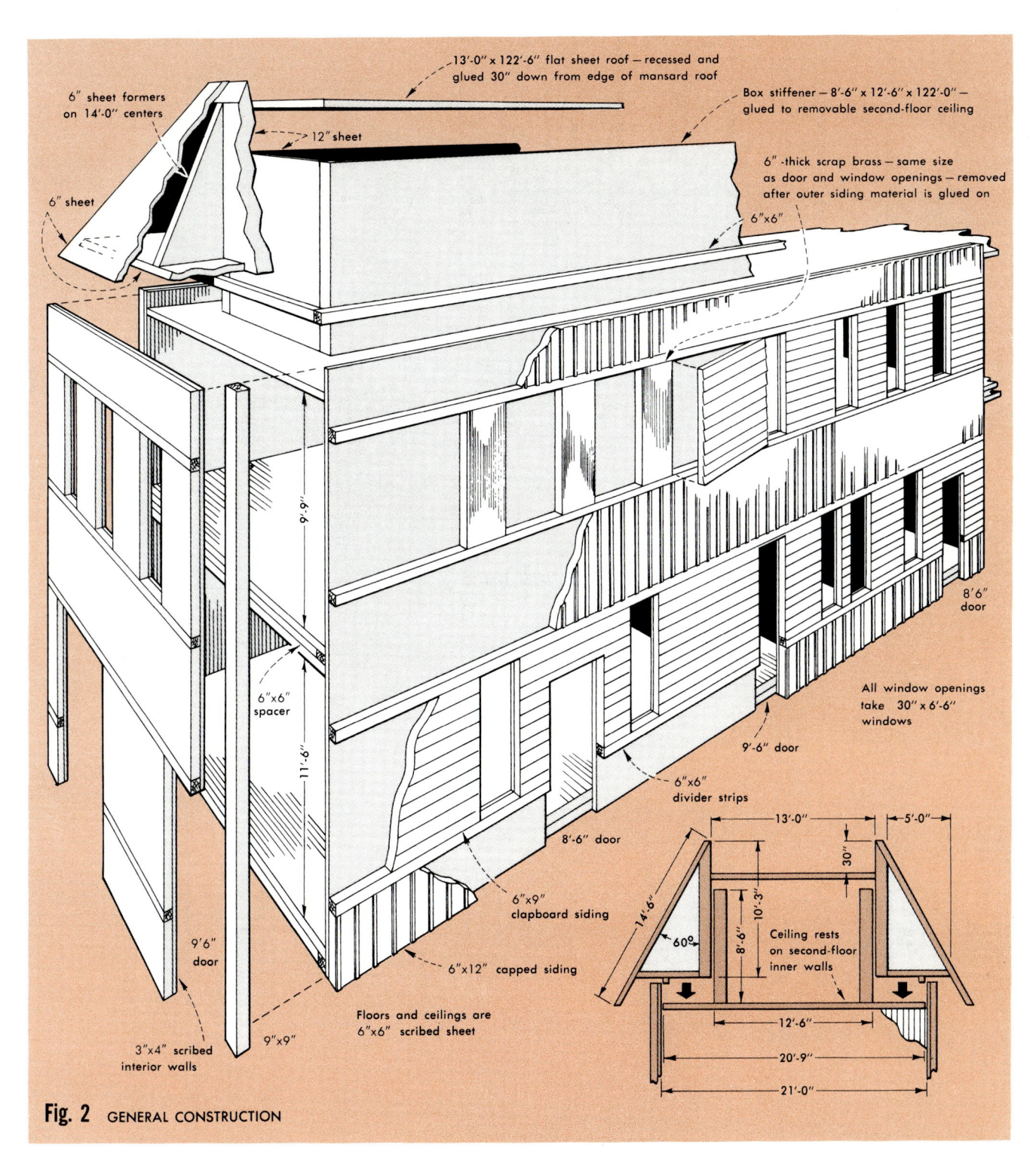

counting the bay window for the ticket office: the two ends, the streetside wall, and a left- and a right-hand section for the trackside wall. Fig. 1 shows dimensions for the left trackside wall. If you plan on altering the overall size of the depot to fit your space requirements, this figure will also provide the necessary information for appropriate door and window spacing, and heights of different siding combinations.

Bay window and ticket office

Fig. 3 shows construction of the ticket office. The walls are sandwiches of 6 x 6 studs, headers, and floor joists. Be sure to frame an opening for the ticket-office grill: This can be fashioned from wood, cardstock, styrene, or metal in any appropriate design, depending on how much time and effort you wish to put into this feature. Note that the 3" inner ticket-office walls project 9", which allows them to cover the stub ends of the two trackside walls to provide an unbroken interior wall.

The bay window for the ticket office on the first-floor and the second-floor dispatcher's office is assembled in a unit with the floors and ceilings fastened to the walls, but it is not glued to the station trackside walls. Instead, it has a force-fit tongue which extends from the first-floor ceiling. This tongue fits between the first-floor ceiling and the second-story floor, and allows the bay window to be removed as a unit for

Stations built to fit

67

STREET SIDE

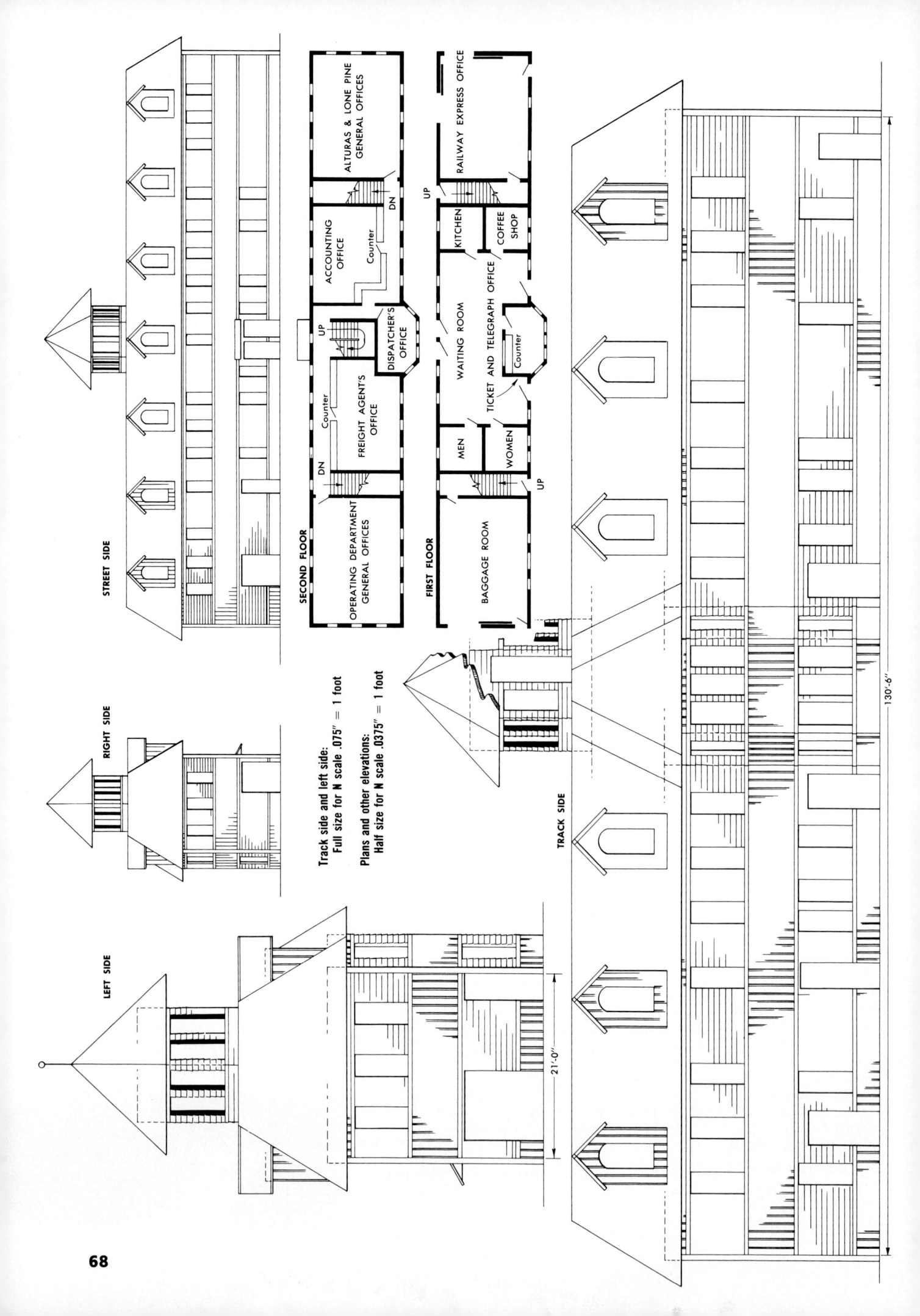

SECOND FLOOR

ALTURAS & LONE PINE GENERAL OFFICES

ACCOUNTING OFFICE

DN

UP

DISPATCHER'S OFFICE

Counter

FREIGHT AGENT'S OFFICE

DN

OPERATING DEPARTMENT GENERAL OFFICES

FIRST FLOOR

RAILWAY EXPRESS OFFICE

UP

KITCHEN

COFFEE SHOP

WAITING ROOM

TICKET AND TELEGRAPH OFFICE

Counter

MEN

WOMEN

UP

BAGGAGE ROOM

RIGHT SIDE

Track side and left side:
Full size for N scale .075" = 1 foot

Plans and other elevations:
Half size for N scale .0375" = 1 foot

TRACK SIDE

130'-6"

LEFT SIDE

21'-0"

68

Fig. 5 DORMER AND CUPOLA CONSTRUCTION

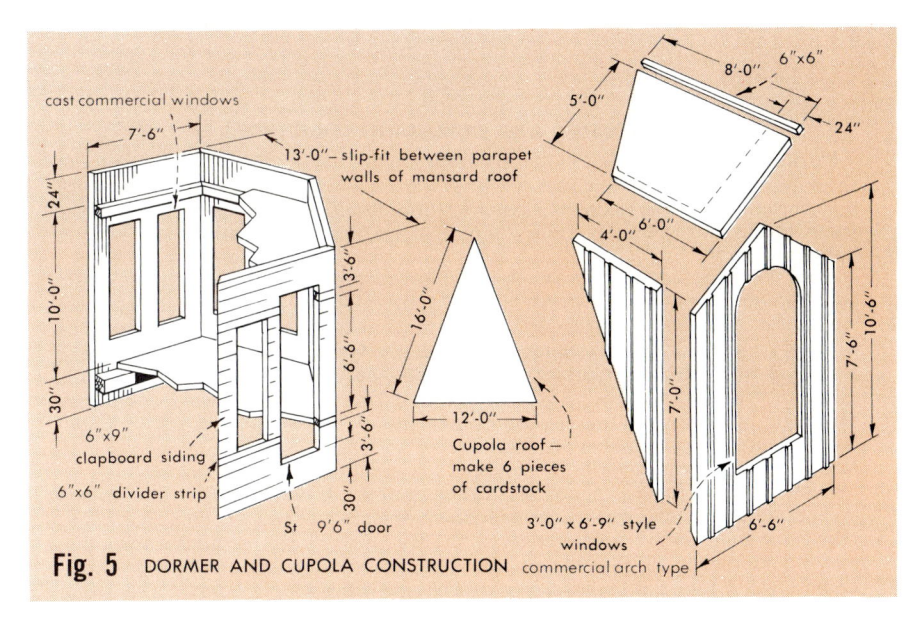

Fig. 4 BAY WINDOW CONSTRUCTION

changing lights and detailing the interior.

Foundation, floors, and ceilings

The building foundation is a simulated concrete slab with concrete walkways and train platforms for two tracks. There is space to handle ten 85-foot passenger cars. The "concrete" on my model was made of thick Strathmore board, heavily scribed with a sharp pencil to simulate the 3 x 3-foot poured sections. Your loading platform obviously must conform to your track plan.

The floor is 6" scribed sheathing with 6 x 6 framing to raise the floor a scale 12" above the concrete subfloor. The second floor also uses a 6" spacer between it and the first-floor ceiling to allow hidden wiring for illumination. I used grain-of-wheat bulbs encased in brass tubing. I placed at least one bulb in each room and used more for the larger rooms.

The second-floor ceiling is similar to that of the first. I left the third floor unfinished behind the roof slopes, ostensibly for the storage of records. It serves as a sort of terminal box for storing all lighting wiring. Wires from the first-floor ceiling lights run up the interior walls to the third floor.

After all the walls are built up, glue the first floor and its floor joists to the end walls, then add the interior walls. Next, glue the first-floor ceiling to the interior and end walls. Fit the second-story floor in place, but don't glue it—it must be removable to get at the first-floor light wiring.

I glued the second-story interior walls to the floor, but did not attach the ceiling. This upper ceiling has a box stiffener that is hidden inside the roof, fig. 2. I wanted to be able to lift it out to get at the second-floor wiring.

I removed the second-story floor and ceiling so I could glue the trackside walls in place. Because of the interior window trim I had to slide the second-story floor in place from the street side.

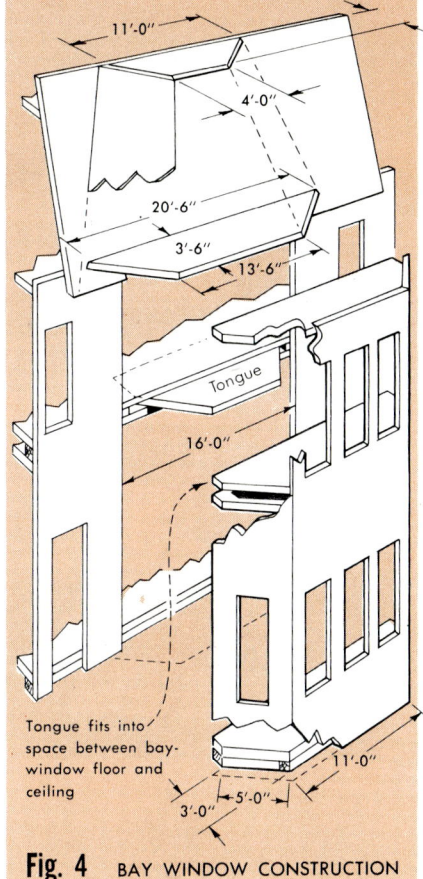

The second-story ceiling, which rests on the interior walls, can be popped into place like a box lid. The box-shaped stiffener projecting into the third story keeps it flat, and provides the weight needed to hold down the second-story floor and walls. The street side wall is quite stiff and is held in place by two small machine screws inserted through the wall. These are threaded into the joists between the first and second stories. Even though the joists are wood the threads are adequate, since it is seldom necessary to remove the wall for access to the interior.

By studying the drawings and detail views of the depot, you'll see how this assembly allows for access to the lights and wiring, and for the addition of more detail.

Roof, dormers, and cupola

Fig. 2 shows a cross section of the roof, which was built up using balsa. Basswood or even a solid wood roof sec-

Stations built to fit

69

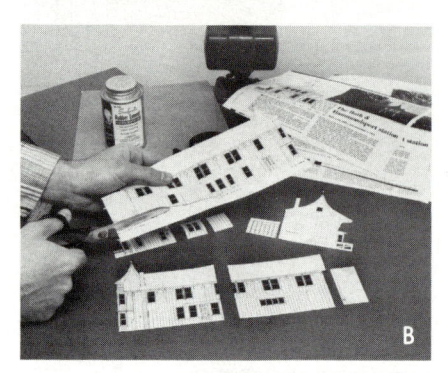

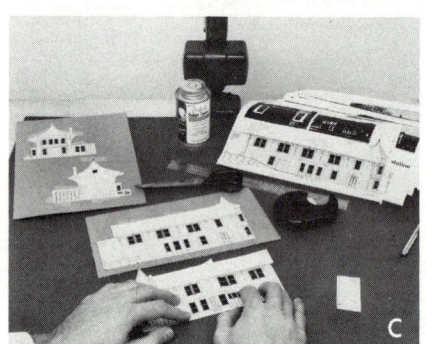

COMPRESSING AND EXPANDING STRUCTURES

Because all but the largest model railroads are built in relatively small spaces, our structures must be small. This does not mean they should be underscale, but they must be sufficiently compact to do their assigned job without overpowering the rest of the scene. Most kit structures are quite compact, as are most of the station models in this book.

How, then, do you start with a likely prototype railroad station—perhaps the one in your hometown—and trim it down to a size appropriate for your layout? The answer is *selective compression*, a process that involves shrinking or eliminating parts of the original structure (or track arrangement, or scenic features, or what-have-you) and modeling only the most important or interesting aspects of the prototype. The overall "look" of the building is not substantially altered. The other side of the coin, *selective expansion*, is more often used by prototype railroads to enlarge a station no longer big enough to meet the needs of its community. Selective expansion could be used in a rare case where your favorite prototype is too small to suit your railroad.

While some modelers can look at a structure or set of drawings for a station and immediately determine how to shrink it down to more manageable bulk, many of us can't. However, there's a cut-and-paste process using photos or photocopies that makes compression easy (A). The number-one tool here is a copy machine, the coin-operated kind found at libraries, post offices, and office-supply stores. Make two or three copies of your drawings, photo, or sketch, and cut one copy into logical sections. For example, separate the structure along division lines, i.e., trim pieces between two types of siding, or panel joints in a building made up of several repeated frames. Or, simply separate it into its various elements —main rectangle, lean-to addition, and so on (B). It's also worthwhile to cut around the outline of the elevations to gain an appreciation of overall proportions and bulk even while working in two dimensions.

Now the fun part: Use a sheet of contrasting paper as a background and overlap your cutout sections, gradually moving the pieces together to assess the impact of varying degrees of compression. After you've developed an attractive condensed version of one elevation, superimpose the cutouts on the opposite side of your building to see the effect of compression there (C). You'll often find that while one wall will compress nicely by lopping off a portion near the end, the opposite wall will look better if you cut a section from the middle. This process thrives on trial and error, so keep at it until you are pleased with the results. Finally, use rubber cement to glue the compressed elevation views to scrap cardboard (D), and build a 3-D mockup. Admittedly, this is extra work, but it is justifiable because you'll be generating a plan of attack for construction while you determine how the structure will fit into your layout. Place the mockup in its ultimate setting, then add trains and other structures to evaluate the impact of their relative sizes and shapes (E).

Finally, make an overall evaluation of the structure before compiling a shopping list of materials. Be critical. Ask yourself whether you've cut away elements or details that attracted you to the building in the first place, whether you've retained parts that add bulk without contributing architectural character, and whether you've preserved the *flavor* of the prototype. Finally, look for places where you can make minor rearrangements to simplify construction—again, without sacrificing the structure's spirit.

Stations built to fit

tion will work. The roof has a flat deck 30" below the top edge, for a parapet wall effect. This flat roof section is the base for the cupola. Note that the flat roof section is attached to the sloping roof, but not to the stiffener extending up from the second-floor ceiling. While not shown in the drawing, knee braces—typical roof-overhang support for structures of the period—have been included on the model. These provide support for the eaves. They are fastened to the building walls, extending down approximately half the window openings on the second story on 10-foot centers.

The roof extension over the bay window is constructed over a pair of for-

70

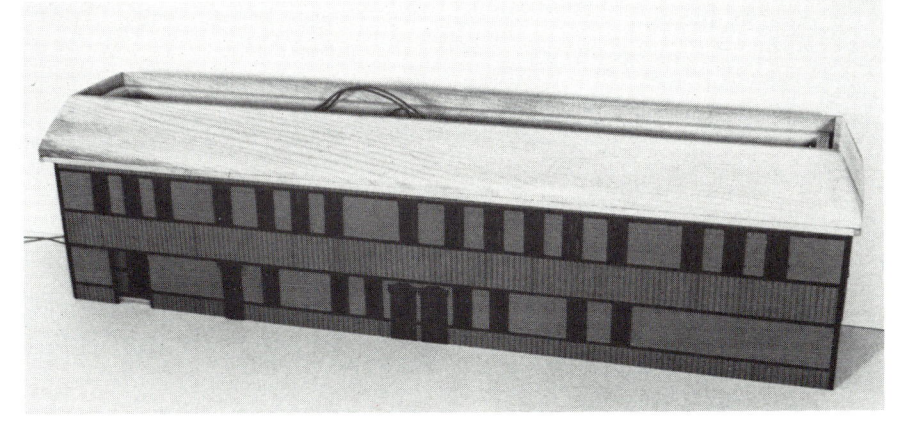

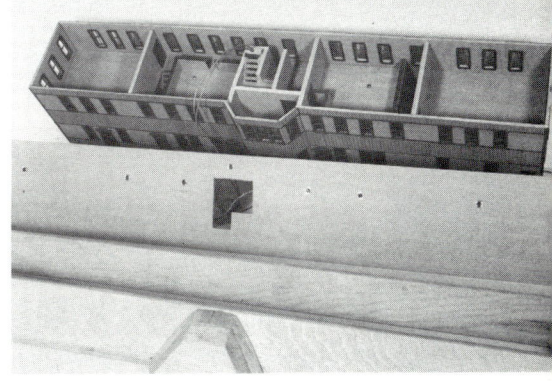

mers, one at the top and one at the bottom. These are sheathed and the resulting dormer is glued directly to the roof, fig. 4.

This style of roof is frequently a copper-sheathed roof, so I painted it with Floquil's jade green, followed by a heavy wash of white and a lighter wash of black to create the streaked, weathered effect of the patina evident after years of service.

Fig. 5 shows the detail for the dormer windows. Glue the windows to the roof after installing the glass. I used .010" acetate sheet for all windows, cutting it to fit the window opening and gluing it flush with the interior walls. For all except the dormers I used a window trim contrasting to the interior walls. I followed ALP standard color practice; interior walls are Floquil dust color, window trim is roof brown. The window trim, made from prepainted strips of 1 x 4, effectively hides the joint and provides a pleasing contrast to the station walls.

The cupola, fig. 5, is known as Whit's Tower. My private office—from which I can oversee the operation of Alturas Yard—is supposedly located in this tower. These walls utilize sandwich-type construction, with the finished hexagonal shape fitted to the inside of the parapet walls. Not shown on the plan is a stairway cut into the floor on the street side. It leads through the mess of wiring to the ceiling of the second floor. With care, a scale figure can make his way down and buy a ticket for Lone Pine on the ALP *Flyer*.

The ALP management is still debating the advisability of roofs for station platforms. While I am not averse to protecting ALP customers from the elements, platform roofs on a model station create two rather serious drawbacks:

● They hide much of the first story of the depot, as well as the passenger tracks.

● The sheds can seriously handicap an operator's ability to read car numbers, check couplers—even rerail equipment or nudge a reluctant locomotive into action—important considerations for modelers who use their railroads in heavy operation.

Stations built to fit

71

All photos by John Allen.

Two-level station

This attractive space saver can be built using your favorite materials; the instructions tell how to tailor a similar station to your railroad

NOW

by Jim Findley

WHILE on a trip to California it was my good fortune to spend an extended visit with John Allen. Among the many subjects we discussed was a two-level station he planned for Cross Junction on his Gorre & Daphetid Railroad. I was impressed by the wide assortment of problems the project entailed, and offered to build the structure. It proved to be a wonderfully educational job, and I learned a number of invaluable lessons. In the end, the GD Line had an acceptable shelter for passengers and freight passing through the towns of Corsa and Cross Junction. (Corsa is located just above Cross Junction on the GD).

The topography at Cross Junction was unique, and you are not likely to find a location exactly like it on your own model railroad. To widen the scope of the project and to make it most useful to you, I intend to discuss several possible modifications to the configuration of the station's principal components. I'll also discuss techniques that apply to adapting any station structure to specific requirements on your pike. These notes are intended as guides rather than as hard and fast specifications for building design.

Two-level track arrangements

Probably the two most common track arrangements that would be served by a two-level station are one in which the upper track roughly parallels the lower (fig. 1), and one in which the upper track crosses over the lower at an angle (fig. 2). The lower level at Cross Junction has two routes crossing at grade, a combination of the two situations.

For the moment let us confine ourselves to the problem of roughly parallel tracks on two levels. Bear in mind that all factors and modifications we consider also apply to the crossed-tracks arrangement.

No matter what size and style are chosen for the structure, thoughtful study reveals that the critical part of the design will be the end elevation of the

Stations built to fit

72

THEN

building. This, in turn, is dependent upon the difference in track elevations. The difference is 26 feet at Cross Junction, but there is only a remote possibility that the separation is the same on your railroad, so you must make adjustments.

The station for Cross Junction has a high platform along the low-level track. The face of the building along this platform is one story high. From the ceiling level of the first story the roof extends broadly upward and back to near the edge of the second-level station platform. The building extends a few feet under the edge of the upper platform at the widest part.

The roof is dominated by a cupola leading onto this rooftop platform extension, while partway down the roof is a second-story dormer. At the end of the building is a one-story brick wing that serves as a waiting room. Its flat roof doubles as the midway landing for the stairway between levels, and a door leads from it into the second story of the main building.

All these elements can be adjusted in height and position to accommodate track separations ranging from 12 to 30 feet, fig. 3. The situation at Cross Junction/Corsa is shown in A in the series. The building proper in this diagram has a 10-foot height at the front wall, and is 22 feet high at the peak of the roof. As is, this would accommodate a track separation of 22 feet, but by raising the level of the lower platform (and the building with it) up to 4 feet, we gain the amount needed for our 26-foot difference. Platforms up to 4 feet above rails are in use by the prototype, particularly in the East.

Now let's consider modifying the building to accommodate a track separation greater than 26 feet. One method is to increase the height without changing the 20-foot depth of the building. This results in an increased roof pitch, fig. 3B.

Because the total height of the building is now 30 feet, there is more freedom in establishing the floor level for the second story, and the dormer can be slid up and down the roof for the best effect. (The doorway from the stairway might ordinarily determine the level of the second-story floor, but there could be steps inside the building if the floor and doorway differ.)

An alternate means of increasing building height is to use the old roof pitch but increase the 20-foot depth. The dormer can be moved as in the above method to its best position. Keep in mind that ceilings are usually at least 8 feet above the floor and, in station buildings, often much more. For a 30-foot height with the original roof pitch, the building would have to be increased to about 24-foot depth. If this is done, the brick waiting-room wing will either have to be moved along with the retaining wall or be made deeper.

Suppose we wish to accommodate less than 22-foot track separation. We can

ABOUT DUO STATION DESIGN
by John Allen

In prototype railroading, two-level stations aren't very common; although they do exist, I doubt if any ever had different station names for the two elevations. The distance between Cross Junction and Corsa is about 45 feet by rail—that's 9 smiles (short miles) by GD Line measurement. Other than in model railroad imagineering, only in amusement parks or on a fantrip would someone take a train rather than walk the two flights of stairs!

Bilevel stations have much value in model railroad practice, where looping over and under is common, because they allow for schematic featuring of two stations while cluttering up the right of way with only one structure. Such stations save on construction time as well as space.

On the GD Line, local passenger and mail trains stop at both stations; to conserve space one structure was designed to serve both. The original tiny Cross Junction station was moved to another point on the line. Space was at a premium, and though the new Cross Junction platform is generous, the actual layout area occupied by the building is only about 8 square inches. By designing three levels into the station and using a large visible roof area, the station gains the appearance of a structure much larger than it is.

Stations built to fit

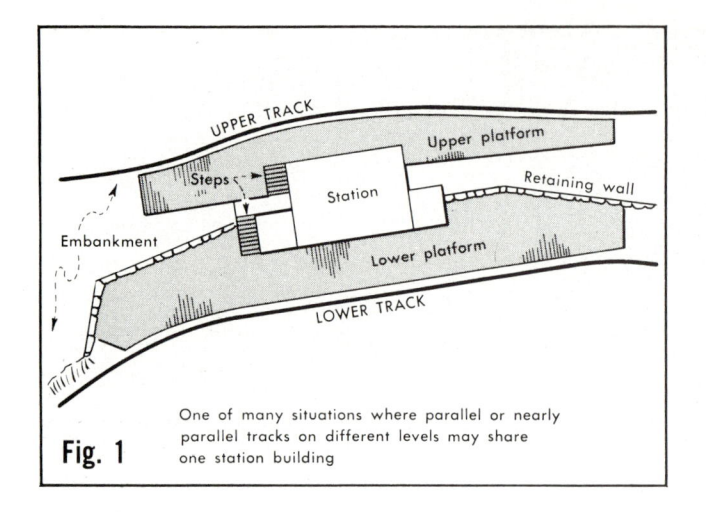

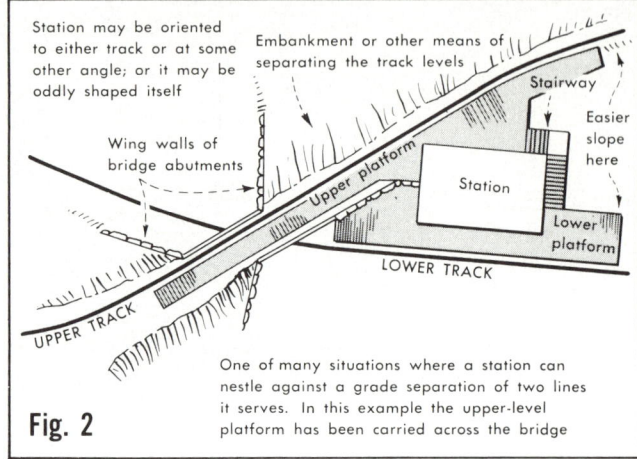

Fig. 1 One of many situations where parallel or nearly parallel tracks on different levels may share one station building

Fig. 2 One of many situations where a station can nestle against a grade separation of two lines it serves. In this example the upper-level platform has been carried across the bridge

easily lower the roof level of the second story by as much as 3 feet. To accomplish this, the dormer window must be moved down and toward the front face of the station, fig. 3C. Three feet is the limit for this "shortening" operation; more than that will give the second floor an unduly squat appearance. Besides, we cannot move the front wall of the dormer forward of the lower-level front walk. The cupola can also be moved forward. We will discuss the location of this component later.

With a separation of less than 19 feet, it is necessary to introduce a peaked roof for the main station, fig. 3D. An upper-level platform of 12 feet is the minimum practical track separation for a two-level station. The peak location will be determined by your upper-platform height. We can move the second-floor door to the left, but below the 17-foot level it will have to be eliminated.

The peaked-roof idea can, of course, be used to advantage at a 19-foot or slightly higher level. However, with any peaked roof we must eliminate the widened part of the upper platform, and relocate the top end of the stairs. The stairs can simply be reversed from the arrangement shown in the main drawing, and end at a small platform opposite an opening in the railing at the top of the retaining wall.

Our last effort to increase the elasticity of our station accommodates greater track separation by introducing another floor level between the first floor and the dormer, fig. 4. The new floor needs windows, and a suggested grouping is shown. This arrangement can be used from about 34 feet to 38 or 39 feet of track level difference. Between 30 feet and 34 feet we can use this same arrangement but must drop the lower platform to the ground again.

There are any number of these sketches that may suit you better, such as those shown in fig. 4 but using the peaked roof in fig. 3D to arrive at a separation of 32 feet. We could also extrapolate greater separations, accommodated by additional floor levels. If we go much higher, though, we'd better make room for an elevator.

Where tracks are not parallel

Angles created by variations from parallel upper- and lower-level tracks can be handled comfortably by changing the platform configuration at either or both levels. We'll talk about that a little later, when we get ready to build the platforms.

Now let's investigate how to use our station at a location where the upper level crosses the lower track at an angle. This is a surprisingly easy adaptation. This was the situation at Cross Junction with respect to that second track at the lower level. On the GD this track comes out of—or enters, as you choose—a tunnel, but it takes only a slight exercise of the imagination to visualize the Corsa main crossing this track on a bridge or trestle. An examination of the photographs shows another interesting fact: The tracks do not cross at right angles, but the lower platform allows for this irregularity so neatly that it goes almost unnoticed.

To increase the versatility of our design, look at fig. 5 to see how the basic components can be repositioned to cover more terrain and track layouts. Note that the bay window has been moved to the end of the main building, facing the track served by the bottom platform. This same arrangement is also shown by dotted lines in fig. 4.

Construction

Several techniques and materials can be used for the project. You may prefer board-and-batten siding instead of clapboard, corrugated metal roof rather than shingles—even a brick retaining wall. Because of this I will touch only on actual construction to the extent that it is unique to the two-level station.

The shape of the foundations and lower rear profile of the sides will be dictated by the cross section of the terrain. If your scenery is already in place you have two choices: You can carefully remove part of the scenery, making a recess for the station, or you can fit the building to existing terrain. Begin by making a template, fig. 6. Cut a piece of heavy cardstock, purposely leaving a sizable gap between the card and the scenery. Hold the cardstock in place, and cement "probes" as required to provide a topographical contour where they touch the embankment. Transfer this contour to the side of the building and cut the side walls to fit.

If the area is not scenicked, you can put the building in place and add scenery later. If you plan to light the building, be sure it is removable to save a lot of grief when a bulb must be replaced.

Walls, windows, and roof

You must prepaint the siding and trim material if you want clean lines between the two. Cross Junction is yellow with maroon trim, the standard color scheme for GD-owned buildings. Aside from the family appearance your railroad acquires when you establish your own color scheme, any leftover prepainted materials can be kept on hand for small "quickie" buildings like a crossing shanty.

One long wall of $1/16$" or thicker cardstock can serve as the back of the main building, the rear of the waiting-room wing, and even as the backing for the "stone" retaining wall. Thus, the main building needs only two end walls and one front wall.

On the front wall of the station, locate and cut out all window and door openings, including the bay window. If time is scarce, a large assortment of plastic or metal cast doors and windows are available. They are easily installed and can even be used in the bay window. Commercial doors and windows should be painted before installation. Otherwise,

Stations built to fit

74

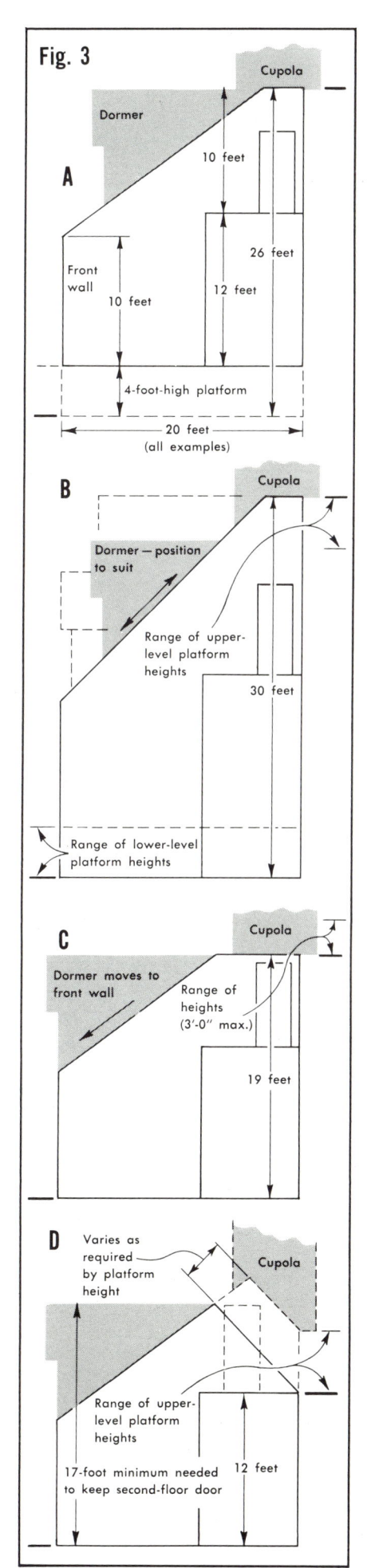

Fig. 3

A
Dormer
Cupola
Front wall 10 feet
10 feet
26 feet
12 feet
4-foot-high platform
20 feet (all examples)

B
Cupola
Dormer — position to suit
Range of upper-level platform heights
30 feet
Range of lower-level platform heights

C
Cupola
Dormer moves to front wall
Range of heights (3'-0" max.)
19 feet

D
Varies as required by platform height
Cupola
Range of upper-level platform heights
17-foot minimum needed to keep second-floor door
12 feet

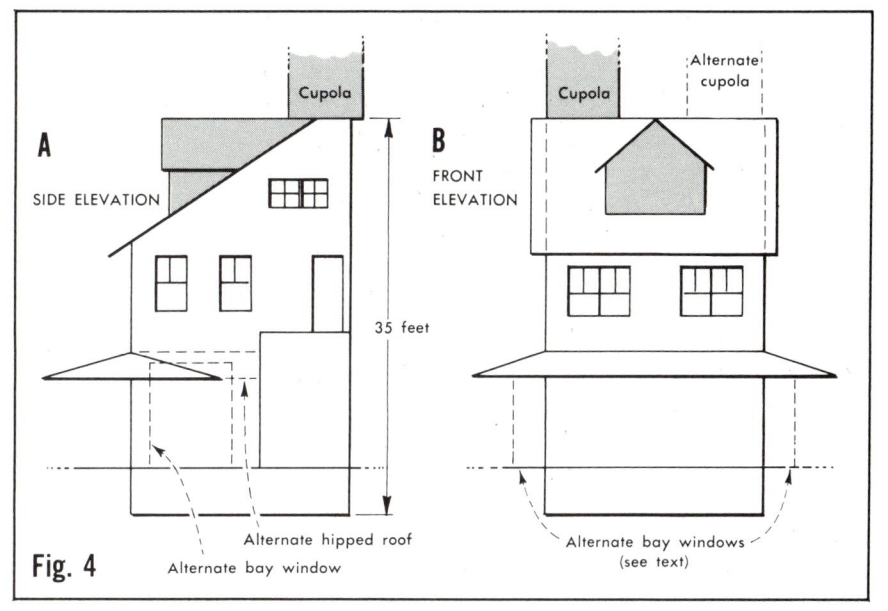

Fig. 4

A SIDE ELEVATION
Cupola
35 feet
Alternate hipped roof
Alternate bay window

B FRONT ELEVATION
Cupola
Alternate cupola
Alternate bay windows (see text)

begin window-building by framing the openings with Z-shaped strips as shown in fig. 7. Don't frame the bay-window opening. Add the doors, making them from two laminations of Strathmore bristol board as indicated in figs. 8 and 9. You may wish to leave a door partially open, or a window raised, as I did. If you leave a door open be sure to add a scrap of interior flooring to the visible area, especially if the station is positioned in a well-lighted area. The bay window must be built before the sides can be assembled, fig. 10. As mentioned, its location will be determined by the location of your lower track.

With windows and doors framed and installed and the bay completed, assemble the basic structure. Assembly differs from the usual braced-corner method (with 6 x 6 trim at each corner) only at the rear wall. As already mentioned, the cardstock used for the rear wall of the main building extends past the side of the station to form the rear wall of the brick addition and to provide backing for the simulated stone retaining wall. Check the structure assembly to be sure it is square, and move on to the roof, fig. 11.

I chose to speed roof construction by using precut commercial shingles and the cardstock that comes with them. If you cut and stain your own shingles use scribed wood instead of cardstock. It will provide guidelines for your shingles. No shingles should be applied until all of the roof sections are in place on the building.

Cut the large main roof from one piece. Its upper portion is 23 feet long, allowing 18" overhang at the sides. The depth of this main section from eaves to peak can be ascertained by measuring the sloping part of the top edge of one side wall. Cut the hipped (flared) section as a part of this same piece, score it, and bend it into position. This flared section measures 23 feet at the top to match the main roof, 49 feet at the bottom, and 8 feet wide.

Fig. 11 shows a rectangular flap cut—on three sides—at the center of the main roof in the area that will be occupied by the dormer window. Folded down into a vertical position, this flap serves as a back wall visible through the windows. Since a light will be installed over the bay window—with an opening in the front wall to allow light to fall inside the station—paint the flap a light color to reflect light into the dormer. Install two formers made of basswood flush against the sides of the building, fig. 11, to brace the flared lower roof section. When cutting the rear pieces of the flared lower roof, remember they must butt against the building walls 18" inside the main roof overhang.

The two triangular end sections can be cut from subroof material now, taking dimensions for the triangular sides from those sections already in place and bearing in mind that the shingle guidelines must be kept horizontal and match the guidelines of the sections already installed.

The dormer is constructed next. The pitch of the main roof determines the dormer side shape and height of the front, fig. 12. First cut out the window opening and frame the windows with Z-stock, adding clear plastic panes and 1 x 2 sashes. Use the same type of corners as for the main station, but substitute a 12 x 12 for the rear wall. This strip is to hold the upper rear corners of the sides

Stations built to fit

75

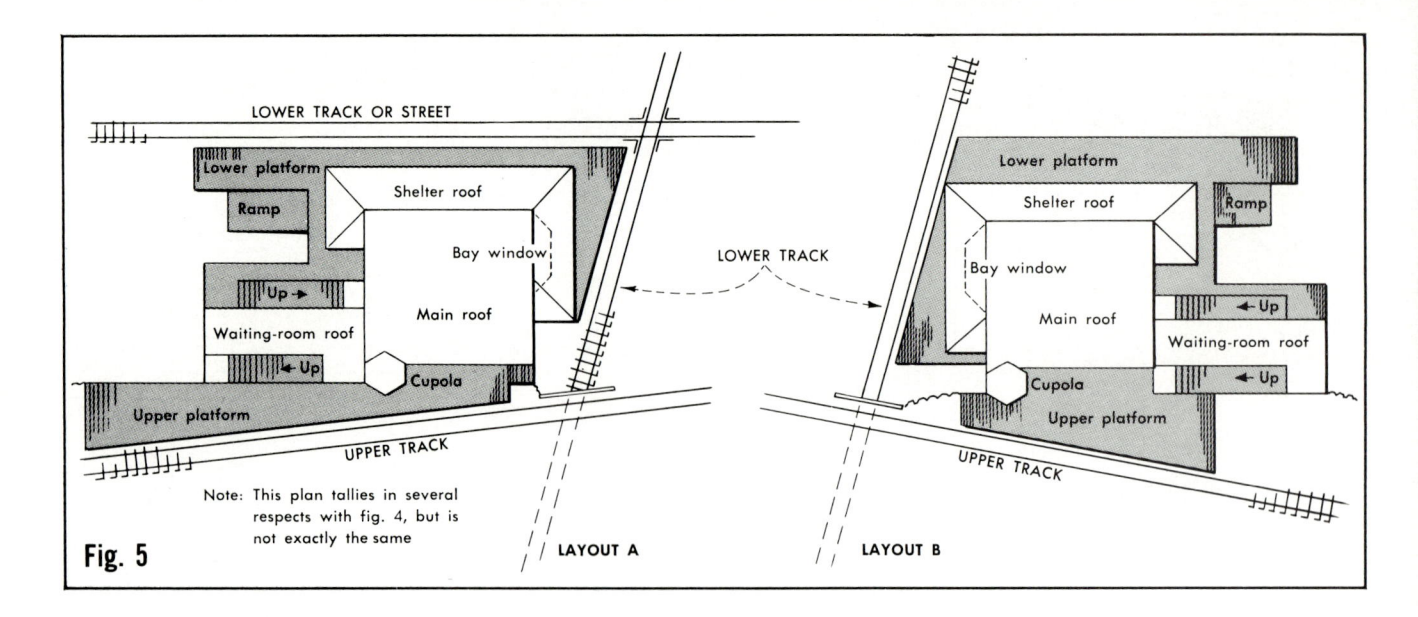

Fig. 5 — Note: This plan tallies in several respects with fig. 4, but is not exactly the same. LAYOUT A / LAYOUT B

Fig. 6

the proper distance apart. The unit must be squared as it is assembled. Cement the dormer to the roof and add the ridgepole, making sure it is exactly horizontal and at right angles to the front station wall.

Cutting and fitting the two halves of the dormer roof is, by and large, a trim-and-try—then trim-and-try again—operation. Every effort must be made to keep the shingle guidelines horizontal. Most of the dimensions are taken from those pieces already in place. Refer to the photographs for eave overhang at front and sides.

Whether you use commercial shingles as I did, or cut and stain your own shingle strips, apply them starting at the eaves and working upward. Bend some shingles at random with a needle; this will emphasize the effect of individual shingles. This procedure is time-consuming, but the result is well worth the effort.

Waiting room and platforms

The waiting-room addition can be assembled quickly. It consists of three pieces of hard balsa, 9" thick, cut to the shape shown in the elevation drawings. The third piece is the roof. Cover the walls with brick paper. Fold the paper into the window and door openings at a 90-degree angle to give depth to the wall. Frame the door and window with 1 x 5 prepainted stripwood. Cement brick paper to two-ply Strathmore and cut it to the width of a half brick (4"); apply this strip across the tops of the openings.

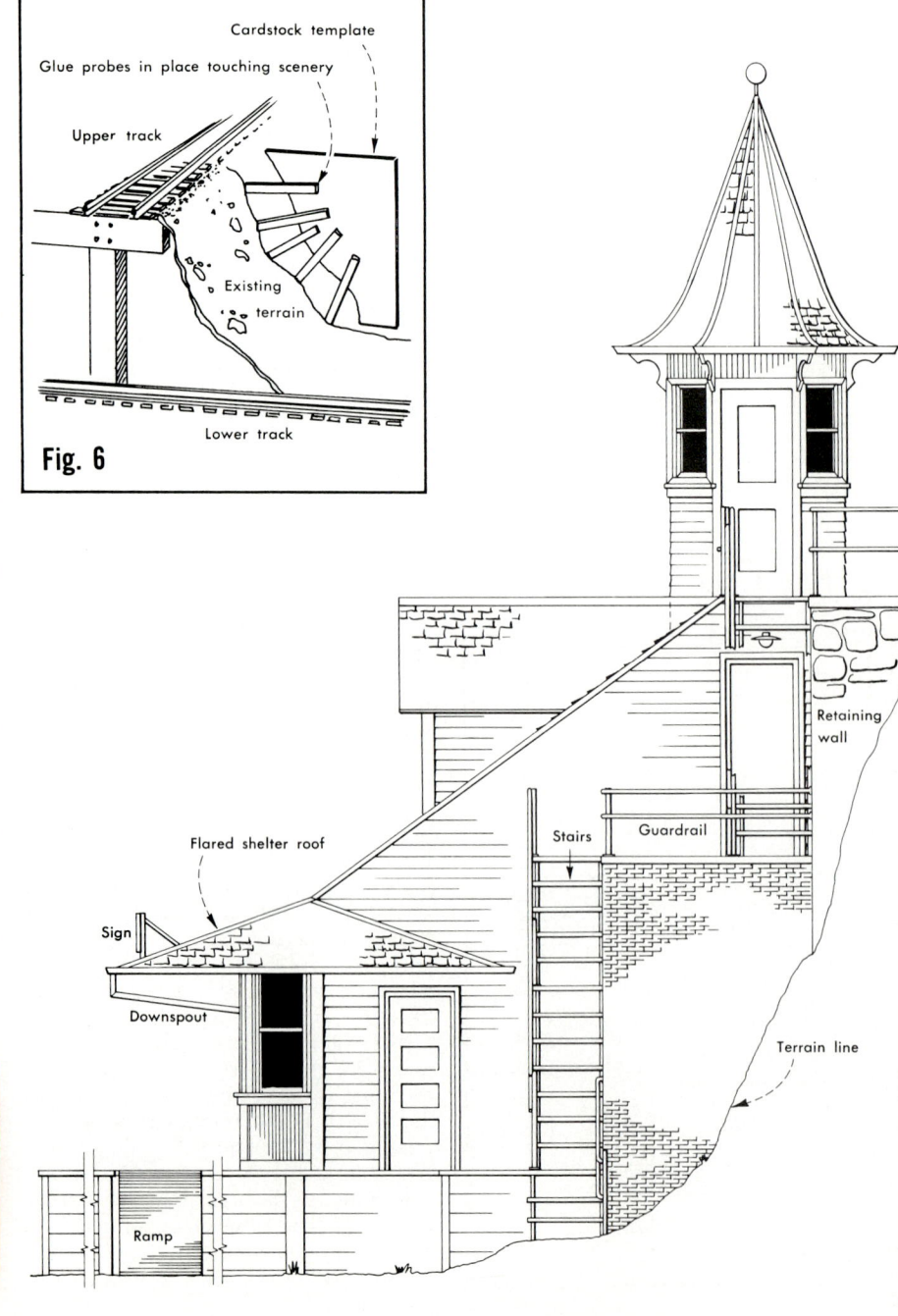

Stations built to fit

76

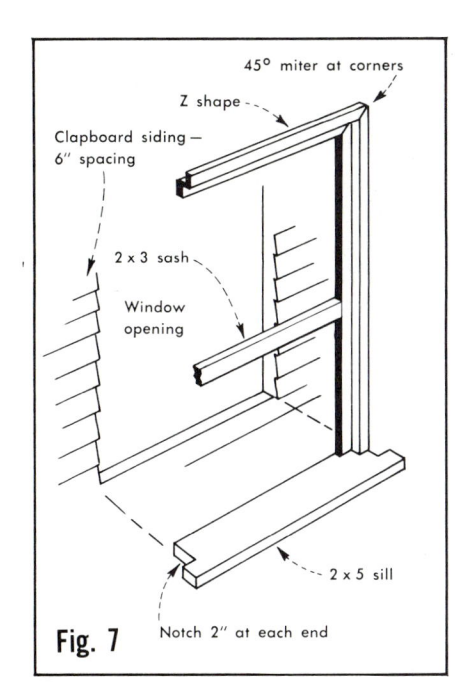

Fig. 7 — 45° miter at corners; Z shape; Clapboard siding — 6" spacing; 2 x 3 sash; Window opening; 2 x 5 sill; Notch 2" at each end.

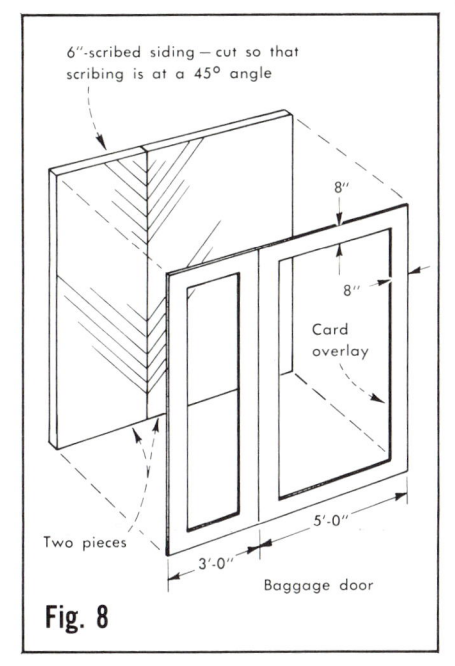

Fig. 8 — 6"-scribed siding — cut so that scribing is at a 45° angle; 8"; 8"; Card overlay; Two pieces; 5'-0"; 3'-0"; Baggage door.

Fig. 9 — Typical door; Celluloid; Paper lamination; Card overlay; 24", 10", 26", 8", 10", 36".

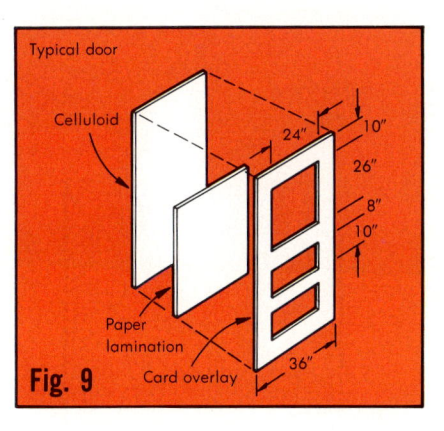

Note the end wall is fitted against the front wall to form a pilaster section projecting 4" past the front wall surface. The door is two laminations of cardstock, with celluloid backing the upper section to form a window, fig. 9.

Before assembly, cement in clear plastic glazing and add the window muntins. The muntins can be painted on with a ruling pen, but painted thread can be used to give the illusion of depth. If thread is used, paint it and let it hang to dry with a weight clipped to the bottom to hold it taut. A neat and simple way to apply a thread muntin after it is cut to length is to lay it in place and touch it with a toothpick dipped in thinner. This will temporarily soften the paint and cause it to adhere to the acetate pane. Now assemble the two walls and roof, fig. 13.

The roof of the waiting-room wing was painted with a thick coat of texture paint in a color I call off-black; that is,

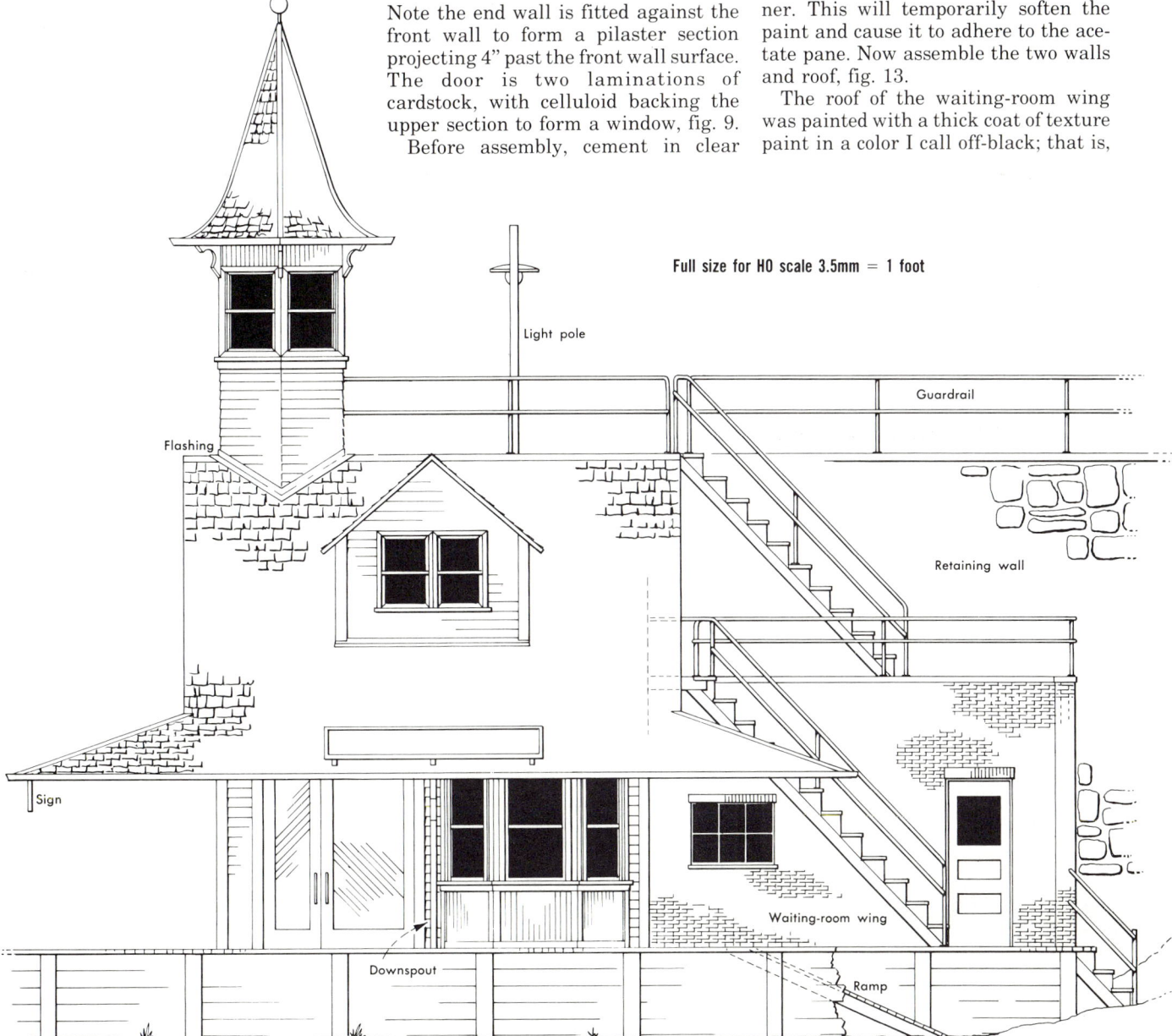

Full size for HO scale 3.5mm = 1 foot

Light pole; Guardrail; Flashing; Retaining wall; Sign; Downspout; Waiting-room wing; Ramp

77

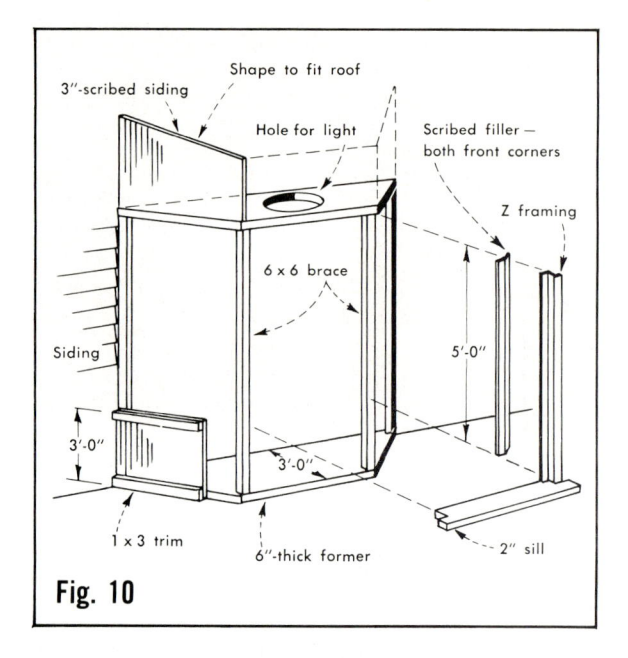

Fig. 10 — 3"-scribed siding; Shape to fit roof; Hole for light; Scribed filler — both front corners; Z framing; 6 x 6 brace; Siding; 5'-0"; 3'-0"; 3'-0"; 1 x 3 trim; 6"-thick former; 2" sill

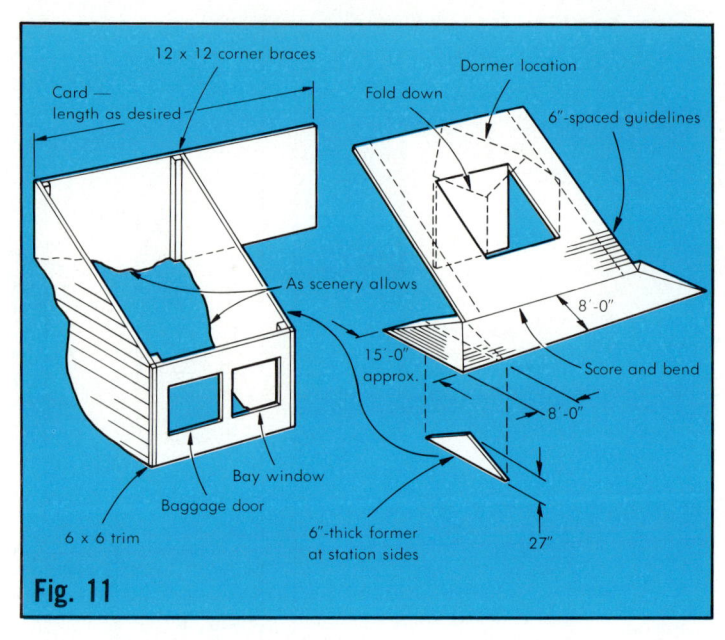

Fig. 11 — 12 x 12 corner braces; Card — length as desired; Dormer location; Fold down; 6"-spaced guidelines; As scenery allows; 8'-0"; 15'-0" approx.; Score and bend; 8'-0"; Bay window; Baggage door; 6 x 6 trim; 6"-thick former at station sides; 27"

Fig. 12 — Flap wall and reflector; Ridgepole (horizontal); Spacer; Shingle guidelines; Complete all window framing before assembly

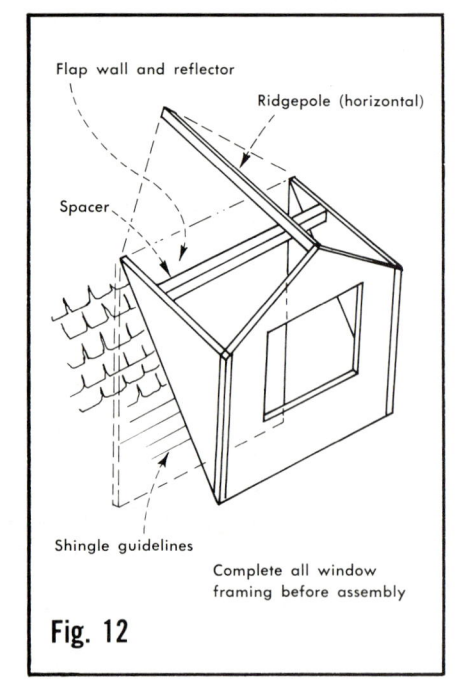

Fig. 13 — Brick paper on cardstock; Texcote or emery cloth for roof cover; 1 x 5 frame; Roof; 2" sill; Muntin — see text; Fold brick paper at door sides; Brick paper — three sides, folded at corners

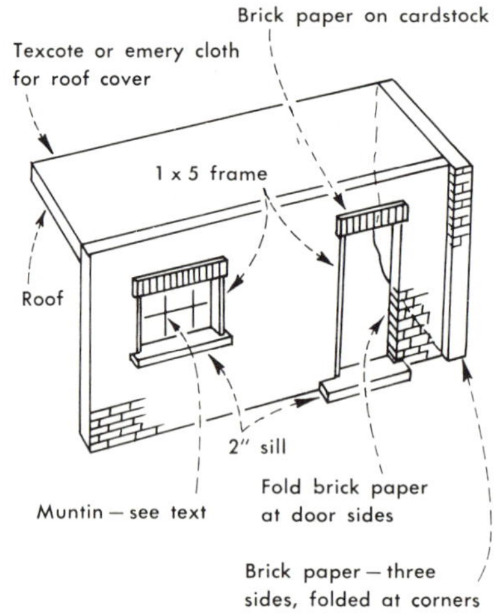

Fig. 14 — Cardstock; 6 x 12; Bevel to 2" thickness

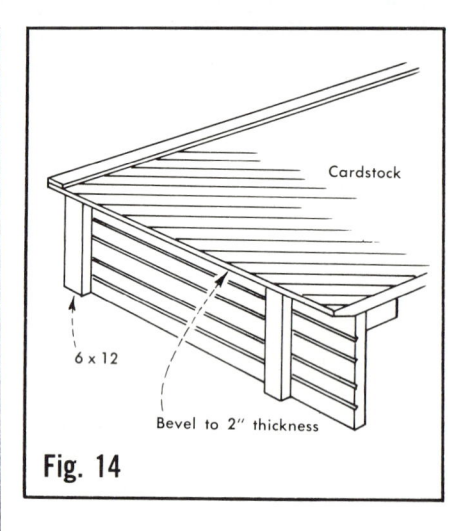

lightened several shades from a deep, full black. An alternate way to add texture would be to cut the exact form of the roof, including the small projecting area at the corner, from fine-grade emery paper, cement it in place, and brush-streak it with white or gray powder.

Now cement the addition to the main building and the card retaining wall, and trim and fit the end wall to the terrain shape where it fits against the embankment. Any acute case of "gaposis" here can be hidden effectively with lichen bushes when the station is in place on the layout.

The retaining wall was covered with commercial stone paper that comes embossed to give a low-relief representation of stones. You may choose to use another material or just paint the wall with concrete-gray texture paint.

Add prestained 9" angle stock to represent flashing along the line where the retaining wall meets the waiting-room roof and along the edge of the roof touching the main station.

Next add the upper and lower station platforms. Make a template to determine the exact size and shape of these platforms. Be sure to observe NMRA clearances from the tracks. Random-scribed siding can be used for the platforms. The thickness of the platform material is not critical, since the edges can be beveled along the bottom to produce an acceptable visible thickness of 2" or 3". The material should be stained before cutting it to exact shape; prestain enough to also furnish the vertical planked section extending from under the platform edge to the ground. Fig. 14 shows how the platform ends are made. The distance between the posts should be between 4 and 6 feet.

If you include a ramp, and are working with cardstock, cut and scribe the ramp as part of the platform. Cut along both sides, score where it joins the platform, and fold this section down to touch the ground. After staining unevenly, scribe the cardstock with a sharp No. 2 pencil. Space the lines at random between 6" and 12" spacing. If the corner is at an angle other than 90 degrees, a strip three or four boards wide should be scribed along the angled edge.

The stairs are, in a manner of speaking, mass-produced using a system that works for flights of stairs of any reasonable length. Draw a straight line a short distance from one edge of a sheet of two-ply Strathmore stock. To make stair stringers, cut along this line with a pair of pinking shears. Check the shears first to be sure that the teeth cut right angles. Not all pinking shears cut 90-degree angles. Trim the pieces on either

Stations built to fit

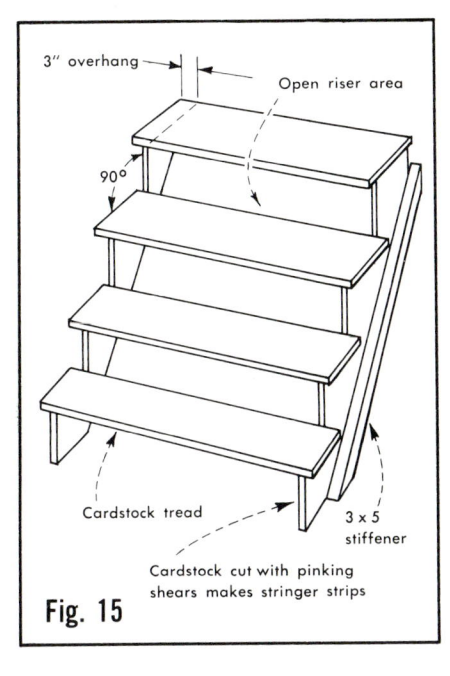

Fig. 15 — 3" overhang; Open riser area; 90°; Cardstock tread; 3 x 5 stiffener; Cardstock cut with pinking shears makes stringer strips

side of the cut to a straight line 5" back of the extreme depth of the serrations. Cement a piece of 3 x 5 basswood along the straight edge of each stringer as a stiffener. Pin the two stiffened stringers 2'-6" apart—and parallel—on a smooth, level surface. Cut the treads from two-ply Strathmore; the job can be done quickly and uniformly on a paper cutter. Each of the treads is 3 feet long, and broad enough to project 3" beyond the serration cuts into which they are cemented. Both stringers and stair treads can be prepainted.

The small landing platforms at the top of the stairs are made of prestained 3"-scribed basswood with joists at either end. A little jockeying around with the angles of the stringers as they are installed will allow full step height at both top and bottom of the stairway.

The cupola

The last of the major components is the hexagonal cupola for the upper level, fig. 16.

First cut the hexagonal floor former, making each side the width of the window you have selected. Now cut a piece of clapboard siding 3 feet wide and at least 10 feet long. From this make three of the sides long enough to fit exactly along three sides of the former; bevel the pieces for a neat corner joint. Cut two more sides, adding about 2 feet more to the total height. This excess will extend at the bottom (below the former)

Stations built to fit

79

Fig. 17

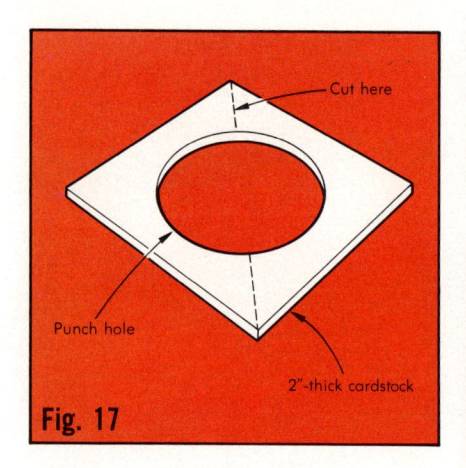

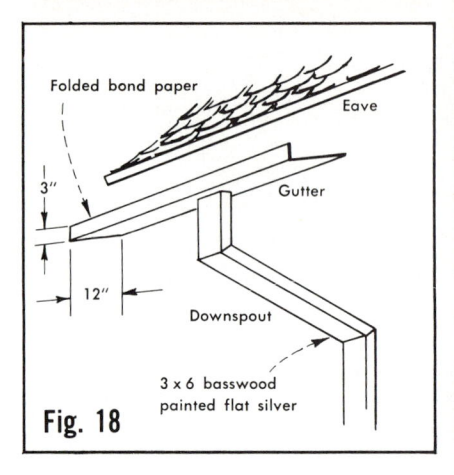

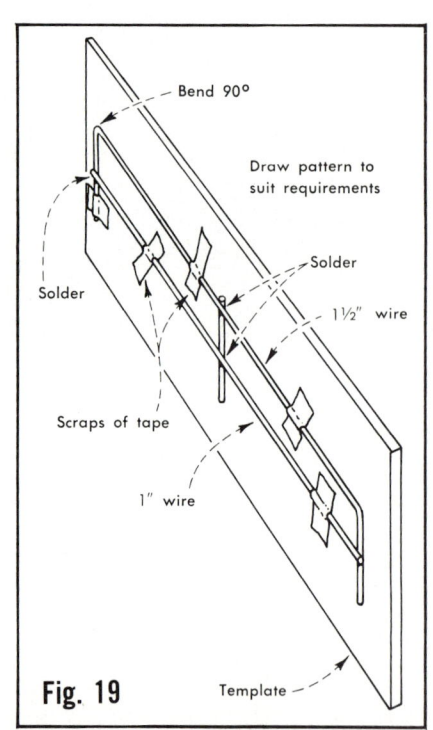

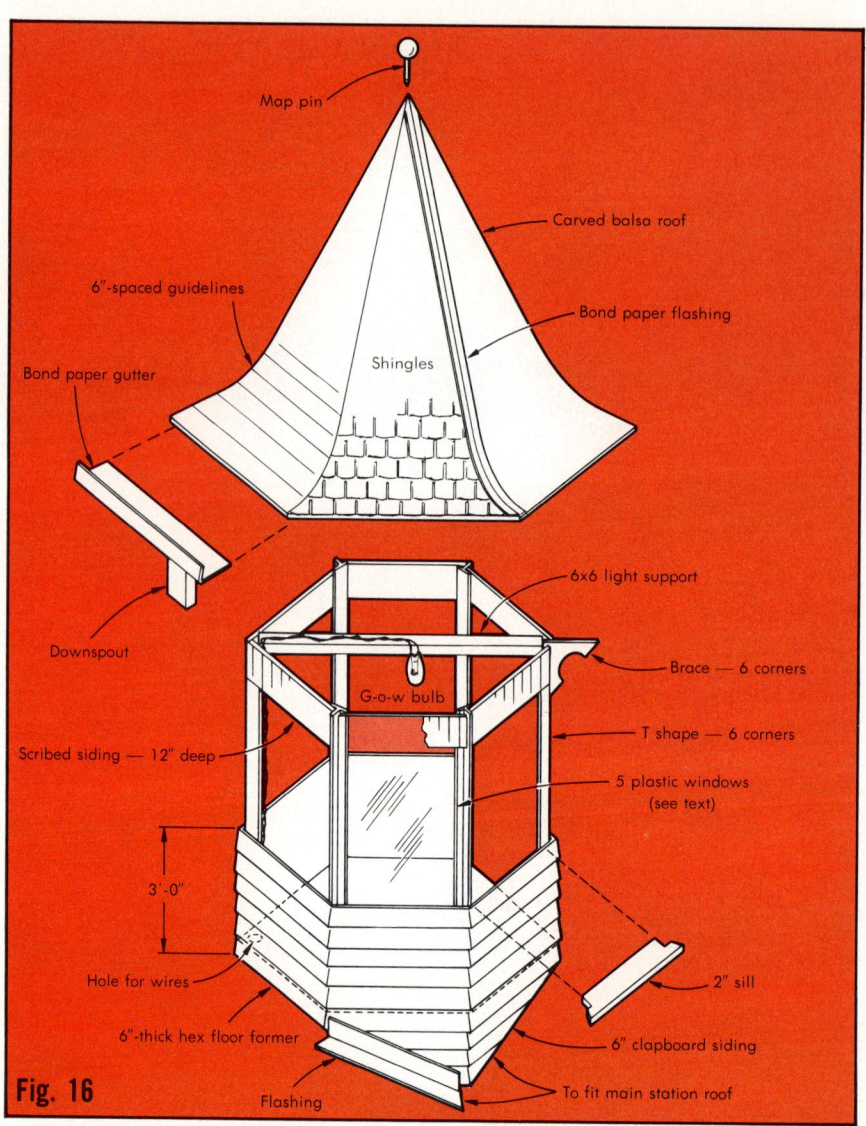

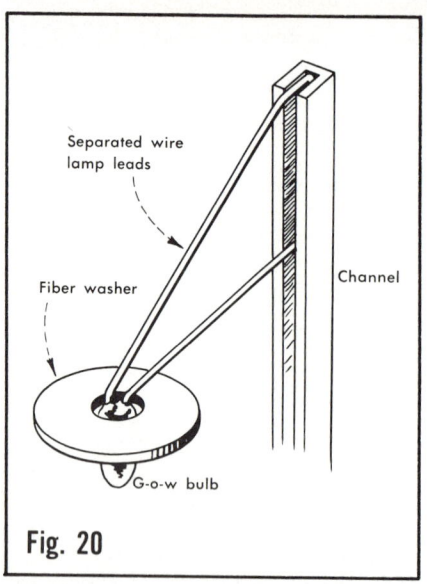

Fig. 18

Fig. 19

Fig. 16

Fig. 20

Stations built to fit

to allow for fitting to the main roof. Cement these five sides to the former piece; the sixth side will be the door. Check to see that all sides are square with the floor.

Now cut six pieces 9 feet long from a length of 6" T-section. Remove the long leg of the T from the lower 4 feet of each upright and cement the uprights into the six corners formed by the clapboard sides. Next cement acetate rectangles into the five window sides, placing them in the angles on either side of the T sections. Cut and install the sills; trim the ends at an angle to match the T-section leg. Cut a 12" strip of 3"-scribed siding and cement it across the top of all sections between the T uprights. Frame the windows with prepainted 1 x 4 stripwood; use 1 x 2 material for the sash. The cupola windows can also be framed with Z-shaped material as were the main station windows; this would ensure a uniform appearance.

At this point the door can be installed. Fig. 17 shows how the fancy eave braces at each of the corners can be made two at a time. Cement a 6 x 6 strip between two of the corners to support the grain-of-wheat lamp. Drill a small hole for the lamp leads through the floor former at a corner directly under one end of the bulb-support piece.

Before starting construction of the station, John and I referred to the cupola roof as "the witch's hat" for want

railings in place with a tiny dab of adhesive. Paint the railings off-black before installation.

Add the retaining wall end that runs from the retaining wall proper back to the embankment. Cut this section to fit from heavy cardstock; miter both pieces at 45 degrees for a neat fit where the end and the main wall come together.

You may not care to go as far in lighting your station as I did with Cross Junction: It has a total of eight bulbs. There is a bulb under each end of the flared roof section over the lower platform, two bulbs inside the station (one directly over the bay window, with a hole cut in the bay window top former, and the front wall removed between the light and the main station interior), a light in the cupola, another over the door opening onto the station addition roof, one over the station addition door, and the eighth mounted on a pole located on the top platform as shown in fig. 20. All light leads go to a terminal strip arrangement to expedite replacing defective bulbs.

Finishing

Station name signs were typed in caps on cardstock and handshaded. These were framed with 3 x 3's, with diagonal braces added to the ones on the roofs. The other signs such as Railway Express Agency, baggage, and train arrival/departure board are a matter of personal taste both as to size and location.

Cross Junction station was weathered by brushing on dry colors. A train-order stand was added to the lower platform. You'll probably want to add the usual clutter of boxes, barrels, and drums to both of the platforms.

At the outset I mentioned having learned some invaluable lessons from this structure. The most impressive new bit of knowledge is the fact that in 99 per cent of all scratchbuilding, correct-to-scale sizes of material are just as easy to work with as oversize material. Another insight gained is that most of our buildings are viewed from above, and the more plausible the detail added for overhead viewing, the better the appearance of the structure. However, the lasting lesson is that no dimension, method of fabrication, or type of material is sacrosanct; each can and should be altered to suit circumstances and the individual modeler's abilities and tastes.

---

of a better term. The roof is made from a block of medium-hard balsa. Make a template of heavy cardstock for the curve of the roof sections by taking the profile of the witch's hat from the elevation drawing. Draw a hexagon to the proper size on the end of your balsa stock. Carefully whittle it to the desired shape, and sand it smooth. Draw lines onto each section at 6" spacing for shingles, the same as used on the other roofs. Apply the shingles, again starting at the eaves and working toward the top. A strip of flashing at each of the six corners will cover any raggedness. Cut a small hexagonal groove in the bottom of the cupola roof to accommodate the top 3" of the cupola walls. This groove makes the roof easy to position and leaves it removable for light-bulb replacement.

All "sheet metal" flashing used on the station is made from bond paper painted flat silver. Fold the prepainted paper into straight creases, then, using a straightedge, cut 3" in from the creases to form a strip of flashing 6" wide, creased in the center. Cement these along the corners of the cupola roof and the flared section of the main roof.

The rain gutters are also made from bond paper, prepainted silver on both sides and creased. Make cuts 3" on one side of the crease and 15" on the other side of the crease. Apply a gutter all around the cupola eaves and add a rectangular basswood downspout 12" to 15" long at the front corner over the main roof. Also add a gutter around the flared section of the main roof. Fig. 18 shows how the downspout is made. It is located at the front center of the station. Flashing 12" wide (as against the 6" width used elsewhere), creased in the middle, should be cemented to the line formed by the junction of the front two sections of the cupola and the main station roof.

Railings and lighting

Take measurements and draw patterns for all of the various guardrails and handrails you need. Make these by bending wire (.020" for the HO model) to shape for the top rail and supports. The center rail is slightly thinner (.015" in HO). Tape all of the wire pieces directly on the pattern, then touch the joints with a soldering iron. Use a needle to make holes for the posts and install the

Stations built to fit

81

C. T. Steeb.

Baggage-handling equipment

Baggage handling equipment is a vital part of the realism in any station scene. Here are drawings and construction notes for baggage wagons and carts in any scale

by Bob Hayden

FEW passengers traveled light in the halcyon days of rail transportation, and a string of overloaded baggage trucks groaning under the combined weight of luggage, steamer trunks, express parcels, and an occasional bass fiddle in its shipping case was a commonplace of the depot scene. The creak and clatter of an iron-tired baggage wagon rolling—if you could call it rolling—across a platform or station concourse dredges up visions of trips to the far corners of the country. No station model is complete without at least one example of wheeled baggage-handling equipment.

All sorts of wagons, trucks, carts, and barrows have been used to move baggage and express parcels between station and train. The most familiar variety is the four-wheeled baggage wagon, fig. 1. The basic design of this flatbed stake truck was well established by the 1800's, and it did not change appreciably for almost 75 years. When changes did come they were minor and incremental; wooden spokes and rims gave way to iron wheels, then to solid rubber treads, and finally to automobile-style pneumatic tires. Even so, a glimpse around a modern passenger terminal finds many of the old wooden- and iron-wheeled monsters still in service.

Not as common as the wagon type, two-wheeled baggage barrows were also found nationwide. Figs. 2 and 3 show a

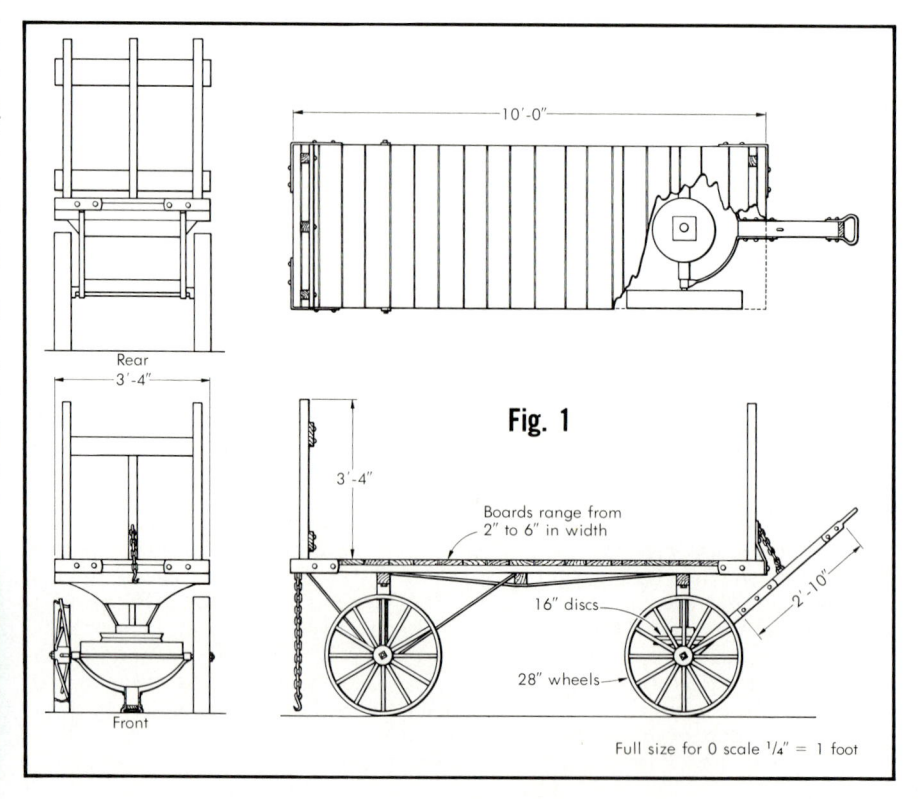

Completing the station scene

82

Bob Hayden.

Bob Hayden.

Fig. 2 — Full size for O scale ¼" = 1 foot. 4" metal tires. Metal strip along both edges. Metal rod. Chamfer edges. Chamfer on edges of vertical posts. Wood block axle support with metal band around it. 9'-10". 3'-1".

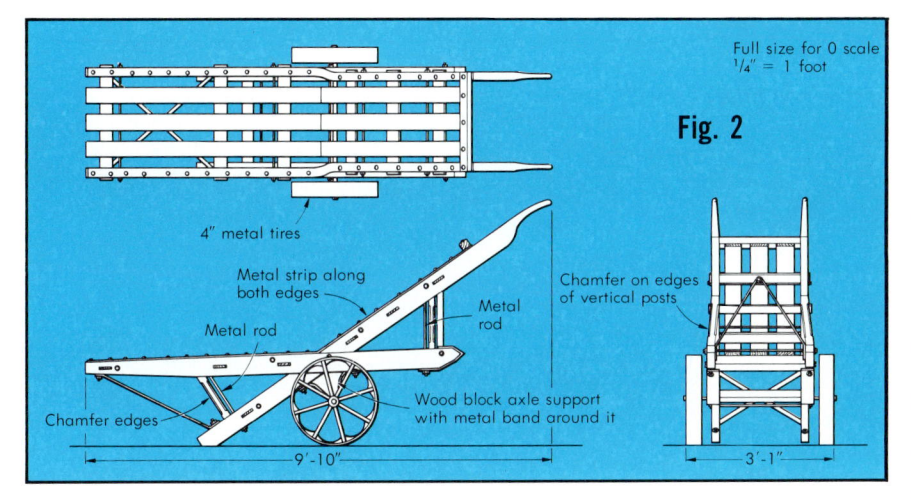

Bob Hayden.

Ward Kimball.

pair of barrow designs. These two-wheeled carts could not carry as much as the wagons, but they had greater maneuverability. This advantage made them well-suited to small stations with narrow platforms.

Large terminal stations use a variety of mechanized equipment for baggage and express handling, some of it similar to what we see at airports today. Modern wagons are built for either hand or tractor hauling, and include such refinements as roller bearings on all wheels—including the fifth wheel, or front axle pivot—and a rounded front end to minimize damage to train sides, fig. 4.

Modeling baggage equipment

Several excellent pieces of scale baggage-handling equipment are available commercially. The four-wheeled wood wagon is offered by at least two manufacturers in HO, and one in O. A two-wheeled barrow is available in HO, and models of simple hand trucks are sold for most of the indoor modeling scales.

The most difficult aspect of scratchbuilding baggage equipment is making the wheels. The easiest way around this problem is to obtain the wheels from inexpensive automobile, military miniature, and even circus models. Keep in mind that you can cross scales without problems here—that an HO circus wheel, for example, may work out perfectly as an O scale barrow wheel, or that an HO brake wheel might work on an N scale baggage truck. Also keep in mind that your model will be stationary, so the wheels need not work. Don't even consider the extra work and thought required to make the wheels

Completing the station scene

83

roll. Chances are you'll never bother to move them after the wagon is placed on the railroad, and it's a sure bet your miniature figures won't be tugging the baggage around.

A fast and simple way to model a baggage wagon that looks quite different from the commercial versions is to "modernize" one of the kitbuilt jobs by adding tires from a scale automobile or military vehicle. The conversion of the HO model shown in the photo took no more time than that required to build the original Grandt Line HO wagon, yet the appearance is very different. The same change could easily be made on any commercial models.

To begin, I found a jeep-type imported HO military vehicle with the proper size tires (24" - 28" diameter) for my model and carefully removed the wheels. After cutting away the fat hubs cast on the rear of the wheels I painted them and added them to the prepainted baggage truck body. The body only required one modification: the addition of a length of

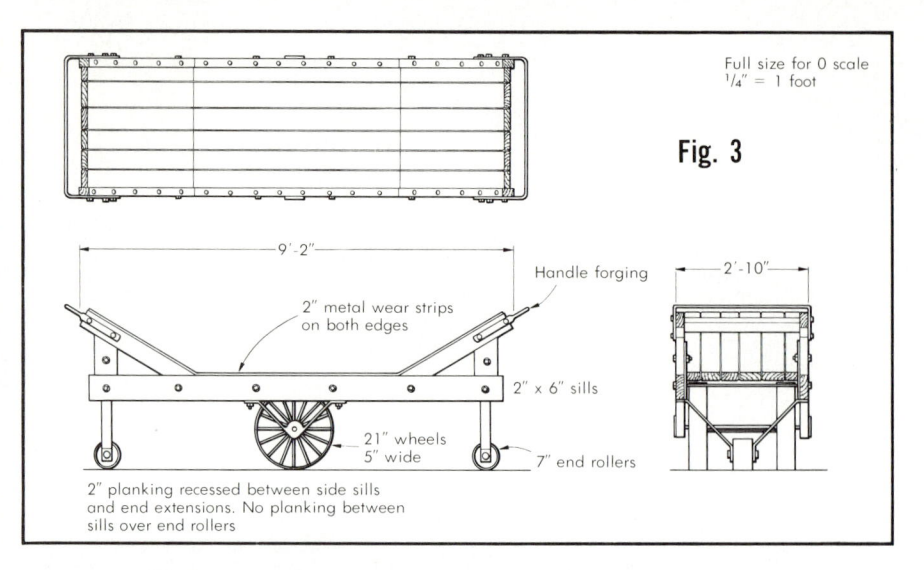

KALMBACH BOOKS: A. L. Schmidt.

These items are some of the baggage handling equipment available commercially. From left to right—Jordan Products HO baggage wagon, Grandt Line HO and O baggage wagons, and SS Ltd. HO baggage barrow and hand truck. All these models are simple kits.

Kelsey-Hayes Wheel Co.

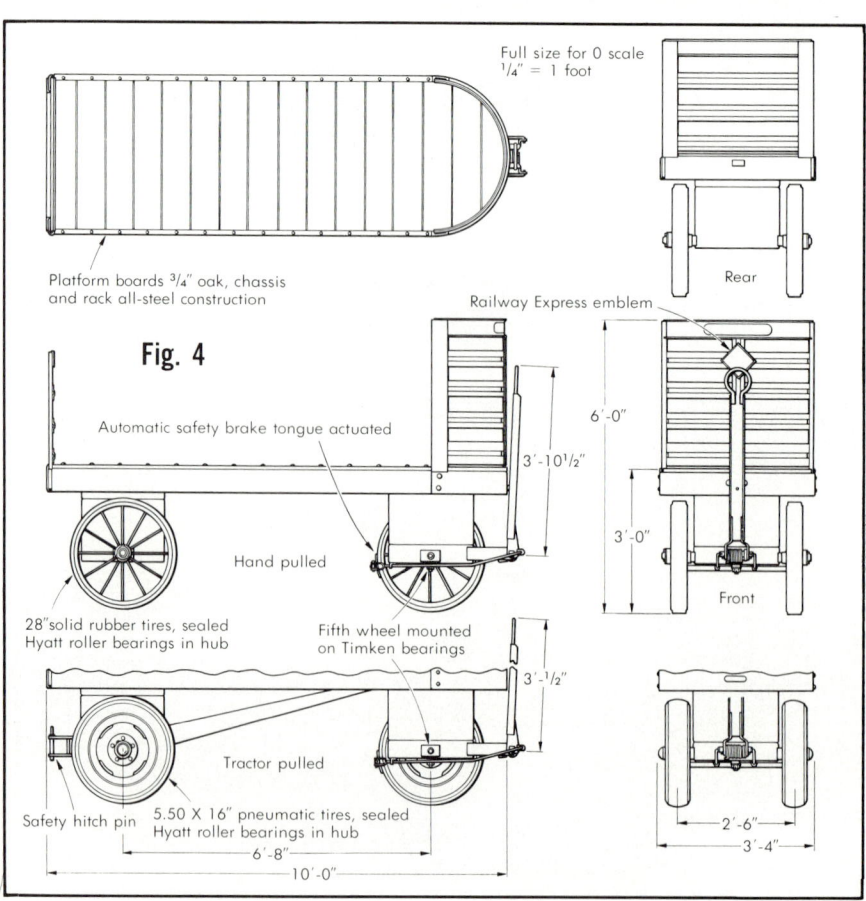

Completing the station scene

Fig. 3

Full size for O scale ¼" = 1 foot

9'-2"
2" metal wear strips on both edges
Handle forging
2" x 6" sills
21" wheels 5" wide
7" end rollers
2'-10"
2" planking recessed between side sills and end extensions. No planking between sills over end rollers

Bob Hayden.

Fig. 4

Full size for O scale ¼" = 1 foot

Platform boards ¾" oak, chassis and rack all-steel construction
Railway Express emblem
Rear
Automatic safety brake tongue actuated
6'-0"
3'-10½"
Hand pulled
3'-0"
Front
28" solid rubber tires, sealed Hyatt roller bearings in hub
Fifth wheel mounted on Timken bearings
3'-½"
Tractor pulled
Safety hitch pin
5.50 X 16" pneumatic tires, sealed Hyatt roller bearings in hub
6'-8"
10'-0"
2'-6"
3'-4"

84

Above—An unmodified Grandt wagon and a "modernized" version with rubber tires. **Right**—Some of the HO military vehicles that can supply wheels and other parts.

Both photos, KALMBACH BOOKS, A. L. Schmidt.

Fig. 5 BAGGAGE WAGON TONGUE ASSEMBLY

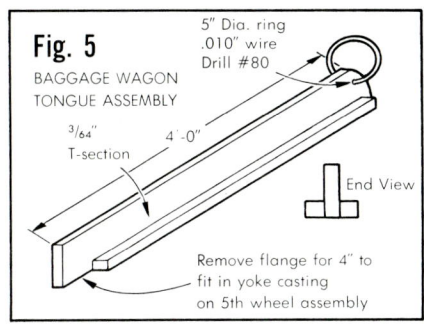

5" Dia. ring .010" wire Drill #80
3/64" T-section
4'-0"
End View
Remove flange for 4" to fit in yoke casting on 5th wheel assembly

Fig. 6 FRONT AXLE & FIFTH WHEEL ASSEMBLY

3" Dia. Axle
4 x 4
2'-8"
1'-9"
Yoke made from Jeep machine gun mount
6" x 6"
Pad 1" thick
1'-6" Dia. steering or brake wheel sanded to 2" thick
1 x 2
1'-4"
8"
4" stock
1'-10"
3/64" ABS T-section
3'-3"
Space for 4" stock between T-section uprights

REAR AXLE ASSEMBLY

3" Dia. Axle
2'-8"
4 x 4
1'-9"
1 x 2
1'-3"
4" stock
12"
2'-1"
1 x 2
3'-3"
3/64" ABS T-section
Space for 4" stock between T-section uprights

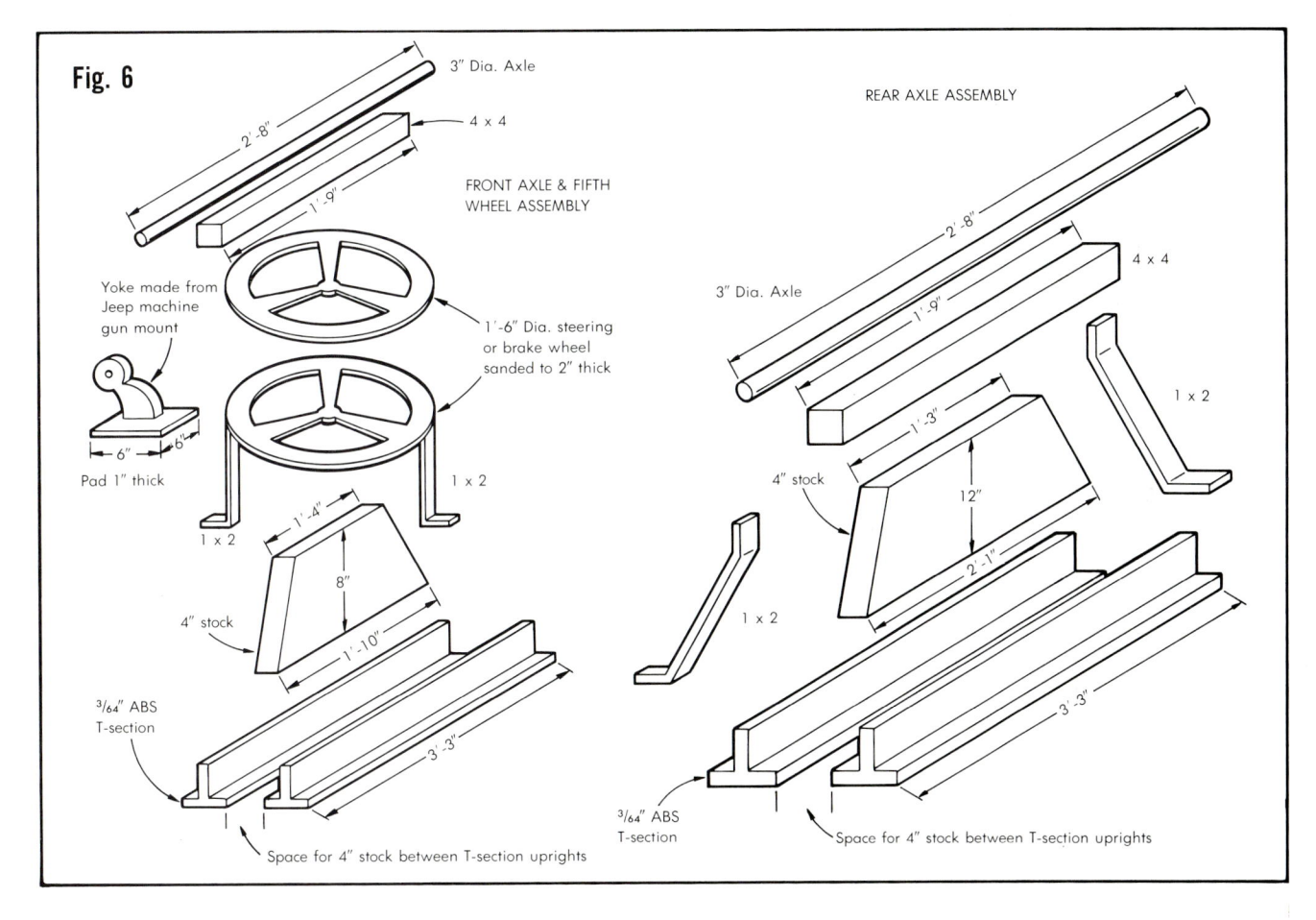

scale 4 x 4 stock between the rear axle support and the body so that the truck bed remains horizontal. I made some cosmetic changes by omitting the rear stake assembly, adding some facing boards to the front stakes, and installing two extra 2 x 4 cross braces on the underframe. The finishing touch is a diamond-shaped Railway Express label on the front stakes.

"Semi-scratchbuilt" baggage wagon

For a more ambitious project I set out to see just how quickly I could scratch-build a convincing HO baggage wagon. I chose a free-lance design patterned after a pair of photos in an old magazine, and used dimensions from the drawings presented here. While it would have been possible to build the model from wood strips and metal, I selected styrene strip and sheet stock for speed and ease of assembly. Once again I went hunting for a suitable source of wheels and odd parts, and once again I came home with an HO military vehicle—another jeep, for under a dollar. I gave a hard look to the rest of the parts, and found I could use the steering wheels—my model came with two of them—as parts of the fifth wheel assembly, a machine gun bracket as the tongue pivot casting, and another machine gun part as a towing ring for the rear end. The only other items required for the job are a swatch of scale 2"-thick styrene sheet, 1 x 4, 2 x 4, and 4 x 4 styrene strips, a short length of 3/64" (actual) plastic T-section, and a scrap of .035" wire. I also used a little piece of .010" wire and two scraps of fine chain, but these are optional.

Start by making the wagon bed. I cut the decking from a 3'-3" x 10'-0" piece of 2"-thick styrene scribed to represent scale 5"-wide flooring. Add a piece of 2 x 4 to the bottom of the floor across one

KALMBACH BOOKS: A. L. Schmidt.

Completing the station scene

85

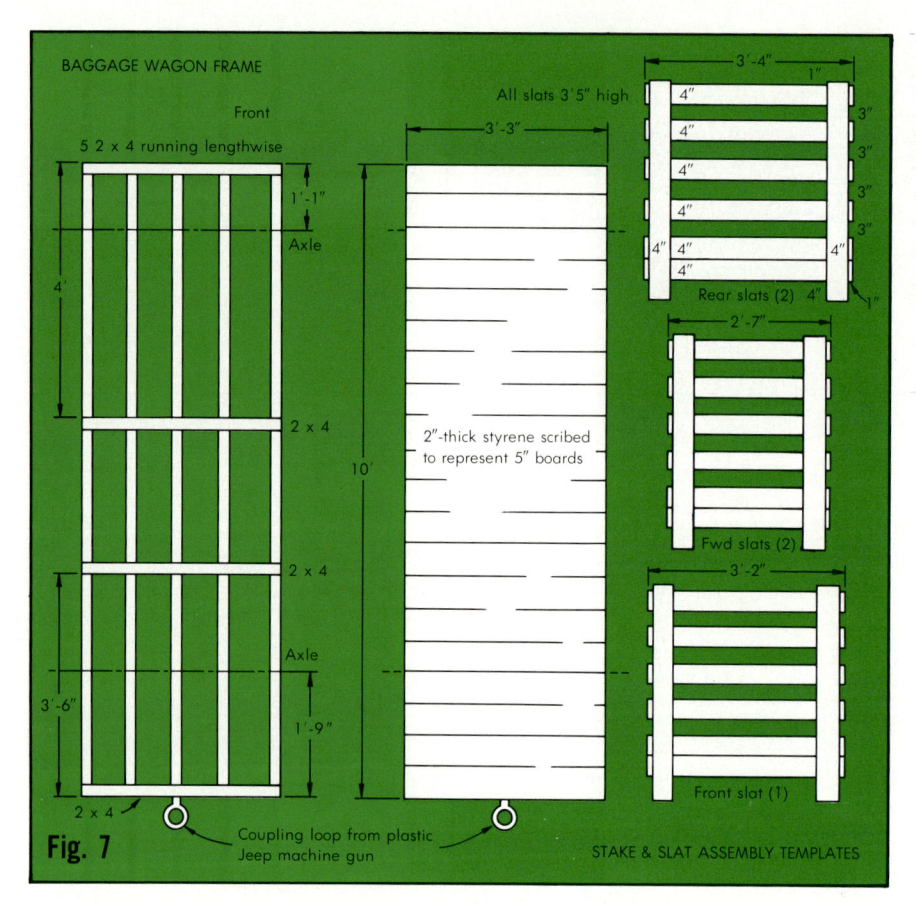

BAGGAGE WAGON FRAME

Front
5 2 x 4 running lengthwise
1'-1"
Axle
4'
2 x 4
10'
2 x 4
Axle
3'-6"
1'-9"
2 x 4
Coupling loop from plastic Jeep machine gun

2"-thick styrene scribed to represent 5" boards
3'-3"

All slats 3'5" high
3'-4" 1"
4"
4"
4"
4"
4"
4" 4"   4"
4"
Rear slats (2) 4" 1"

2'-7"
Fwd slats (2)

3'-2"
Front slat (1)

STAKE & SLAT ASSEMBLY TEMPLATES

Fig. 7

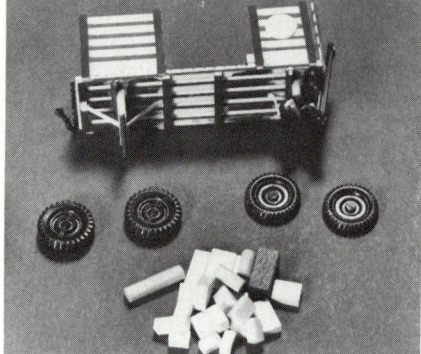

KALMBACH BOOKS: A. L. Schmidt.

From left to right—Unmodified Grandt Line HO baggage wagon, updated pneumatic tire version of the same kit, and the styrene "semi-scratchbuilt" model.

KALMBACH BOOKS: A. L. Schmidt.

fits into the fifth wheel yoke casting, and shape the top end as shown. Drill a No. 80 hole and add a loop of .010" wire as a handle if desired. Do not install the tongue until the stake assemblies are complete and in place—otherwise you'll knock it off the model several times.

To complete the bed and undercarriage detail, add front and rear braces to both axles. Make these from 1 x 2 strips. I installed only a single brace at each location on the centerline, but prototype wagons had as many as three on each side of each axle support. Add a tow ring to the rear of the frame and put it aside while you build some rack sections.

The five rack pieces are built up from 2 x 4 uprights and 1 x 4 slats, fig. 7. I find it's easier to build up assemblies like these if one size of styrene strip is prepainted a color to contrast with the other stock, so I used prepainted 2 x 4. There is one disadvantage to this technique: The paint must be scraped away on a joining surface now and then.

Add the completed rack sections to the frame and install the tongue. Cut two axles from .035" wire 2'-8" long and install them. I added two 14" circular signboards to the side slats; these were made by simply punching .010" styrene stock with a 5/32"-diameter leatherworking punch. The express parcels and other boxes in the "load" were made by cutting irregular lengths of styrene strip stock, stripwood, and a cotton swab stick and painting them to represent cardboard boxes. After painting I cut a few tiny bits of paper and added them to the "boxes" as labels. This kind of detail may not be breathtaking, but it is convincing in a photo or at the normal viewing distances on your railroad.

Complete your wagon by painting it. Common Railway Express colors in at least one era called for a dark green body and slatting with red wheels, while some wagons were painted to match the colors of a railroad's crack passenger trains. Touch the wheel tires with some dull black, then glue the wheels to the frame and the job is done—a detailed and delicate-looking item of baggage gear built for a total investment of an evening and—if you were thrifty when choosing the wheels—less cash than any similar commercial item.

end, and then cut five 9'-4"-long pieces of 2 x 4 and install them running lengthwise. Add another 2 x 4 running crosswise to complete the frame, then add two more cross braces on top of the framing. Place one of these 4'-0" from the end of the planked section, and the other 3'-6" in from the opposite end.

Build up the rear axle support as shown in fig. 6. Cut the parts to size, and sandwich the 4 x 10 support block between the T-sections. Then top with a short piece of 4 x 4 stock. Build up the front axle assembly as you did the rear, substituting a 4 x 8 block. Sand two steering or brake wheels to a thickness of 2" and add them to the support block to simulate the fifth wheel unit. Add another short section of 4 x 4 to the fifth wheel to support the front axle. Cement a 6" square of 1"-thick stock to the front half of the fifth wheel to support the pivot yoke for the wagon tongue; I made the pivot yoke from a part of my jeep, but you could easily make a simple U-shaped plastic piece that would work as well. This type of tongue mounting yoke is similar to that shown in fig. 4.

Make the wagon tongue from a length of 3/64" T-section stock, fig. 5. Cut away the flange at the point where the tongue

Completing the station scene

All photos by the author unless otherwise credited.

Train-order signals

One of the oldest—and most photogenic—signals is a functional part of the station scene: the "board" that tells the train crew that the station operator has orders for it from the dispatcher

by Paul Larson

THE train-order signal is commonplace to railroading, as traditional a part of the station scene as the image of the brave engineer with a hand on the throttle and a determined glint in his eye. At one time, virtually every station included one of these "boards" for instructing train crews to slow or stop, or to pick up orders from the operator. Nowadays, of course, many stations don't need train-order boards because traffic movements are controlled by automatic or dispatcher-controlled signaling and even by orders issued over radio circuits. But the signals remain. They are a natural for dressing up a station and for making it look its part: a vital operational cog in the overall railroad scheme. In the same vein, they are the perfect project for the modeler who wants to build a signal once in a while, but who doesn't want to build a complete, complicated signaling system.

Probably because they were among the earliest forms of signaling and train control, train-order signals escaped much of the onrush of standardization. Design, construction, and operation of these signals varies from one railroad to another, and even from one station to

Completing the station scene

87

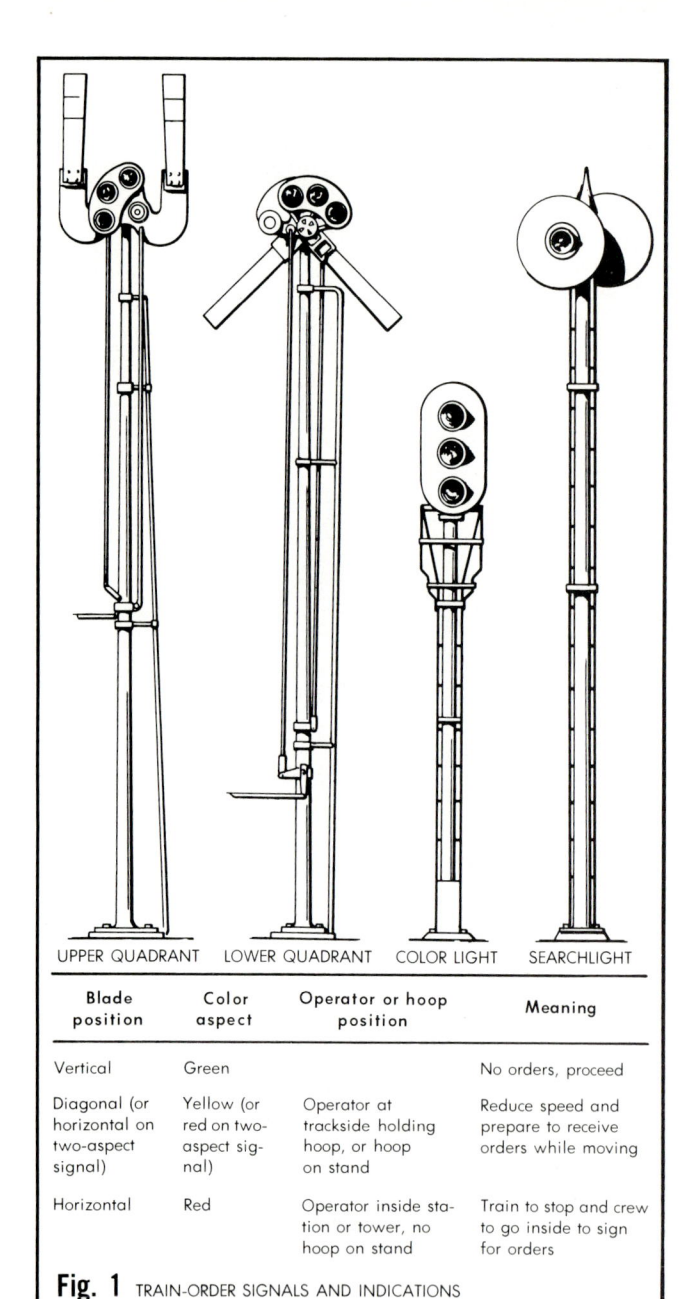

Fig. 1 TRAIN-ORDER SIGNALS AND INDICATIONS

Blade position	Color aspect	Operator or hoop position	Meaning
Vertical	Green		No orders, proceed
Diagonal (or horizontal on two-aspect signal)	Yellow (or red on two-aspect signal)	Operator at trackside holding hoop, or hoop on stand	Reduce speed and prepare to receive orders while moving
Horizontal	Red	Operator inside station or tower, no hoop on stand	Train to stop and crew to go inside to sign for orders

UPPER QUADRANT — LOWER QUADRANT — COLOR LIGHT — SEARCHLIGHT

KALMBACH BOOKS: A. L. Schmidt.

Above—Parts and kits for train-order signals are available in several scales. **Below**—This is the lever-frame actuator used to operate the author's semaphore signal.

another on the same road. Some signals have upper-quadrant semaphores; some use lower-quadrant. Some more modern installations use color light or searchlight types. Certain roads use only two indications; others use three blade positions or three colors, fig. 1. The "slow" or "caution" indication means Form 19 orders, orders which can be picked up on the fly (without a signature), while the "stop" board usually means the crew must sign the operator's receipt for Form 31 (restricting) orders.

Completing the station scene

88

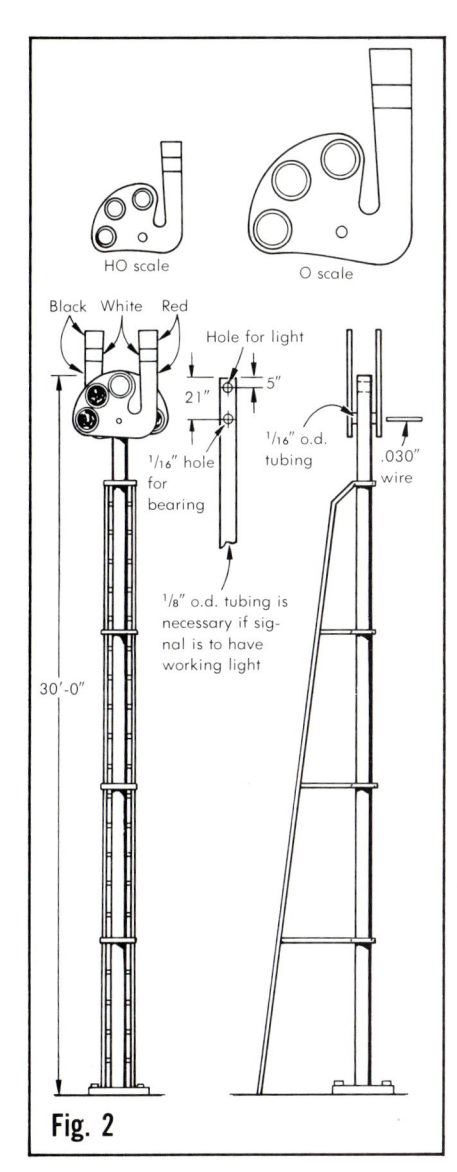

Many years ago, primarily in the late 1800's and early 1900's, the train-order signal was used as a part of the manual-block system of train control. After a train passed his station, the operator would set the signal at red, and would not clear it to the green "proceed" indication until he received permission to do so over the telegraph from the dispatcher.

Constructing a semaphore order board

While several nonworking train-order signals are available commercially, I wanted to incorporate train-order operation into my layout and chose to build a working model. Fig. 2 shows the general arrangement of the signal I built in HO scale, and includes templates for the semaphore head and blade assembly in HO and O scales. In the HO model I had to sacrifice some detail between the blades to permit installation of a short horizontal section of 1/8" o.d. brass tubing to house the grain-of-wheat bulb.

Construction of the model signal is not difficult, but there is some fussy work required in the final assembly. Make the mast from a length of tubing (1/8" o.d. is acceptable in HO, but 3/32" o.d. has a more authentic, spindly look), and the ladder from punched brass ladder stock. Drill all mounting and pivot holes in the mast stock before adding the ladder and the three braces that wrap around the mast to hold it in place. Make these braces from lengths of 1/64" x 1/32" brass strip.

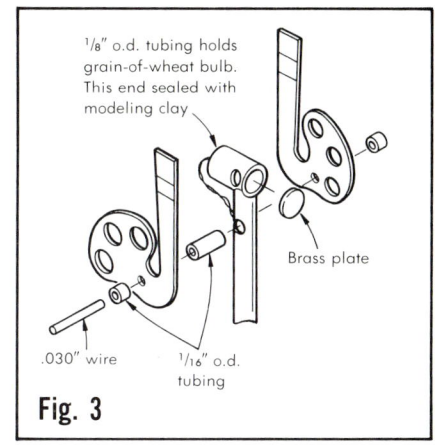

The base of the signal is a scale 12"-long section of larger tubing slipped over the bottom of the mast. Make the mast 3/4" longer than the actual above-ground height of the signal so that it extends down into the baseboard. Size up the location for the signal on your railroad before cutting the mast to length, as many prototype applications on curves or in cluttered locations require extra-tall signals for improved visibility.

I made the blades for my order board from .015" sheet brass. Shaping the blades is probably the least enjoyable part of the project. Drill the lens openings *before* cutting out the blades and save at least a couple of headaches. The lenses are bits of colored acetate cemented to the rear of the blades. Because my railroad uses only two-aspect boards (for simplicity), I blanked out the hole for the third lens by soldering a bit of metal over it—a practice similar to that used to modify prototype signals. Lay out the outline of the blades on the brass stock with dividers and a scriber, and cut the blades to approximate shape with thin-billed metal shears. Then file the blades judiciously to final shape.

Assembly and installation

Fig. 3 shows how the blades are attached to the mast. The blades are retained on the pivot wire by short bits of small tubing soldered onto the wire at either end. The soldering job is a bit tricky, because you don't want the solder to run along the wire and bind the blades in place. I forced a piece of paper over the wire ends before slipping the short pieces of tubing in place. The paper should prevent excess solder flow. After soldering, the paper can be torn loose and removed.

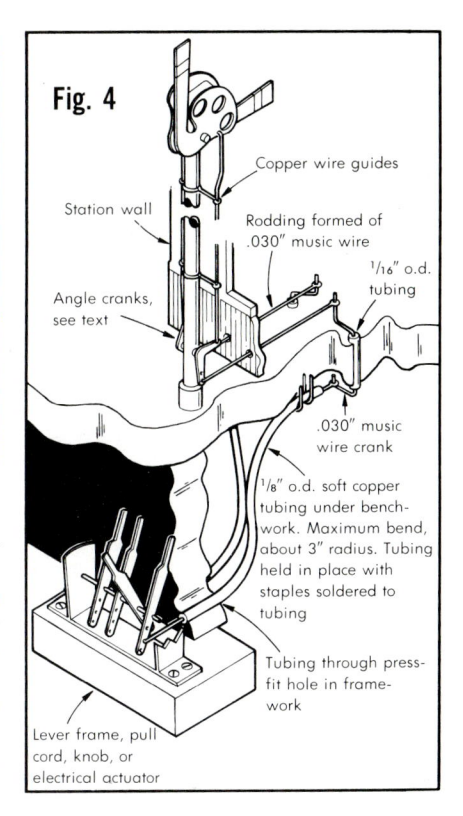

Fig. 4 will give you an idea of how I installed the rodding and linkages to operate the blades. This is the fussy part of the project that I mentioned above, and there is some careful adjustment required to get the semaphore blades to travel through their full throws. You may have to alter the angle cranks by shortening or lengthening to achieve the right amount of blade movement. In any case, it's a simple mechanism and the resulting animation is well worth the effort.

My signal is actuated by a lever frame (fig. 4), a commercial item sold for turnout linkages and the like. A pull cord, knob, or electrical actuator could also be used. Once you've finalized the actuator and rodding arrangements, the signal can easily be installed in front of the station. I made the holes in the station wall slightly oversize to minimize the possibility of the rodding contacting the wall and binding.

I painted my signal black, with red blades and a white stripe near the end of each. The backs of the blades are also black. Alternative prototype colors are yellow blades with black stripes, and yellow or white blade backing.

Completing the station scene

The Canadian National commuter station at Val Royal, Que., wears a modern sign that displays the company logo. *William D. Middleton.*

"Kiski" Junction on the Pennsylvania. This cast metal sign with raised letters and border was a standard Pennsy type. *C. E. Starr.*

Above—A cast sign on a light standard at Benwood Jct., W. Va., on the B&O. Below—Campbell Hall, N. Y., on the New York, Ontario & Western. *TRAINS: Linn H. Westcott.*

Frank Quin.

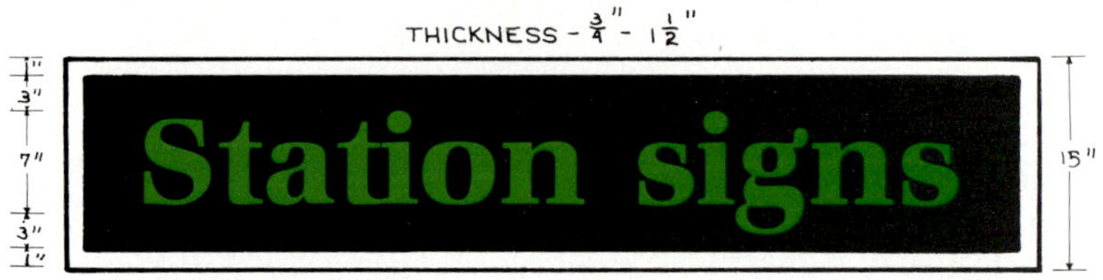

Station signs

Because they are vital to the operation of your railroad, legible station signs are necessary detail. Here's how to make them with dry-transfer lettering

by Bob Hayden

THERE is more to modeling a railroad station than building the structure, and the first thing you should add after the walls and roof are completed is at least one appropriate station sign. This label declares the name of your station to viewers and operators, and goes a long way toward establishing the idea of a separate place on your pike. The sign, in fact, has more to do with the place than does the building, and some early prototype railroads carried this idea so far as to erect a sign in many places *without* a station, hoping that in time the passenger and freight business would grow to require a structure.

The photographs featured above illustrate a few of the many types and shapes of station nameboards. Most railroads used a standardized color scheme for their signs, and many issued standardized drawings—similar to the one at the top of this page—to be used whenever a new sign was needed. Big roads, like the Pennsylvania, made cast iron signs with raised letters for most stations but adorned insignificant stops with similar designs done in wood or even painted directly on the station wall. Large terminal stations often had nonstandard signs to reflect their importance or to blend with their architectural style.

With few exceptions, station signs are lettered with simple, legible typefaces, usually all capitals, and—thankfully for those of us modeling them—without punctuation. Color combinations are chosen for prominence and readability. Recommended color combinations include white, yellow, or aluminum letters on a black or dark-blue ground, and black letters on white or buff. At least one company, the Ingram-Richardson Mfg. Co. of Beaver Falls, Pa., manufactured porcelain enameled iron signs to order. These signs—most often white letters on a blue background—were made by baking several layers of enamel onto a steel backing. The signs were guaranteed to last 10 years but they frequently outlasted the station, and many of them are still to be found in service or in museums. Truly modern practice calls for reflectorized signs; these are similar to highway signs, with either glass bead reflectors, small lenslike inserts, or patented reflective lettering material.

Making signs in miniature

There are many effective ways to make model station signs. Hand lettering requires practice and a good deal of skill, so most modelers opt for an easier way. Stencils, rubber stamps, and commercial photo reduction techniques have been used effectively, but all are relatively expensive when only two or three identical signs are required. Likewise, draftsman's lettering guides can be used, but they, too, are expensive for only a few signs, and the available typefaces are limited. By far the easiest and least costly methods of making station nameboards utilize alphabet transfers—sets of individual letters printed on decal film or dry-transfer sheets.

Most modelers are familiar with decal techniques, so let's focus our discussion on dry-transfer signmaking. The dry transfers themselves are a relatively modern innovation. They are made by depositing letters or designs onto the back of a clear carrier sheet with a tacky, waxlike coating that will release the letters when the carrier is rubbed gently from the front side. The letters contain a pressure-sensitive adhesive substance that adheres to any clean, dry

Completing the station scene

George G. Weiss.

Left—The station name and the Santa Fe logo are painted on the wall of the station at Presidio, Tex. Above—Scarborough, Ont., on the Canadian National.

Everett L. DeGolyer Jr.

John B. Corns collection.

The Pennsylvania Railroad's famous keystone is part of this passenger platform sign at Canton, Ohio.

Keith Pritchard.

Southern Pacific.

Modern signs on modern stations. Above—North Cairo, Ill., on Gulf, Mobile & Ohio. Below—Galesburg, Ill., on the Santa Fe.

Above—A modern Amtrak platform sign at Rochester, N. Y. Below—Middletown, N. Y., on the New York, Ontario & Western.

Above—This sign at Loomis, Calif., on the Southern Pacific included mainline mileage statistics. Below—Katy, Tex., on the M-K-T.

Santa Fe.

Jim Shaughnessy.

J. Parker Lamb Jr.

surface. To apply the letters, you hold the carrier sheet over the area to be lettered and rub a portion of the sheet over a letter. The waxlike carrier sheet coating releases, transferring the letter without any film or residue. The process is fast and neat, and the transfers are inexpensive compared to the signmaking methods mentioned above.

Dry-transfer alphabet sets are available in most hobby shops. Stationery, office-supply, art-supply, and blueprint-, drafting-, and engineering-supply houses also stock transfers. There are several name brands, among them Chartpak, Letraset, Normatype, and Prestype, and there are many sizes and typefaces.

You'll need only a few tools and materials to make scale station nameboards with dry transfers. In addition to a lettering set in the proper size and style, you should have some .020" styrene sheet stock, model paints, tweezers, a modeling knife, scissors, and a wide, soft-bristled brush. You'll also need a soft No. 0 pencil to rub down the lettering, or you can use one of the fancy burnishing tools sold especially for the job. A needle held in a pin vise or glued into the end of a short dowel handle makes a handy positioning aid, and a binocular visor or other hands-free magnifier is helpful with the smaller lettering sizes. The last items for your list are a straightedge, a sheet of graph paper, and a roll of Scotch brand Magic Tape No. 810, used to remove improperly applied letters.

Sign layout

Some of the most important steps in any lettering job come before you start applying letters. Measure your letters, count the characters in the sign, and check to see that the sign will fit on your model. Note that all letters do not take up the same amount of space; I's, for example, take up only one-third the space of W's. Straight-sided vertical letters—M, N, H, etc.—are placed farther apart, while rounded and slope-sided letters—O, V, A, etc.—should be brought closer to their neighbors. Refer to a photo of the prototype sign, newspaper headlines, or book titles as guides when spacing letters.

In some cases you'll find it handy to prepare a template from scrap cardstock. This approach works particularly well for arched or curved lettering layouts. If the job looks complex, make a practice sign, and then use it as a guide for your finished versions. If your sign will be applied directly to the station wall, be sure to start the lettering job at the center of the sign and work toward the ends.

Method A: Direct dry transfer

If you are able to find dry-transfer lettering in the proper color and size for your sign, start by coloring a sheet of .020" styrene stock with your background color. An airbrush or spray can does the job quickly and easily, but if you are brushing, be sure to use a plastic-compatible paint. Even if you are making only one sign, color a large sheet of the styrene. The extra will become your reserve sign stock, making the job a lot easier next time and standardizing your sign color scheme.

When the sign stock is thoroughly dry—a couple days or at least overnight—place a piece of graph paper underneath it (for alignment reference) and tape it to your work surface. Dust off the sign stock with a soft-bristled brush and wash your hands thoroughly; any dirt or grime on the sign will be well-nigh impossible to remove, and if the sign isn't neat, the most carefully built model will look bad.

Next, write down the station name on a scrap of paper and check it against a map, atlas, or other source. I speak from

Completing the station scene

All photos, KALMBACH BOOKS: A. L. Schmidt.

METHOD A

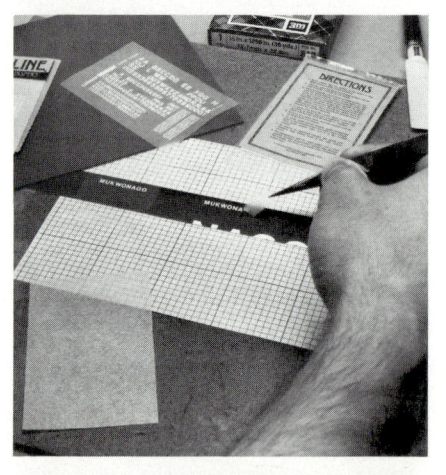

experience here, having painstakingly lettered more than one sign only to find the station name misspelled. Verify the spelling and place the correctly written name on the workbench in front of you.

Now—at last—apply the transfer lettering. Align each character carefully with the graph paper lines and the preceding letters and transfer it by burnishing with up and down strokes, scanning slowly back and forth across the character. Never burnish with a random or circular motion, as this can stretch, distort, and tear the letters. If a letter has not transferred completely when you peel away the carrier sheet, carefully align the carrier and try again.

Temperature is a factor in the correct application of some brands of dry transfers, and sometimes it helps to hold the carrier sheet near an incandescent bulb for a few seconds to warm it slightly before transferring the letters. After transferring each letter examine it critically. Then place the paper that backs the carrier sheet over each letter and burnish it down again. Be fussy. If a letter is crooked, out of line, or improperly spaced, remove it with the No. 810 tape and start again—a neat result is worth the effort. Discipline yourself to use a soft-bristle brush frequently to whisk away stray dust or lint fibers so they are not trapped in place by the lettering, and refer back to your scrap of paper after every transfer operation to check the spelling. Be forewarned that a long signmaking session can make your eyes cross, hands shake, and nerves tighten, so do only a little at a time and occasionally move on to another project to "rest" before continuing.

When all letters for one sign are transferred and you are satisfied with the spacing and alignment, burnish the entire sign once more, again placing the carrier sheet backing paper over the letters. If you plan to make a second identical sign, cover the first one with a small sheet of material cut from a clear polyethylene bag to protect it while you refer back to it for a spacing guide. This is particularly helpful because you can place the sheet of transfers over the completed sign and note the proper relationships between letters instead of taking the time to determine the spacing all over again.

To protect the finished signs, apply a single coat of clear flat finish over the lettering. A few brands of flat finish will attack the lettering, so test the paint on a spare letter before using it on the entire sign. Here again, a spray finish is fastest and easiest, but brushing will yield excellent results. Let the clear finish dry several days before cutting out the sign and adding it to your structure.

Method B: Masking with dry transfers

Now let's take a look at a little different case, the situation where you can get the size and style of dry transfer you need, but not the right color. Here we'll

Completing the station scene

92

use the lettering as a mask and remove it after painting the background color. This method is easy if you want white lettering, since you can use the color of the unpainted styrene sheet to provide the white, and paint only the background. In the situation where you need a lettering color other than white you must paint the sign stock, mask with transfers, and paint again with the background color. The letters are then removed with No. 810 tape—just as we removed incorrect lettering in the direct transfer process—leaving the desired color combination.

After applying your lettering color to the sign stock and allowing it to cure a couple of days, rub on the dry transfers, but omit the final burnishing step. Paint the entire sign with the background color using a paint that will not attack the styrene, the lettering color, or the dry-transfer film. When this paint coat is dry to the touch, try lifting the paint film at an edge with No. 810 tape. If the paint does not lift, the sign is dry enough to proceed. Using the No. 810 tape, lift off the transfers and expose the lettering color.

Admittedly, this technique takes some getting used to, and I can't say just how long you should let the paint dry, as brands, methods of application, and even weather conditions will change this. You don't want to let the background paint coat cure fully before attempting to lift the letters, because the paint will form a tough film across the letters that won't break cleanly as the transfers are removed. If you don't wait long enough, you run the risk of pulling up some of the background color with the tape. I have achieved excellent results by waiting 3 to 5 hours after applying the background color before pulling up the transfer masks.

Method C: Make your own decals

While it is far easier to letter your signs before attaching them to the station, some prototypes—Santa Fe among them—call for applying the sign to the structure walls. This presents some problems, among them the difficulty of applying dry transfers over the irregular surface textures and the awkwardness of working with a completed or nearly completed model. The ability of a decal to conform to an irregular surface and to be applied "all at once" is what we need here, so let's *make* a decal.

For this signmaking method we'll need some blank decal paper. You may find this in the railroad section of the hobby shop, but also ask at the scale auto and airplane counters, as it is widely used in those hobbies. As long as your signs are small, you can use the blank margins from printed decal sheets.

Lay out and transfer the lettering to the decal paper just as you would to a signboard, then burnish, dust, and cover it with a clear coating to seal the letters to the decal film. Let this coating dry, and apply your finished sign using conventional decal techniques. I find it helpful to cut a small section of the decal paper and use it as a test sample to determine how fast the decal will loosen from the backing when soaked with water—this prevents poking and pulling on the homemade decal, which is just a shade more delicate than commercial ones. Apply a decal setting fluid to make the film settle down over your irregular surface and "disappear."

A further extension of Method C is application of both a background color and dry-transfer lettering to the decal film. In the same vein, there is no reason why the dry-transfer masking technique should not work on decal film, but I hesitate to recommend it because I haven't tried it myself.

Finishing and mounting station signs

Not all station nameboards require a border, but you can make very neat white trim around the edges of Method A and B signs by scraping away the background color with the edge of a razor blade. Cut the signboard to width—the vertical dimension—first, then place your steel straightedge over the body of the sign and the lettering, allowing only the narrow band that will become the white border to protrude. Press down hard on the straightedge and draw the razor blade along it, scraping away the paint until a clean white border remains. Several strokes may be necessary, but try not to wear away too much of the plastic or the border will be recessed. Continue with the top and bottom edges, then cut the signboard to length and scrape the end borders. One hint: Do some trial scraping on a section of the sign that will be trimmed off. This will give you a feel for how a particular batch of paint, flat finish, and sign stock will respond to the razor scraping.

Borders for Method B signs are easily made by masking the lettering color with No. 810 tape when you apply the dry-transfer lettering. Mask the borders wider than required and trim the edges of the sign with a knife for the neatest results. Three-dimensional framing can be added using pre-colored wood or styrene strips.

Prototype railroads mounted nameboards in a variety of locations. The most common scheme used signs at each end of the station building, mounted on the roof, hung from the eaves, or tacked to the wall of the structure. When a single sign was used, it was usually positioned on the station wall or hung from the eaves facing the track. As an alternative to mounting the boards on the building, consider a free-standing arrangement using a post or pair of posts.

METHOD B

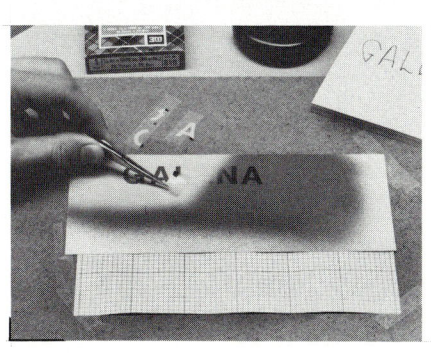

Above — For a two-color sign, the styrene is painted with the lettering color, the dry-transfer mask applied, and the letters removed after adding the background color. Below — Another "Method B" sign, using the white of the styrene as the contrasting lettering color.

Completing the station scene

Variety in station platforms

Prototype data and modeling techniques for several types of platforms

by Bob Hayden

CONSTRUCTION dates for station buildings and station platforms offer a case of the old chicken-and-egg dilemma. In many cases the platform came first, and the railroad waited until the stop proved itself before erecting a costly structure. In other cases, old photos show newly completed rights of way and yet-unpainted stations without platforms; the good footing apparently came later when railroad management budgeted the money to quash passenger complaints of muddy shoes and damp baggage. Although you are unlikely to have such complaints on your model railroad, your station buildings need platforms in order to look complete.

Completing the station scene

Prototype practices and dimensions

The purpose of any platform structure is to elevate passengers, baggage, express parcels, mail, and baggage-handling equipment above dirt and moisture, and to a convenient level relative to the track. Fig. 1 is a composite platform section derived from several railroad engineering drawings and NMRA clearance standards. In general, passenger platforms are built low—from 2" to 18" above the top of the rail—and are a minimum of 12 feet wide in front of the station building proper. The extensions of the passenger platforms along the track can be as narrow as 4 to 6 feet, and as long as necessary to accommodate the expected train length. As passenger business grew, platforms were extended to accommodate new train lengths, and it's not unusual for a platform to include sections built from different materials at different times.

Freight platforms are built high—between 3'-6" and 4'-0" from the railhead—to coincide with freight-car floor heights. Freight platform width generally exceeds that of the passenger platforms because of the bulk of the items to be handled and the larger size of the associated handling equipment. Likewise, freight platforms are constructed from heavier materials. The preferred method of transition between freight and passenger platform heights is a ramp that allows movement of wheeled vehicles. All platforms slope away from the station building for proper drainage, and platforms between tracks are built with a crown similar to that used in highway construction.

Types of platforms

Almost any type of load-supporting structure can be used—and has been used—to bring platform height up to the required level. The prototype railroads sought to match the construction and cost of the platform materials to the importance of the station. Planked timber platforms were the rule in early railroad construction because wood was inexpensive and did not require specialized building skills. A second low-cost type is the filled platform, constructed with a curb or coping of heavy timbers, concrete, or cut stone that retains a bed of screened cinders or crushed rock, fig. 2.

Heavy baggage and freight traffic re-

94

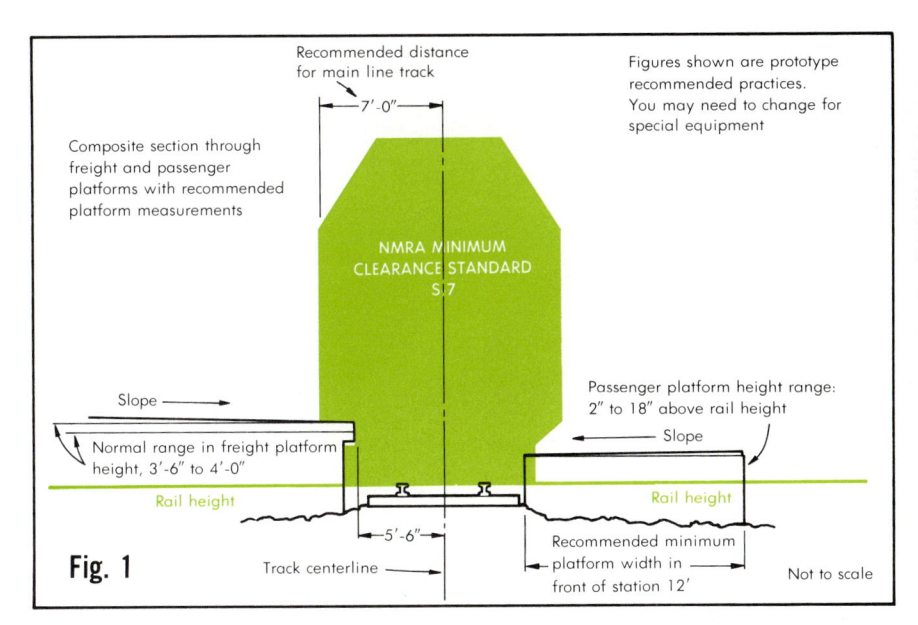

Fig. 1

- Composite section through freight and passenger platforms with recommended platform measurements
- Recommended distance for main line track: 7'-0"
- Figures shown are prototype recommended practices. You may need to change for special equipment
- NMRA MINIMUM CLEARANCE STANDARD S-7
- Slope
- Normal range in freight platform height, 3'-6" to 4'-0"
- Passenger platform height range: 2" to 18" above rail height
- Slope
- Rail height
- Track centerline — 5'-6"
- Recommended minimum platform width in front of station 12'
- Not to scale

Bob Hayden.

This typical passenger step box is on the station platform at Durango, Colo., on the line of the narrow-gauge Silverton train. Note the safety stripe.

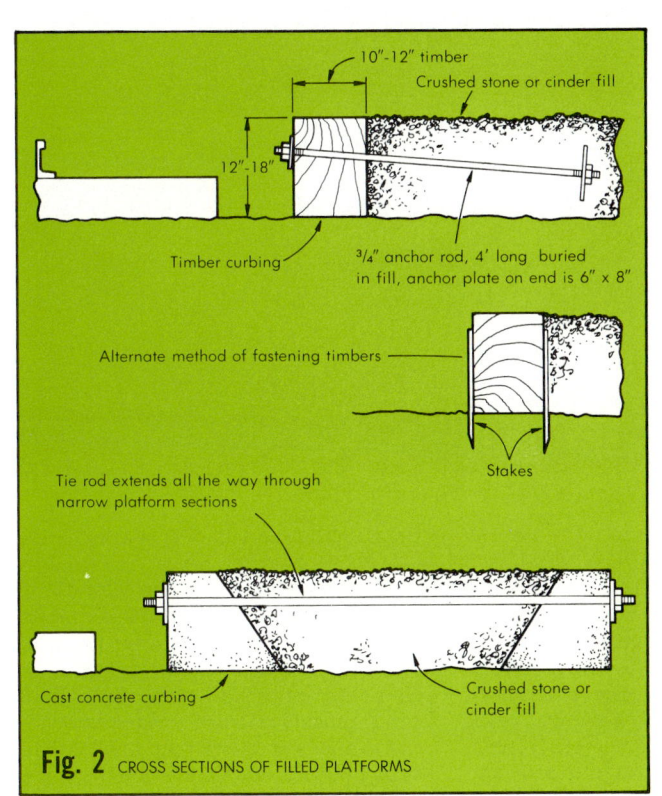

Fig. 2 CROSS SECTIONS OF FILLED PLATFORMS

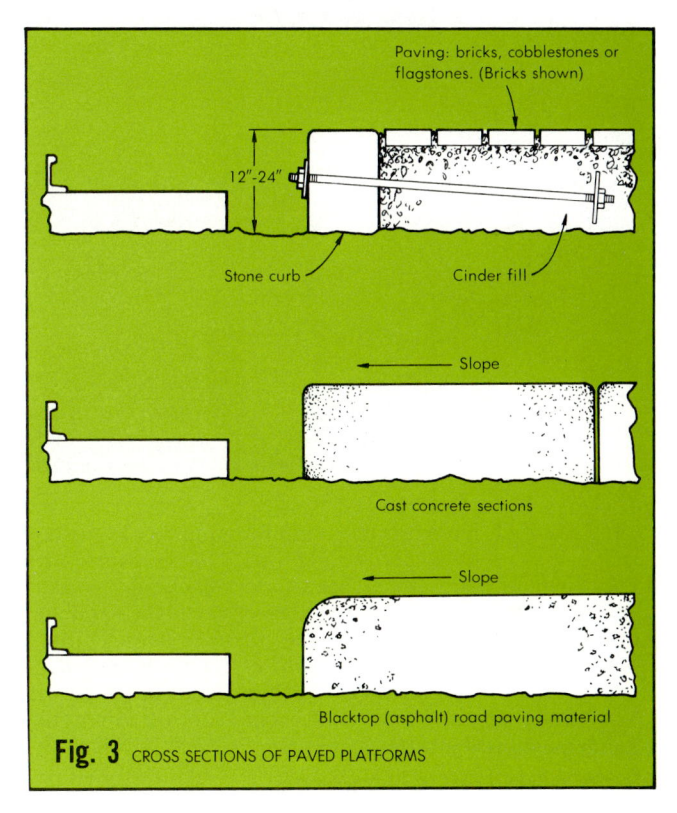

- 10"-12" timber
- Crushed stone or cinder fill
- 12"-18"
- Timber curbing
- 3/4" anchor rod, 4' long buried in fill, anchor plate on end is 6" x 8"
- Alternate method of fastening timbers
- Stakes
- Tie rod extends all the way through narrow platform sections
- Cast concrete curbing
- Crushed stone or cinder fill

Fig. 3 CROSS SECTIONS OF PAVED PLATFORMS

- Paving: bricks, cobblestones or flagstones. (Bricks shown)
- 12"-24"
- Stone curb
- Cinder fill
- Slope
- Cast concrete sections
- Slope
- Blacktop (asphalt) road paving material

At left are a few of the wide variety of commercially made station platform detail parts. From left to right, O scale luggage and steamer trunk (3 pieces), HO scale step box, HO scale steamer trunk, HO scale baggage set (6 pieces), HO scale wood-slat bench, and HO scale barrel and oil drums. All parts are soft-metal castings except the barrel and drums, which are turned wood.

Completing the station scene

95

quires a harder, more durable platform surface to withstand the weight and wear of handling equipment. Some form of paving is usually the answer. Paved platforms include those made of brick—with a curb similar to that of filled platforms—concrete—either poured or precast sections—cobblestone, and asphalt, fig. 3.

Model platform construction

Timber platform construction is discussed at least once in each section of this book, and the "Mail-Order Station" project includes detailed instructions for making a filled platform, so let's look at paved types. Brick, cobblestone, or flagstone surfaces are best simulated with a commercial three-dimensional texture sheet. Determine the size and shape of your platform and cut a stiff material like plywood, styrene, or heavy illustration board to serve as a backing for the sheet material. For realism, sand, gouge, or build up areas of the backing to represent sections where moisture and temperature changes have caused the surface to buckle. Prepaint the stone or brick sheet stock with a base color, let dry, and rub mortar-color paint into the cracks with a rag. Cement the sheet to the backing with a contact-type adhesive, trim the edges, and touch up with paint, and this type of platform is complete.

The photo sequence shows the simple steps involved in making a convincing asphalt (blacktop) platform. The paving material is ready-mixed vinyl or acrylic spackling paste mixed with sand and acrylic paint. The spackling compound—sold in hardware stores—has good binding and working qualities, doesn't shrink, dries quickly to a flat finish, and cleans up with water. Two brands are shown in the photos; neither contains excessive moisture, so the compound won't swell or warp the base of a wood or cardstock station.

After determining where to place your station and the size of the platform, mix a small quantity of spackling paste with about twice as much fine sand or other texture material. The color of the texture material doesn't matter since we are going to color it anyway. Add some black acrylic color—artists' tube colors, flat latex wall paint, or Polly-S brand model railroad colors will all work—and stir until you have a uniform mixture. Don't use much of the paint because the mixture may turn out too black. Depending on the brand of paste you use you may want to add a few drops of water to make the mixture more workable.

Trowel the mixture into place and use a butter knife, cake-frosting spatula, or artists' palette knife to spread and shape the material to the desired contours. Do your best to make a smooth, level surface, but don't use a guide or template, because the irregularities induced by "eyeballing" the paving job are part of the realism of the technique. Don't make the surface too smooth or you will destroy the open-grained texture effect; if the platform looks too uniform, lightly draw the edge of the knife across the surface to make the surface pebbly again. Use a piece of scrap wood or cardstock as a temporary form

Completing the station scene

against which to make the platform edges and then round the edges slightly with the knife after removing the form. According to my experience the spackling and sand mixture is workable for about 15 minutes, but you can extend the working life slightly by rewetting the surface with a few drops of water.

Continue mixing and applying small batches of your paving mixture until your platform is complete. Work in a few surface irregularities like pockmarks and potholes, but be careful—too much weathering and deterioration can make your station look as if it's been abandoned. Allow the platform to dry thoroughly overnight and color it with thin washes of earth and mud paints to represent dust and dirt that have worked into the porous texture. The platform shown in the photos was detailed one step further by adding a narrow yellow safety line with decal striping. These stripes are usually 5 to 7 feet from the inner rail, should you decide to add similar detail to your model.

There are a number of ways to make a cast or poured concrete platform. I suggest you build a wood form similar to the coping on a filled platform and pour in soupy plaster of paris. When the plaster has thickened and set (allow 15 to 20 minutes) remove the form and add joint lines, cracks, and crumbling edges by scribing and picking the plaster with the tip of a knife blade. Then stain a light gray.

Platform details

You can go as far as you like with platform detailing. Baggage-handling equipment is discussed elsewhere in this section. Items like benches, luggage and trunks, scales, and step boxes are available from manufacturers in several scales, and each will increase the realism of the overall station scene. The list of possible additions goes on and on—vending machines, newspaper stands, light fixtures, mail boxes, caution signs, fences, even phone booths—depending on the era of your railroad. Finally, add some scale figures to represent the passengers that your trains—and your stations—serve so efficiently.

Completing the station scene

97

Scratchbuilders' Glossary

Architectural and modelbuilding terms

ABS: a resilient plastic similar to styrene, but more resistant to chemicals and solvents used in paints. Available in sheets, strips, and structural shapes. One brand is Plastruct.

ACC, alphacyanoacrylate, cyanoacrylate, "super glue": a one-part liquid adhesive that combines great holding power with extremely fast setting. Recommended for nonporous materials; some types are also formulated for wood and paper. ACC has great strength in tension and compression joints, but low shear and peel resistance. It bonds skin and must be used with care. Joined fingers, excess glue, and improperly positioned joints may be softened with acetone or nail polish remover.

Acetate-base cement, cellulose cement, household cement, model airplane cement: a heavy-bodied adhesive suitable for wood, cardstock, and other porous materials, and particularly good for cardstock laminations. It is relatively slow-drying, and most brands have a strong solvent odor. Excess adhesive may be removed by brushing with acetone or liquid plastic cement. Common brands are Ambroid Cement and Duco Household Cement.

Acetate, cellulose acetate: a plastic available in several forms. In modeling it is commonly used in thin clear sheets for window glazing.

Airbrush: a miniature paint sprayer used by modelmakers and artists. An airbrush is variable in both air pressure and paint volume, produces a fine atomized spray, and requires compressed gas for operation.

Basswood: the most common modelbuilding wood. Basswood comes from linden trees, and is heavier, harder, stronger, and finer grained than balsa. It is widely available in sheets, strips, scale lumber, structural shapes, and milled structure siding.

Battens, bats, board-and-batten siding: narrow strips of wood or metal nailed over the joints of wall or roof sheathing to keep out the weather.

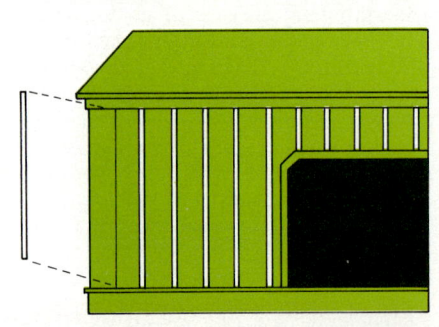

Bond paper: high-quality smooth-texture stationery paper from .003" to .005" thick. The bond paper called for in construction projects is single-ply paper with no finish or gloss, similar to that used for business envelopes.

Bristol board: see *Strathmore*.

Capillary action: the tendency of a thin fluid to flow along and be drawn into a joint.

Card, cardstock: stiff pressed paper stock available in a variety of thicknesses, textures, and qualities. Where a project calls for card without specifying a type, use medium-weight file card, manila folder, or Strathmore with a smooth finish where it will be visible. See also *Strathmore, mounting board*.

Chamfer: a bevel or angle cut on the edge of a piece of stock or the lip of a hole.

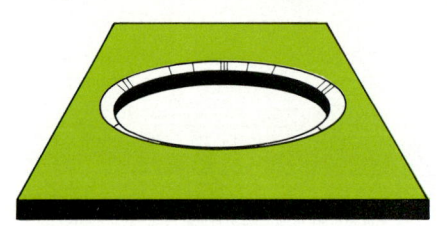

Clear plastic glazing: thin transparent plastic used to simulate window glass, usually acetate or clear styrene .010"-.020" thick.

Contact-type adhesive: a flexible, rubber-like cement suitable for both porous and nonporous materials. Very neat joints are possible by using this adhesive in the *contact process:* applying a thin coat of cement to each surface to be joined, letting dry a short time, and pressing together. Common brands are Goodyear Pliobond, Hobsco Goo, and Weldwood Contact Cement; they can be thinned or removed with liquid plastic cement or their own special solvents.

Coping: a capping for the top edge of a wall to protect the wall material from the weather.

Corbel: a projection from the face of a wall supporting a weight. A common form of corbel is a series of stone or brick courses, each projecting slightly beyond the next lower course.

Crazing: the formation of minute cracks on a finished surface due to moisture (in a paint surface) or incompatible solvent action (on plastic). The etched, orange peel effect on plastic can be avoided by using the proper paints. See *plastic-compatible paint*.

Dormer: an extension of an attic room that protrudes through a sloping roof to allow a vertical window opening into the room.

Dry-brushing: a painting and weathering technique in which most of the pigment or paint is removed from the brush before the brush is touched to the model. The "dry brush," with only a little damp color on the tips of the bristles, is stroked lightly over the model to bring out raised details, textures, and panel joints.

Dry-transfer lettering: a lettering material made of thin plastic with pressure-sensitive adhesive, supplied on a waxed carrier sheet that releases the letters when rubbed, transferring them to the model.

Eaves: the lower borders of a roof, the parts that overhang the walls.

Elevation view: a drawing of a structure on a plane perpendicular to the horizon, showing the side and end views. See *plan view*.

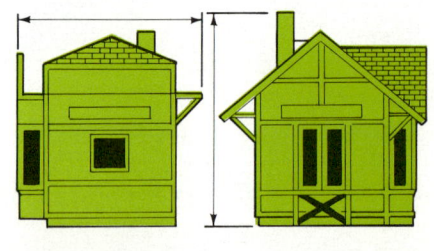

Epoxy adhesive: any one of a large number of two-part resin and catalyst adhesives suitable for porous and nonporous materials. Epoxies cure rather than dry, and make strong bonds. Most are heavy-bodied and do not shrink, and are waterproof after setting. The most useful for modeling are the 5-minute setting types.

Fascia, fascia boards: boards or other flat material placed at or near the upper edge of a wall, usually as trim and frequently covering the joint between the top of the wall and the projecting eaves.

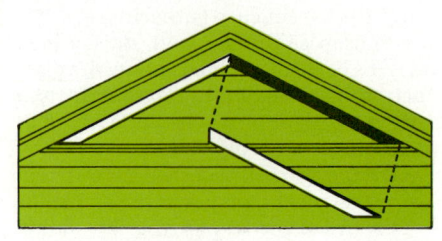

98

Flashing: sheet metal or other material used in roof and wall construction to protect the building from water seepage.

Free-lance project: a model or design without a specific prototype, but incorporating features from several prototypes or conforming to standard practices for similar items. Free-lance departures from prototype dimensions are usually minor, but allow the modeler much more latitude in choosing materials and construction methods.

Gable: the triangular upper portion of the end wall of a building, from the level of the cornice or eaves up to the apex of the roof.

Glazing: glasswork. See *clear plastic glazing*.

Household cement: see *acetate-base cement*.

I.d.: inside diameter.

Injection-moldings: parts made by forcing hot plastic or metal into hollow dies or molds. Most plastic kits and parts are manufactured by this process.

Kitbashing, kitlancing, cross-kitting: combining parts from kits to produce models unlike the straight kitbuilt versions.

Kraft tape: a heavy, strong brown paper gummed tape approximately .007" thick used for package wrapping and sealing. The adhesive must be moistened with water. One brand is NeaTape.

Lintel: the horizontal member over a door or window opening that supports the weight over the opening.

Liquid plastic cement: a solvent used to cement plastic by dissolving a thin layer of the surfaces to be joined and fusing them together as it evaporates. Applied with a brush or needle applicator, it has no body and distributes itself along joints by capillary action, leaving very neat results. Common brands include Testors Plastic Cement, Plastic Weld, and Micro Weld.

Mounting board: an inexpensive cardboard about .050" thick that consists of thin high-finish outer plies with a softer gray filler stock sandwiched between them. Used for strength in formers and for backing parts, but not for finished surfaces.

Mullions: the thin upright bars dividing and supporting the panels of windows, screens, or similar frames.

Muntins: vertical or horizontal strip members separating the panes of glass in a door or window sash.

N-B-W, nut-bolt-washer castings: small moldings in plastic, soft metal, or brass that represent the end of a bolt or threaded rod.

NMRA: the National Model Railroad Association, a U.S. based worldwide organization of hobbyists who gather to exchange information and promote creative development and fellowship in model railroading. NMRA researches and establishes standards and recommended practices that ensure compatibility of mechanical and electrical components from different model railroad manufacturers.

O.d.: outside diameter.

Parapet: a low wall or wall extension along the edge of a roof, designed to hide the edge of the sloping roof and to prevent people and objects from falling. Usually topped by a *coping*.

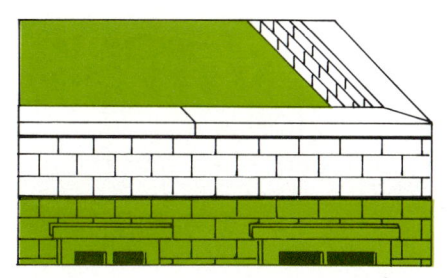

Plan view: a top view drawing, showing a structure as it would be seen from above; a floor plan or ground plan. See *elevation view*.

Plastic-compatible paint: a paint that will not etch or craze the surface of a plastic model regardless of the method of application. These paints include enamels (Humbrol, Pactra, Testors are common brands) and water-soluble latex or acrylic finishes (Polly-S).

Press-type: see *dry-transfer lettering*.

Purlin: a member of a roof frame that rests horizontally on the main roof truss members to support rafters and roof covering.

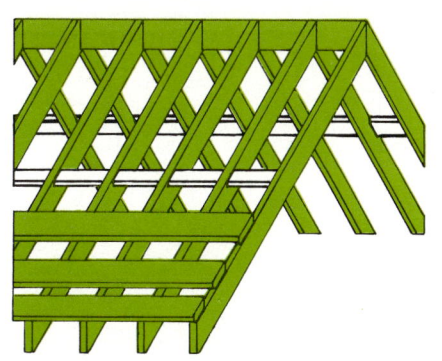

Scale lumber: wood strips manufactured to inch sizes in a designated scale (HO 2 x 4, O 6 x 8, etc.) rather than decimal or fractional inch dimensions (.012" x 1/16", 1/8" square, etc.). See *stripwood*.

Scribed wood: thin wood sheet, usually basswood or soft pine, with milled grooves to represent board sheathing or planking. Available in several thicknesses and groove spacings.

Selective compression: the process of incorporating the most interesting or unique qualities of the prototype and discarding others to reduce the bulk of a model into a scaled-down version of manageable size.

Soffit: the underside of the members of a building, such as overhangs, staircases, cornices, beams, and arches.

Solvent cement: see *liquid plastic cement*.

Sprue: the treelike molded framework to which injection-molded plastic parts are attached. Often many small castings come attached to a common sprue.

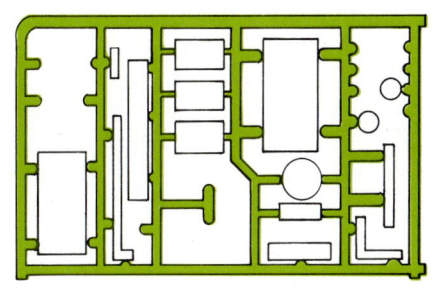

Stain: a thinned pigment, in a vehicle, intended to be absorbed into the surface of a porous material or to settle on the surface as a semitransparent overcoat to dull or modify the underlying color. Most stains in the construction projects in this book are made by thinning model paints.

Strathmore, Strathmore paper: a high-quality artists' material and drafting paper well suited to finish modelwork. Strathmore consists of one or more plies of hard white paper with a smooth or matte finish, and ranges in thickness from .005" (1-ply) to .025" (5-ply).

Stripwood, fractional stripwood: wood strips, usually basswood or sugar pine, manufactured in decimal or fractional inch sizes for modelbuilding. See *scale lumber*.

Styrene, polystyrene: a soft, grainless thermoplastic that can be formed and fabricated easily with both hand and machine tools. Styrene is the material for most injection-molded parts, kits, and ready-to-run equipment, and is available in opaque and clear sheets, precut strips, milled structure siding, rods, and tubes.

"Super glue": see *ACC*.

Transom: a movable window placed over a door for light and ventilation.

Wainscoting: a wall finish of wood or other material covering the bottom fourth of a wall, usually from 3 to 4 feet high and finished with a projecting cap molding.

White glue: any of a number of polyvinyl acetate resin adhesives that are water soluble and milky white in liquid form, but that dry clear. White glue is suitable for porous materials but has limited holding power on metal and plastic. Its advantages are low cost, water cleanup and thinning, and lack of strong solvent or chemical odors. Common brands are Elmer's Glue-All, Ambroid SeCurlt, and Slomon's Sobo Glue.

99

Index of techniques

Boldface numerals indicate comprehensive discussion or illustration of the subject

A

Acrylic matte medium, 60
Actuator, lever, 89
Adhesives, see *Gluing techniques* and **Glossary**
Aging, see *Weathering*

B

Bay window, 11, **45**, 67, 78
Brick, **42**, 76

C

Cardstock, see *Strathmore*
Castings, 37, **51**
Catalog modeling, **50**
Ceilings, 8, **69**
Chimneys, 6, 14, **28**, 38, **47**, 59
Commercial parts, **51**
Compressing structures, **70**
Cupola, **69**, 79
Cutting guide, 14

D

Decals, homemade, **93**
Designing stations, 22, **65**, **70**, **72**, **73**
Doors:
    Baggage room, 5, 17, 62, **77**
    Prefabricated units, **37**
    Strathmore, 4, **44**, **75**
    Working, **7**, **16**
Dormers, **69**, **75**
Drawings, making your own, **50**
Dry-transfer lettering, **90**

E

Eave braces, 6, 17, **37**
Eave gauge block, 27

F

Flashing, 39, **49**, 59, 81
Flooring, 5, 8, 69
Foundations, **44**, 69

G

Gluing techniques:
    Contact, 4, **5**, 6
    Dry preassembly, **11**
    Prepainted parts, 11
    Solvent, **23**, 36
    Two-step (ACC/epoxy), **54**
Gussets, **37**
Gutters and downspouts, 21, **80**

I

Interior detail, 48
Interior walls, 66

J

Jigs:
    Pin, **21**
    Rafter end, **15**
    Railing, **80**
    Roof bracket, **16**
    Window muntin, **16**
    Window opening plug, 7, **43**

K

Kitbashing, 30, **41**

L

Laminating, Strathmore, 4
Liftoff buildings, **9**, 17
Lighting, 17, 48, 69, **80**
Linkage, **89**

O

Order box, **49**
Ornamental detail:
    Brickwork, **46**, 59
    Gable trim, 14
    Grillwork, 29
Outhouse, 14

P

Painting:
    Before assembly, 2, 7, **10**
    Castings, 51
    Stonework, **56**, 59
Styrene, 29
Planning, 31
Plaster, see *Stucco*
Plastic, see *Styrene* and *Kitbashing*
Platforms:
    Clearances, **95**
    Filled, **59**, **94**
    Freight loading dock, 63
    Lamps, **80**
    Paved, 21, 29, **95**
    Planked, 6, 8, **39**, **78**
    Roofs, 71
    Safety line, **97**
    Shelters, **18**

R

Railings, **80**
Roof brackets, jig, **16**
Roofing:
    Asphalt, tarpaper roll, 21, **28**, 63
    Copper-sheathed, **71**
    Gable, 13
    Hip, 57
    Peaked (dunce or witch's cap), **58**, **80**
    Removable, 13
    Sheet metal, **38**, **46**
    Shingle, **5**, 27, 37, **48**, 58
    Texture paint, 77

S

Sandwich-style part making, **38**, **59**
Sandwich wall construction, **66**
Scribing:
    Strathmore, 4
    Styrene, **25**
Selective compression and expansion, **70**
Signal indications, **88**
Signals, 49, **87**
Signs, 17, 40, 81, **90**
Spackling compound, **96**
Staining Strathmore, **4**
Stairs, **78**
Stonework, 54
Stonework mortar color, 59
Strathmore, 4
Stucco, **61**
Styrene, 23

T

Template, ground contour, **74**
Ticket office, **67**
Timber (log cabin) construction, 7
Trim:
    Cardstock (Strathmore), 4
    Roof, **49**
    Styrene, **38**
Two-level station design, **73**

V

Ventilators, **47**

W

Walls:
    Increasing thickness around windows, 2
    Stone, 54
    Strathmore, 2
    Stucco, **61**
    Styrene, 24
    Wood, **11**, 66
Weathering:
    Chalks, 49, 81
    Dry-brushing, 59
    Stains, 39
    Washes, 39
Wetting agent, 60
Wheels (for baggage wagons), sources, 83
Windows:
    Boarded-up, 2
    Double-hung, 16
    Operating, **8**
    Pattern block for openings, 7, **43**, 66
    Plexiglas, 62
    Pre-glazed, 37
    Shades, **37**, 46
    Using castings, **51**, **54**, 59
    Z-section frames, **75**
Window mullions/muntins:
    Jig, **16**
    Paint, 43
    Thread, **16**, 77
    Wood, 3
Wood:
    General construction, **10**
    Siding styles, **65**